DON'T WASTE YOUR TIME® IN THE
BC COAST MOUNTAINS

BOOT-TESTED AND WRITTEN BY
KATHY AND CRAIG COPELAND

VOICE IN THE WILDERNESS PRESS

AN OPINIONATED HIKING GUIDE

TO HELP YOU GET THE MOST FROM THIS **MAGNIFICENT WILDERNESS**

Dedicated to helping people
more easily appreciate
mountain grandeur, in hope
that it will enrich their lives
and inspire their commitment
to preserve what little
wilderness remains.

Photos by authors
Cover design by Matthew Clark
Maps and Typesetting by C.J. Chiarizia

Published in Canada by
Voice in the Wilderness Press, Inc.
P.O. Box 71, Riondel, British Columbia V0B 2B0

♻ Printed on recycled paper, 20% post-consumer fibre

Canadian Cataloguing in Publication Data

Copeland, Kathy, 1959-
    Don't waste your time in the B.C. Coast Mountains

    Includes index.
ISBN 0-9698016-3-7

    1. Trails—Coast Mountains (B.C. and Alaska)—Guidebooks.
2. Hiking—Coast Mountains (B.C. and Alaska)—Guidebooks. 3.
Coast Mountains (B.C. and Alaska)—Guidebooks. I. Copeland,
Craig, 1955- II. Title.
GV 199.44.C22C7415 1997   796.52'2'097111   C97-910119-0

Front cover photo: On Tabletop Mountain, near the Stein Divide (Trip 28)
Back cover photo: Rainbow Lake (Trip 32)

Contents

Your Safety is Your Responsibility

    Hiking and camping in the wilderness can be dangerous. Experience and preparation reduce risk, but will never eliminate it. The unique details of your specific situation and the decisions you make at that time will determine the outcome. This book is not a substitute for common sense or sound judgment. If you doubt your ability to negotiate mountain terrain, respond to wild animals, or handle sudden, extreme weather changes, hike only in a group led by a competent guide. The authors and the publisher disclaim liability for any loss or injury incurred by anyone using information in this book.

Area Covered by This Book

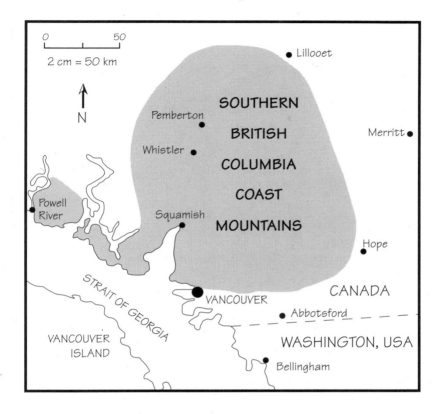

The B.C. Coast Mountains extend nearly the entire length of the province, from Vancouver to the Northwest Territories. That's 1400 km (870 mi). Technically, the southern B.C. Coast Mountains are the bottom half of the range: a stretch continuing about as far north as Smithers. Trails are few and far between, however, northwest of the Southern Chilcotin (Trip 29), as well as between Powell River and the Squamish River Valley. So this book only covers the extreme southern end of the range. That's where the trails are concentrated—within striking distance of B.C.'s biggest cities. The rest of the range is well worth exploring and includes several wild provincial parks. But backcountry travel there is rarely just hiking. It truly is exploration, requiring exceptional skills and determination.

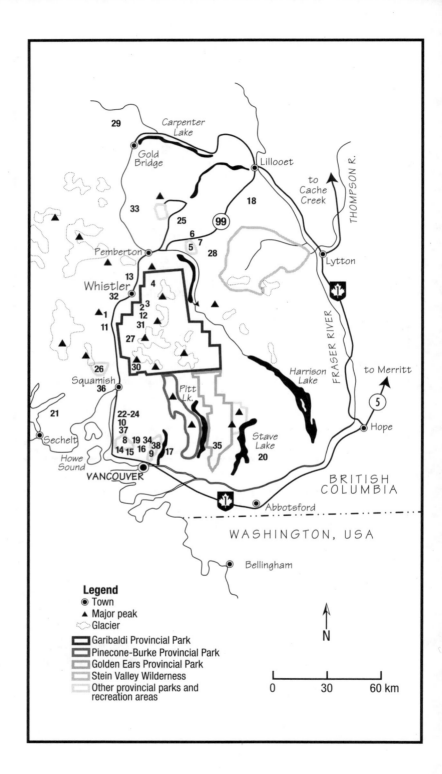

29

Carpenter
Lake

Gold
Bridge

Lillooet

to
Cache
Creek

THOMPSON R.

33

18

25

99

6
5 7

28

Pemberton

Lytton

13
Whistler
32

4

2 3
12
31

1

11

27

30

26
Squamish
36

Pitt
Lk.

Harrison
Lake

FRASER RIVER

to Merritt

5

Hope

21

Sechelt

22-24
10
37
8 19 34
16 38
14 15 9 17

Stave
Lake

20

35

Howe
Sound

VANCOUVER

BRITISH
COLUMBIA

Abbotsford

WASHINGTON, USA

Bellingham

Legend
◉ Town
▲ Major peak
⬡ Glacier
▮ Garibaldi Provincial Park
▮ Pinecone-Burke Provincial Park
▯ Golden Ears Provincial Park
▯ Stein Valley Wilderness
▯ Other provincial parks and
  recreation areas

N

0   30   60 km

Summer Trip Locations

1 Brandywine Meadows
2 Musical Bumps
3 Blackcomb Peak
4 Wedgemount Lake
5 Joffre Lakes
6 Rohr Lake / Marriott Basin
7 Cerise Creek
8 Mt. Strachan
9 Mt. Seymour
10 The Lions
11 Brew Lake
12 Fitzsimmons Creek / Russet Lake
13 Cougar Mountain Cedar Grove
14 Black Mountain
15 Unnecessary Mountain from Cypress Ski Area
16 Goat Mountain / Hanes Creek
17 Eagle Ridge / Dilly Dally Peak
18 Blowdown Pass / Gott Peak
19 Crown Mountain
20 Mt. St. Benedict
21 Mt. Steele
22 Unnecessary Mountain from Lions Bay
23 Deeks and Brunswick Lakes
24 Deeks Peak
25 Place Glacier
26 Lake Lovely Water
27 Garibaldi Lake / Black Tusk / Panorama Ridge
28 Stein Divide
29 Southern Chilcotin / Taylor Basin
30 Elfin Lakes / Mamquam Lake
31 Helm Creek
32 Rainbow Lake
33 Tenquille Lake
34 Coliseum Mountain
35 Golden Ears
36 Sylvia Lake / Mt. Roderick
37 Howe Sound Crest
38 Elsay Lake

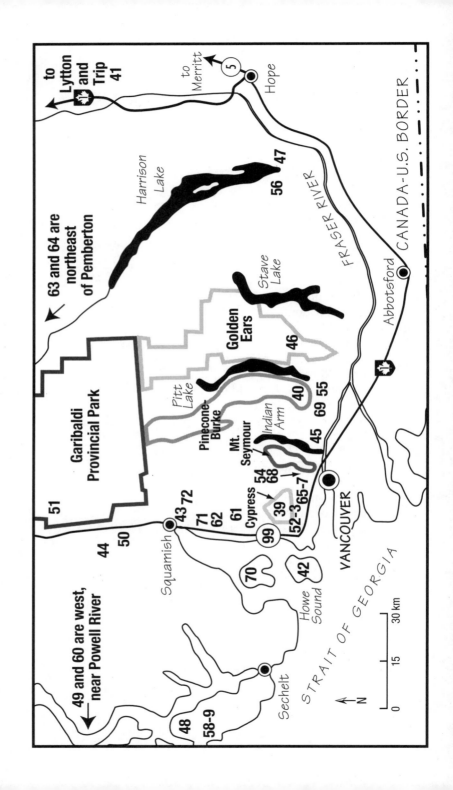

Shoulder-Season Trip Locations

Traversing Tabletop Mountain (Trip 28)

Time Is Precious

A disappointing trip leaves a psychic dent. Sometimes it can't be helped. But often it can, by knowing where to go instead of guessing. Too many people toil up scenically deprived trails to lackluster destinations when they could be dancing with delight before one of North America's premier mountain panoramas. That's been our motivation: to save you from wasting your precious time. Even in this glorious mountain kingdom, not all scenery is created equal. Some places are simply more striking, more intriguing, more inspiring than others. Now you can be certain you're choosing a rewarding trail for your weekend or vacation.

These are our boot-tested opinions on which are the best hikes in the southern B.C. Coast Mountains, which ones you should avoid, and why. We rate the hikes **Premier, Outstanding, Worthwhile,** or **Don't Do.**

This kind of advice is available only from the *Don't Waste Your Time®* guidebook series. Think of it as an honest friend who has vast hiking experience and wants you to enjoy a memorable adventure. With other guidebooks, deciphering which hikes offer superior scenery, then choosing one, can be a slow, difficult process. We've made it fast, easy and enjoyable.

Our opinions are strong, but they're based on widely shared, common-sense criteria. To help you understand our commentary, here are our preferences:

• A hike isn't emotionally rewarding solely because of the destination. Variety is what we're after. We want to be wowed along the way by mammoth trees, luxuriant understory, profuse wildflowers, plunging gorges, rocky escarpments. We're deeply moved by sacred, ancient forests. We find solitude to be a sustaining necessity of life. Watching a stream charge on its journey excites us. The closer we get to gleaming glaciers and piercing peaks, the more ecstatic we feel. High, awe-inspiring, soul-expanding perches thrill us most of all.

• Spending a sunny summer day entirely in forest, even ancient forest, doesn't appeal to us. We're discouraged by views of only rounded, forest-shrouded, nondescript mountains. Long stretches of trail through disenchanted forest (scraggly trees, particularly second-growth) are downright depressing.

When the scenery gets monotonous and the trail cantankerous, it's trudgery; all we want to do is finish. Although we'll push ourselves far higher for jolting scenery, we don't like climbing over 1070 meters (3500 feet) a day for anything less.

This is the guidebook we wish we'd had when we moved to Vancouver. After spending years in the Canadian Rockies, an inviting range where massive glaciers and soaring rock faces are frequently visible from the road, we were discouraged by the southern B.C. Coast Mountains. Peering up at 1220 vertical meters (4000 feet) of uninterrupted forest was daunting. It was hard to imagine penetrating those thick bastions and enjoying it.

We've long since learned the Coast Mountains are a world of wonders for hikers of all levels. Mountain magic is here, if you know where to look. Our complete, precise directions will tell you. Our discerning opinions will warn you away from inferior trips and empower you to choose worthier ones.

We also hope our suggestions compel you to get out even more often than you have. Do it to cultivate your wild self. It will give you perspective. Do it because the mountains teach simplicity and self-reliance, qualities that make life more fulfilling. Do it to remind yourself why wilderness needs and deserves your protection. A bolder conservation ethic develops naturally in the mountains. And do it to rediscover the fundamental but easily forgotten truth that there's little of importance outside simple, raw experience.

Ridge above Mamquam Lake (Trip 30), with Mt. Garibaldi in view

Trail-Rating System

PREMIER

Here's where you'll enjoy the most spectacular terrain: rugged peaks, sheer cliffs, extensive meadows, tumbling glaciers. The panoramic vistas have startling impact. You'll attain views soon (within 6 km / 3.7 miles on dayhikes, 8 km / 5 miles on backpack trips). Most of the dayhikes are quickly gratifying because they start at higher elevations. The backpack trips lead you into grand alpine terrain, where you're greeted by awesome peaks and surrounded by opportunities for high-elevation exploration. You'll want to come back again and again.

OUTSTANDING

These are exhilarating destinations, but overall the trips are not superlative. Either you have to work harder and longer to achieve astounding views, or the scenery never reaches an intense climax. They might have earned a Premier rating if the backpack trips felt wilder, or the dayhikes led you closer to glaciers and cliffs.

WORTHWHILE

You'll see beautiful scenery here, just not the kind that leaves an image blazed in your memory. The dayhikes are enjoyable, revealing a special aspect of the area. The backpack trips are very demanding, and you'll trek a long way before it's obvious why you came, but you'll be glad you did.

DON'T DO

We have nothing good to say about these cursed trails. They're tedious and have little interesting scenery, or too miserably demanding for the reward they offer. Repeat a Premier or an Outstanding hike rather than waste your time here.

Shoulder-Season Hiking

Shoulder season is a term used by airlines and travel agencies. It refers to the months before and after the popular, main season. We use it to describe spring and late-fall hiking. In the Coast Mountains, shoulder-season trips allow you to get outdoors starting in March and stay out through November. Lower elevations and mild, wet weather keep these trails snow-free most of the year. Of course, you'll generally be walking through forest, but it will keep you in shape for summer and, on sunny days, you'll enjoy revitalizing views.

Some shoulder-season dayhikes can also be short backpack trips. Widgeon Lake (Trip 40) and the Stein River Canyon (Trip 41) are long enough trails to offer a fulfilling overnight experience.

Remember: shoulder-season ratings are specific to that time of year; they're not equivalent to ratings for prime hiking season. Many shoulder-season trips are either too short, or require you to spend too much time on logging roads, to feel like an adventure. A Premier shoulder-season trip might be merely Worthwhile in summer. A Worthwhile shoulder-season trip could be a Don't Do in summer.

Shoulder Season: Premier means the trip is pleasing overall. Compared to other choices in spring or late fall, these trails are more enjoyable (except Widgeon Lake, Trip 40) and the scenery more rewarding.

Shoulder Season: Outstanding means the trip offers a special vantage point, but is otherwise typical of spring or late-fall options.

Shoulder Season: Worthwhile means the trip simply provides an opportunity to hike in spring or late fall. The views are not as striking, or not as expansive. Several trails are very short.

Dayhiking Versus Backpacking

To help speed your decision making, we've separated the trips roughly according to round-trip distance. Most backpack trips are longer than 24 km (15 mi). Most dayhikes are shorter than 16 km (10 mi).

Don't necessarily limit yourself to our guidelines. Some dayhikes, like Brandywine Meadows (Trip 1), Rohr Lake (Trip 6), and Russet Lake (Trip 12), make excellent backpack trips if you want or need a shorter option. Many backpack trips are hikeable in a day, if you're swift.

> **Trips at a Glance**
>
> *Trips in each category are listed according to geographic location: starting in the south and moving roughly from west to east, then north. After the trip name, the round-trip distance is listed, followed by the elevation gain.*

Dayhikes at a Glance

PREMIER

1	Brandywine Meadows	13.6 km / 8.4 mi	600 m / 1970 ft
2	Musical Bumps	19 km / 11.8 mi	727 m / 2385 ft
		or 22 km / 13.6 mi	575 m / 1885 ft
3	Blackcomb Peak	9 km / 5.6 mi	355 m / 1164 ft
4	Wedgemount Lake	14 km / 8.7 mi	1160 m / 3805 ft
5	Joffre Lakes	11 km / 6.8 mi	370 m / 1214 ft
6	Rohr Lake /	9 km / 5.6 mi	430 m / 1410 ft
	Marriott Basin	or 16 km / 10 mi	370 m / 1210 ft
7	Cerise Creek	8 km / 5 mi	305 m / 1000 ft

OUTSTANDING

8	Mt. Strachan	10 km / 6.2 mi	534 m / 1752 ft
9	Mt. Seymour	9 km / 5.6 mi	440 m / 1443 ft
10	The Lions	15 km / 9.3 mi	1525 m / 5002 ft
11	Brew Lake	13 km / 8 mi	963 m / 3160 ft
12	Fitzsimmons Creek /		
	Russet Lake	19 km / 11.8 mi	945 m / 3100 ft
13	Cougar Mountain	5 km / 3 mi	150 m / 492 ft
	Cedar Grove		

WORTHWHILE

14	Black Mountain	7.5 km / 4.7 mi	297 m / 974 ft
15	Unnecessary Mountain		
	from Cypress Ski Area	18 km / 11.2 mi	844 m / 2770 ft
16	Goat Mtn. /Hanes Creek	18 km / 11.2 mi	273 m / 895 ft
17	Eagle Ridge /		
	Dilly Dally Peak	24 km / 15 mi	1370 m / 4500 ft
18	Blowdown Pass /		
	Gott Peak	14.4 km / 9 mi	874 m / 2867 ft

DON'T DO

19	Crown Mountain	9.6 km / 6 mi	695 m / 2278 ft
20	Mt. St. Benedict	15 km / 9.3 mi	1279 m / 4195 ft
21	Mt. Steele	18 km / 11.2 mi	543 m / 1781 ft
22	Unnecessary Mountain from Lions Bay	9.5 km / 6 mi	1310 m / 4297 ft
23	Deeks and Brunswick Lakes	14.4 km / 9 mi or 20 km / 12.4 mi	990 m / 3247 ft 1120 m / 3670 ft
24	Deeks Peak	16 km / 10 mi	1613 m / 5291 ft
25	Place Glacier	21 km / 13 mi	1310 m / 4300 ft

Backpack Trips at a Glance

PREMIER

26	Lake Lovely Water	10 km / 6.2 mi	1128 m / 3700 ft
27	Garibaldi Lake / Black Tusk / Panorama Ridge	18 km / 11.2 mi or 35 km / 22 mi	875 m / 2870 ft 2450 m / 8035 ft
28	Stein Divide	28.6 km / 17.7 mi	1265 m / 4150 ft
29	Southern Chilcotin / Taylor Basin	37 km / 23 mi	1340 m / 4400 ft

OUTSTANDING

30	Elfin Lakes / Mamquam Lake	22 km / 13.6 mi or 44 km / 27.2 mi	915 m / 3000 ft 1555 m / 5100 ft
31	Helm Creek	16 km / 10 mi	717 m / 2352 ft
32	Rainbow Lake	16 km / 10 mi	850 m / 2788 ft
33	Tenquille Lake	12 km / 7.5 mi +	457 m / 1500 ft +

WORTHWHILE

34	Coliseum Mountain	24.5 km / 15.2 mi	1239 m / 4064 ft
35	Golden Ears	24 km / 15 mi	1500 m / 4920 ft
36	Sylvia Lake / Mt. Roderick	20 km / 12.4 mi	1476 m / 4840 ft

DON'T DO

37	Howe Sound Crest	30 km / 18.6 mi	1185 m / 3887 ft
38	Elsay Lake	20 km / 12.4 mi	885 m / 2903 ft

Shoulder-Season Trips at a Glance

PREMIER

39	Mt. Hollyburn	8 km / 5 mi	405 m / 1328 ft
40	Widgeon Lake	18.5 km / 11.5 mi	815 m / 2673 ft
41	Stein River Canyon	27 km / 16.7 mi	355 m / 1165 ft
42	Mt. Gardner / Bowen Island	16 km / 10 mi	750 m / 2460 ft
43	Stawamus Chief	6 km / 3.7 mi	612 m / 2007 ft
44	High Falls Creek	12 km / 7.5 mi	640 m / 2100 ft

OUTSTANDING

45	Diez Vistas	13 km / 8 mi	455 m / 1490 ft
46	Alouette Mountain	22.6 km / 14 mi	1116 m / 3660 ft
47	Bear Mountain	17.7 km / 11 mi	1008 m / 3306 ft
48	Mt. Hallowell	15 km / 9.3 mi	1020 m / 3346 ft
49	Tin Hat Mountain	12.5 km / 7.75 mi	732 m / 2400 ft
50	Skyline / Levette Lake	11 km / 6.8 mi	540 m / 1770 ft
51	Cheakamus Lake	12.8 km / 8 mi	negligible

WORTHWHILE

52	Eagle Bluff	12 km / 7.4 mi	974 m / 3195 ft
53	Brothers Creek	10 km / 6.2 mi	437 m / 1433 ft
54	Lynn Valley	9.5 km / 5.9 mi	160 m / 525 ft
55	Dennett Lake /	10 km / 6.2 mi	860 m / 2820 ft
	Burke Ridge	or 15 km / 9.3 mi	1120 m / 3675 ft
56	Mt. Agassiz	7.4 km / 4.6 mi	700 m / 2296 ft
57	Brigade Bluffs	13 km / 8 mi	780 m / 2560 ft
58	Skookumchuck Narrows	8 km / 5 mi	negligible
59	Mt. Daniel	5 km / 3 mi	375 m / 1225 ft
60	Inland Lake	13 km / 8 mi	negligible
61	Deeks Bluffs	9 km / 5.6 mi	395 m / 1296 ft
62	Petgill Lake	11.5 km / 7 mi	665 m / 2181 ft
63	Place Creek Falls	3 km / 2 mi	230 m / 754 ft
64	Birkenhead Lake	3.5 km / 2.2 mi	negligible

DON'T DO

65	Lower Hollyburn Lakes	11 km / 7 mi	427 m / 1400 ft
66	Grouse Grind	5 km / 3 mi	854 m / 2800 ft
67	Mt. Fromme	15 km / 9.3 mi	866 m / 2840 ft
68	Lynn Peak	7.2 km / 4.5 mi	714 m / 2340 ft
69	Burke Ridge	20 km / 12.4 mi	880 m / 2885 ft
70	Mt. Liddell/Gambier Island	14 km / 8.7 mi	903 m / 2963 ft
71	Phyllis and Marion Lakes	16 km / 10 mi	490 m / 1607 ft
72	Stawamus Squaw	14.5 km / 9 mi	570 m / 1870 ft

Trails Not in this Book

We excluded many trails we would have rated Don't Do. It seemed a waste of your time, as well as ours, to fully describe undesirable options you're unlikely to be drawn to anyway. Several are obscure, familiar only to locals. Most are too punishing, tedious, or sketchy, even by outrageous Coast Mountain standards. Some are more disappointing than the Don't Do trips we kept in the book. Few people hike these trails. If you want to, you're on your own, Billy Goat. Specifically, here's why:

(1) Where the scenery doesn't justify it, shredding your knees by climbing over 170 meters per kilometer (558 feet per 0.6 mile) for more than 6.5 km (4 miles) is absurd. Capilano Mountain and Goat Ridge, both rising out of Howe Sound, are examples. Mt. Roderick (Trip 36) barely made it into the book.

(2) Long, rugged approach roads require a serious 4WD vehicle and an experienced driver immune to acrophobia. For instance, Alice Ridge and Brohm Ridge, both on Mt. Garibaldi, off Hwy 99; Seton Ridge, in the Cayoosh Range, southwest of Lillooet; and Eagle Ridge, off Kwoiek Creek logging road, near the Fraser Canyon. To reach Statlu Lake, northwest of Chehalis Lake, you'd spend more time negotiating the miserably jarring 39-km (24-mi) road than you would hiking. All the trails in this book are two-wheel-drive accessible.

(3) Most hikers lack orienteering skills, as well as the mental and physical toughness to bushwhack very far. That eliminates Mt. Price, rising above the southwest shore of Garibaldi Lake, and Van Horlick Pass, on the west side of the Stein Wilderness. To explore Eagle Ridge, mentioned above, you must find your own way up, then locate and follow the fading remnants of an historic trail. Indistinct routes like these we've left to intrepid explorers who don't need guidebooks.

(4) Complicated access keeps trails to remote destinations unmaintained, and out of range for most hikers. One of these is Zenith Lake, in a glorious cirque north of Lake Lovely Water. To get there, you must boat across the Squamish River, then find the overgrown, boot-beaten path and bash your way up. If you're ever lucky enough to boat or fly into Princess Louisa Inlet, try the steep trappers' route starting just east of Loquilts Creek. It leads to a pass overlooking Sims Creek valley.

(5) Resource development, primarily logging but also tourist facility construction, is gnawing away at Coast Mountain wilderness. Typical of this category is the Upper Elaho Valley (reached from the Squamish Valley Road), in the proposed Stoltmann Wilderness. Here, International Forest Products (Interfor) was granted (again in 1996) logging rights to a magnificent ancient forest of giant Douglas firs. The valley hiking route, surveyed and cleared by volunteers of the Western Canada Wilderness Committee (WCWC), could be obliterated, if it hasn't been already. In 1996 the forests of two watersheds—the Clendenning and the Upper Lillooet—gained park status and were protected. But they're separated by the larger area of the Upper Elaho, which was left in the hands of the logging company.

Check with the WCWC (604-683-8220) for current information on how far the logging road has been pushed up the Elaho and whether the Douglas Fir Loop, north of Lava Creek, is still untouched. This is an Outstanding daytrip. When we hiked it in 1996, we encountered a giant Douglas fir every 10 seconds. Trees of this size (up to 10 meters around) will not regenerate. Even if the same climactic conditions existed, it would take a seedling 800 to 1,000 years to achieve this miraculous stature.

The north end of the Stoltmann, near Meager Creek and the Upper Lillooet River, is also threatened. If this area is still intact, plan at least a two-day backpack trip. Be sure to get the WCWC's guide. Head for the Hundred Lakes Plateau, where lakes, ponds and heather meadows enhance views of the huge Elaho Range glaciers. If the valley forest is saved, you could hike 28 km (17 mi) north to south, through the Upper Elaho.

Do your part to save B.C.'s cathedral forests—the Sistine Chapels of the Northwest. Join the voices who are speaking for the trees. Urge the provincial government to save these living monuments.

(6) Some routes are so overgrown most people would recoil in dismay. The Fool's Gold Route in Pinecone-Burke Provincial Park is a prime example. It's accessed north of Coquitlam from Widgeon Creek valley (Trip 40), or east of Squamish via the Mamquam Valley road. The trail through Boise Creek valley to the Cedar Spirit Grove was forged

by the WCWC, who sought provincial park status to protect the area. Only half of the primitive route is cleared. The rest you have to bushwack, following blazes through dense, fiendish brush. If you think misery is too much to pay for a wild wilderness experience, wait until BC Parks or volunteers clear the route. If you're up for a struggle of mythic proportions, purchase WCWC's *Boise Valley Road Access and Recreation Guide.*

Some Coast Mountain trails are just roots.

Challenging Trails

The Coast Mountains will test the mettle of most hikers. It's a more challenging range than others in North America.

The ascents are often excruciatingly steep, rising directly from the sea. Many trails (or the roads that now serve as trails) were hastily constructed by loggers, trappers and miners intent on getting rich, not on providing recreation opportunities. Others were boot-built by climbers unconcerned about who might follow. As a result, the tread is often poorly routed, with insufficient switchbacks. No thought was given to developing a trail network. Trail maintenance is minimal or nonexistent, largely left up to volunteers. Trail construction is a seldom-realized fantasy. A few places, like Garibaldi Park, have remarkably well-groomed trails, but these are rare exceptions.

If your point of reference is the Canadian Rockies, steel yourself for a shock. Here, where the forest and understory are far more luxuriant and the rainfall much heavier, you'll constantly be skirmishing with brush, deadfall, roots and mud. Be prepared to follow metal blazes and ribbon flagging for long distances where the trail is faint or fictional. Even Washington's North Cascades, climactically and geographically similar to the Coast Mountains, allow easier hiking because of superior trail construction, maintenance and marking.

To enjoy hiking the Coast Mountains, physical fitness and mental toughness are requirements. Think of it as your own, private Outward Bound experience.

Physical Capability

Until you gain experience judging your physical capability and that of your companions, these guidelines might be helpful. Anything longer than an 11-km (7-mi) round-trip dayhike can be very taxing for someone who doesn't hike regularly. A 425-m (1400-ft) elevation gain in that distance is challenging but possible for anyone in average physical condition. Very fit hikers are comfortable hiking 18 km (11 mi) or more and gaining 950-plus meters (3100-plus feet) in a single day. Backpacking 18 km (11 mi) in two days is a reasonable goal for most beginners. Hikers who backpack a couple times a season can enjoyably manage 27 km (17 mi) in two days. Avid backpackers should find 38 km (24 mi) in two days no problem. Remember it's always safer to underestimate your limits.

Crowded Trails

The southern Coast Mountains begin in Vancouver's backyard. Many trails are within easy striking distance of this metropolis, as well as Whistler, the resort capital of B.C. That makes solitude difficult to find.

To avoid the throngs, you have several choices: go midweek, hike farther into the mountains than most people do, or set off cross-country. For example, backpack to a place like Garibaldi Lake, then explore ridges and mountains distant from the hive of activity. Or choose a terrifically steep trail like the ones up Deeks Peak (Trip 24), or Coliseum Mountain (Trip 34). We usually prefer to share Premier trails with other hikers than trudge alone and disgruntled through uninspiring and cantankerous terrain.

Don't let the crowds inhibit your enjoyment. Be glad they're out there. People who get close to nature develop reverence—an attitude that could help solve a lot of the world's problems. And the more hikers, the more of us who'll be working together to protect wild lands from development and resource extraction.

Looking toward Fissile Peak from Oboe Summit (Trip 2)

Maps, Elevations, Distances

Various information sources such as maps, books, and brochures often state different elevation and distance figures for the same hike. But the discrepancies are usually small. And most hikers don't care whether an ascent is 914 m (2997 ft) or 920 m (3018 ft), or a trail is 8.7 km (5.4 mi) or 9 km (5.6 mi). Still, we made a supreme effort to give accurate figures. Only fast hikers, however, will agree with most of the point-to-point hiking times in the *On Foot* descriptions; if you're a moderate or slow hiker, extend the estimates according to your pace.

We used the elevation figures on the topographic maps printed by the Department of Energy, Mines and Resources. If the elevation of a lake or peak wasn't printed on the map, we used the contour intervals to calculate a close estimate.

In the trip information boxes, you'll often see ITM maps listed. They're published by International Travel Maps (World Wide Books and Maps) in Vancouver. If there's an ITM map for the area you're hiking, it will be more useful than the government map(s) because it indicates the trails. The trails, however, are not always accurately placed, so keep in mind: the map is not the territory. Even if you hike only a few times a season, get the 1:50 000 maps *Vancouver's Northshore* and *Whistler and Region*, and the 1:100 000 *Garibaldi Region*. The *Lower Mainland Road Map* (1:250 000) will help you identify distant peaks.

Using the 1:50 000 government topographic maps can be frustrating because they don't indicate most trails. They're really only helpful for bushwhacking and identifying peaks. They're also expensive. You can buy them at outdoor stores and at the Geological Survey of Canada: 101-605 Robson Street, Vancouver, BC V6B 5J3. Their phone number is (604) 666-0529.

Request the provincial park brochures from the district offices. The contact numbers are listed under *Information Sources* at the back of this book. Or pick up the brochures from a tourist Infocentre or park kiosk. The maps in these brochures are useful but very sketchy, giving only a general sense of direction, distance and elevation.

Wilderness Ethics

We hope you're already conscientious about respecting nature and other people. If not, don't be a bozo, keep reading.

Let wildflowers live. They blossom for only a few fleeting weeks. Uprooting them doesn't enhance your enjoyment, and it prevents others from seeing them at all. We've heard parents urge a string of children to pick as many different-colored flowers as they could find. It's a mistake to teach kids to entertain themselves by killing nature.

Stay on the trail. Shortcutting causes erosion. You probably won't save time anyway, unless you're incredibly strong.

Roam meadows with your eyes, not your boots. Again, stay on the trail. If it's braided, stick to the main path. When you're compelled to take a photo among the wildflowers, try to walk on rocks.

Leave the land unscarred. Avoid building fires. If you must, use an existing fire ring and keep the fire small. If there are no rings, build your fire on dirt or gravel. Never scorch meadows. Over time, tents can also leave scars. Pitch yours on an existing tent site whenever possible. If none is available, choose a patch of dirt, gravel, or pine needles. Never pitch your tent on grass, no matter how appealing it looks. If you do, and others follow, the grass will soon be gone.

Stein Wilderness forest fire caused by a careless camper

Be quiet at backcountry campsites. Most of us are out there to enjoy tranquility. If you want to party, go to a bar.

Pack out everything you bring. Never leave a scrap of trash any-where. This includes toilet paper, nut shells, even cigarette butts. People who drop butts in the wilderness are buttheads. They're buttheads in the city too, but it's worse in the wilds. Banana and orange peels are also trash. They take years to decompose, and wild animals won't eat them. If you bring fruit on your hike, you're responsible for the peels. And don't just pack out *your* trash. Leave nothing behind, whether you brought it or not. Clean up after others. Don't be hesitant or oblivious. Be proud. We always keep a small plastic bag handy, which makes pick-ing up trash a habit instead of a pain. It's infuriating and disgusting to see what people toss on the trail. Often the tossing is mindless, but sometimes it's intentional. Anyone who leaves a pile of toilet paper and unburied feces should have their nose rubbed in it.

Keep streams and lakes pristine. When brushing your teeth or washing yourself or your dishes with soap, do it well away from water sources, even if you use biodegradable soap. Carry water far enough so the waste water will percolate through soil and break down without directly polluting the wilderness water.

Respect the reverie of other hikers. On busy Coast Mountain trails, don't feel it's necessary to communicate with everyone you pass. Most of us are seeking solitude, not a social scene. A simple greeting is sufficient to convey good will. Obviously, only you can judge what's appropriate at the time. But it's usually presumptuous and annoying to blurt out advice without being asked. "Boy, have you got a long way to go." "The views are much better up there." "Be careful, it gets rougher." If anyone wants to know, they'll ask. Some people are sly. They start by asking where you're going, so they can tell you all about it. Offer unsolicited information only to warn other hikers about conditions ahead that could seriously affect their trip.

Volunteer Trail Maintenance

In the Coast Mountains, where vast expanses of wild land are trailless (though not always roadless), it's often mountaineers, venturing into untracked valleys and up raw mountainsides, who initiate the trail-building process today. Hikers almost always follow someone else's bootprints. Before climbers, true-grit trappers and miners cleared the way for us.

Until BC Parks or the Ministry of Forests can fund more trail crews, grassroots efforts are needed to maintain and increase our trail network. Heavy rainfall and a temperate climate enable brush to grow profusely in the Coast Mountains, swallowing some trails in a single summer. Dense forests mean lots of deadfall. Extremely steep grades allow serious erosion. Help protect our trails. Join a hiking or climbing club. Spend a weekend with a volunteer trail-crew constructing, marking or clearing a trail.

Contact the Federation of Mountain Clubs of British Columbia to get a list of hiking and climbing clubs. Ask them which ones will be doing trail maintenance. The B.C. Mountaineering Club and the North Shore Hikers usually have work projects each summer. You can also contribute to the route-building efforts of the Western Canada Wilderness Committee. Their volunteers survey and construct routes in an effort to save threatened wilderness from logging. They also maintain existing trails. Contact numbers for all these groups are in *Information Sources* at the back of the book.

Deadfall is a common obstacle in the Coast Mountains.

Coast Mountain Climate

The volatile Coast Mountain climate will have you building shrines to placate the weather gods. Storms roll in off the Pacific Ocean, unleashing most of the precipitation on the west side and leaving the east side thirsty. On the west side, conditions can vary radically from day to day. Visibility and temperature can change in a few minutes when clouds move in. Even during summer, it seems to rain half the time. Many of the rain-free days are cloudy. So don't waste clear days on less scenic hikes. When you wake up to a blue sky, head for a Premier trail and zoom up to a grand vista.

In the rainshadow, on the drier, east side of the range, it's often possible to hike under a clear sky while it's raining near the coast. But there are fewer trails there, reaching the trailheads is often difficult, and the mountains are less interesting. We recommend the Stein River Canyon (Trip 41) and the Brigade Bluffs (Trip 57).

Summer daytime maximum temperatures average 24°C (75°F) on the west, 29°C (85°F) on the east. The mercury can soar as high 33°C (92°F) on the west, higher on the east. To avoid the worst heat on the hottest days, hike early or late in the day, or plan to be at higher elevations or under dense forest cover in midday. The sun's power on the west side is often tempered by cloudy skies and abundant shade. Stay away from the east side during summer—it's a furnace.

Enough snow usually melts from high-elevation trails (above 1550 m / 5085 ft) by mid-July to allow hiking. Just one week of clear, sunny weather can greatly increase trail accessibility. Don't count on more than 2 ½ months of high-country hiking.

The large glaciers in the Coast Mountains testify to the area's abundant snowfall and short summers. Snowstorms can hit high elevations the first week of September. An early wave of cold and snow, however, is often followed by warm days into late September. Fall colours usually reach full intensity by late September. Rain or snow predominates by mid-October.

The large glaciers in the Coast Mountains testify to the area's abundant snowfall and short summers.

Scourge of the Coast Mountains

You'll be tired, sweaty, thirsty. You'll stop for a rest. Within seconds, they'll be all over you: fingernail-sized, crunchy-to-the-touch black flies. A dozen or more will assault your legs, attack your arms, land on your neck, strafe your ears, crawl up your nose. And if you don't swat them, you'll feel the sharp, sudden prick of their vicious bite. Because they're sluggish, you'll easily kill many. Whap. Whap. Whap. But they're impossible to vanquish. They just keep coming, wave after endless wave. So you gulp a few sips of water and move on. Perpetual motion is your best defense. But there are a few other tactics you'll find helpful.

Black flies, as well as the larger deerflies and horseflies, usually appear in the Coast Mountains by mid-July. If the weather's been hot, they'll be a nuisance earlier. Along the Coast (Sechelt Peninsula) deerflies and gnats will be pestiferous by June. The blitz will continue until the weather cools, probably in September. Mosquitoes are bothersome too, of course, but no more so here than in most mountain ranges. It's the black flies that will torment you.

In midsummer, when the flies are worst, begin long hikes at sunrise. Flies are aroused as the temperature rises. When the sun's heat penetrates the forest—about 9 A.M.—it's as if the flies hear their starting gun. Cooler temperatures subdue them, so consider starting backpack trips or very short dayhikes after 4 P.M.

Citronella bug repellent or eucalyptus oil might deter flies from biting you, but won't actually disperse them. They'll still swarm. Repellents containing DEET might keep them away, but you have to be desperate to rub anything that poisonous on your skin. A loose, lightweight, tightly-knit, long-sleeve shirt is preferable. Check out bug-net garments. Head covers are especially helpful when you sit for a break.

Bandanas are effective anti-fly weapons. While hiking, you can wave one briskly around your legs, over your shoulders, and around your head. Bring an extra bandana to tuck under your hat so it will drape, Lawrence of Arabia style, over your ears, temples, cheeks and neck, keeping flies away from those otherwise exposed areas.

A small, folding fan is also worth a try. You can use it to whisk away flies and cool yourself at the same time. We've even seen resourceful people waving hemlock or pine boughs as they walk. This works almost as well as a fan, and has the added benefit of providing comic relief for other hikers.

Flies decrease at higher elevations. And a stiff breeze keeps them grounded, just like mosquitoes. So you can look forward to relief at most passes. But getting there requires great mental control if the flies are bad below. Try not to focus your thoughts on them. Stay calm. Don't let them keep you from stopping to drink or rest.

Some hikers adopt a zen attitude. Refusing to be enraged by the abhorrently slow, stupid pests, they simply observe or ignore them. It's a wise approach. All of us should at least appreciate that flies in the Coast Mountains aren't speedy and clever. That would be a truly diabolical torture.

Battling Brush

Brush is a defining characteristic of Coast Mountain valleys and alpine slopes. The term "brush" refers to all the shrubs, bushes, sedges, and grasses that grow rapidly and profusely in this temperate range. "Brush" is also a verb that means to cut and clear. Some trails become choked with vegetation unless they're brushed annually by a work crew. Stinging nettles and devil's club are downright vicious.

To combat brush on trails that haven't been cleared, wear long pants. It's a good solution on cool days, but too hot during warm weather. Tall gaiters are helpful then, though they leave your knees and thighs exposed. Occasionally, we slow down and use both hands to hold large bandanas in front of our legs as deflectors. It helps. Bandanas weigh almost nothing, dry quickly, and have a dozen other uses.

Hantavirus

Hantavirus pulmonary syndrome is related to the 1994 Ebola virus that wiped out more than 200 people in Zaire. Hanta killed 17 in the Four Corners area of the southwest U.S. in 1993, and more recently one person who had just returned from hiking in the Washington Cascades. In B.C., 6 people contracted hantavirus from 1994 through 1996. Four of them died.

Your chances of contracting hanta are infinitesimally small, but possibly increasing. Hikers and campers are at risk because the virus is carried by rodents, especially deer mice. It's usually transmitted to people by airborne fecal matter. A microsecond of breathing infected air could do it—for example, while stepping into a hut or cabin and kicking up a little dust. If you enter one, walk lightly and slowly. Look for rodent droppings. If you see any, leave immediately. Hiking a dusty trail has not been identified as a risk factor for hanta.

Hanta-carrying rodents have been found throughout North

America. The U.S. Centers for Disease Control and Prevention say infected rodents are in at least 20 U.S. national parks and could be in all of them. According to the B.C. Centre for Disease Control, it's possible to contract hanta anywhere in the province.

Warning signs in Washington's North Cascades, first called our attention to the disease. Later, while camping in our van, we were alarmed by rodents scurrying inside the vehicle at night. The amount of feces they leave behind is surprising. We followed the recommended cleaning procedures: wear a face mask and rubber gloves; don't raise dust by vacuuming, sweeping or dry mopping; wipe clean with a bleach-dampened cloth.

People display symptoms within 45 days of exposure to the virus. The initial fever, coughing, headache, and muscle pain resemble the flu. Nausea follows. While victims vomit, internal bleeding begins. Fluid seeps into their lungs and suffocates them.

No antiviral drug cures hanta. Of those who contract the disease, 51% die. But early diagnosis and prompt supportive respiratory care can increase chances of recovery. The best hanta protection is to avoid rodent feces like the plague.

Cougars

You'll probably never see a cougar in the Coast Mountains. But they're here, and they can be dangerous, so you should know a bit about them.

Elsewhere referred to as a puma, mountain lion, or panther, the cougar is an enormous, graceful cat. An adult male can reach the size of a big human: 80 kilos (175 pounds), and 2.4 meters (8 feet) long, including a 1-meter (3-foot) tail. In the Pacific Northwest, they tend to be a tawny grey.

Nocturnal, secretive, solitary creatures, cougars come together only to mate. Each cat establishes a territory of 200 to 280 square kilometers (125 to 175 square miles). They favor dense forest that provides cover while hunting. They also hide among rock outcroppings and in steep canyons.

Habitat loss and aggressive predator-control programs have severely limited the range of this mysterious animal that once thrived across North America. Still, cougars are not considered endangered or threatened. Cougar encounters continue to occur near North Vancouver neighbourhoods.

Cougars are carnivores. They eat everything from mice to elk, but prefer deer. They occasionally stalk people, but rarely attack them. In folklore, cougars are called ghost cats or ghost walkers, and for good reason. They're very shy and typically avoid human contact.

Cougar sightings and encounters are increasing, but it's uncertain whether that's due to a larger cougar population or the growing number of people visiting the wilderness. If you're lucky enough to see a cougar, treasure the experience. Just remember they're unpredictable. Follow these suggestions:

Never hike alone in areas of known cougar sightings. Keep children close to you; pick them up if you see fresh cougar scat or tracks. Never approach a cougar, especially a feeding one. Never flee from a cougar, or even turn your back on it. Sudden movement might trigger an instinctive attack. Avert your gaze and speak to it in a calm, soothing voice. Hold your ground or back away slowly. Always give the animal a way out. If a cougar approaches, spread your arms, open your jacket, do anything you can to enlarge your image. If it acts aggressively, wave your arms, shout, throw rocks or sticks. If attacked, fight back. Don't play dead.

Bears

Bears are not a problem in the Coast Mountains, but oblivious hikers are. Too many people are unaware that these mountains support a healthy population of bears. Unprepared for a bear encounter, and ignorant of how to prevent one, they make bears a more serious threat—to themselves and everyone else.

Backpackers who don't properly hang their food at night are inviting bears into their campsite, greatly increasing the chance of a dangerous encounter. And bears are smart. They quickly learn to associate a particular place, or people in general, with an easy meal. They become habituated and lose their fear of man. A habituated bear is a menace to any hiker within its range.

Black bears are by far the most common species in the southern Coast Mountains. Grizzly bears are also here, but it's unlikely you'll encounter one. There's a better chance you'll see a black bear.

The two species can be difficult for an inexperienced observer to tell apart. Both range in colour from nearly white to cinnamon to black. Full-grown grizzlies are much bigger, but a young grizzly can resemble an adult black bear, so size is not a good indicator. The most obvious differences are that grizzlies have a dished face; big, muscular shoulder humps; and long, curved front claws. Blacks have a straight face; no hump; and shorter, less visible front claws. Grizzlies are potentially more dangerous than black bears, although a black bear sow with cubs can be just as aggressive. Be wary of all bears.

Any bear might attack when surprised. If you're hiking, and forest or brush limits your visibility, you can prevent surprising a bear by making noise. Bears hear about as well as humans and are generally as anxious to avoid an encounter as you are. If you warn them of your presence before they see you, they'll usually clear out. So when you fear a bear encounter, talk to your companions, yodel, sing, make up nonsense words, practice a foreign language. Do it loudly. Shout "Bears beware! We're comin' through!" Don't be embarrassed. Be safe. The sound we've found easiest to project and sustain frequently is the two vowel combination "AY...OH!" Be especially loud near streams so your voice carries over the competing noise. Sound off more frequently when hiking into the wind. That's when bears are least able to hear or smell you coming.

Bears' strongest sense is smell. So never cook in your tent; the fabric might retain odour. Cook as far as possible from where you'll be sleeping. Afterward, hang your remaining food, cooking gear, and anything else that smells (lotion, sunscreen, bug repellent, lip balm, toothpaste, garbage) in a tree, out of reach of bears and other critters. Bring a

If you see a grizzly bear this close, hope you're in your car.

sturdy plastic bag or extra stuff-sack to hang your food in, instead of getting your sleeping-bag stuff-sack smelly. Hoist it at least 5 meters (15 feet) off the ground and 1.5 meters (5 feet) from the tree trunk or other branches, which requires about 12 meters (40 feet) of light nylon cord. Clip the sack to the cord with an ultralight carabiner.

If you see a bear, don't look it in the eyes; it might think you're challenging it. Never run. Be still. If you must move, do it in slow motion. Bears are more likely to attack if you flee, and they're fast, much faster than humans. A grizzly can outsprint a racehorse. Climbing a tree is an option. Some people have saved their lives this way, others have been caught in the process. Despite their ungainly appearance, bears are excellent climbers. To be out of reach of an adult bear, you'd have to climb at least 10 meters (33 feet), something few people are capable of. And you'd probably need to be at least two football fields from the bear to beat it up a tree.

Several bear confrontations (grizzlies as well as blacks) in other ranges have convinced us we're unlikely to provoke an attack as long as we stay calm, retreat slowly, and make soothing sounds to convey a nonthreatening presence. Playing dead is debatable. It used to be the recommended response to a charge, but now some scientists, rangers and surviving victims say it might be better to fight back. It's your call. Every encounter involves different bears and different people, and the results vary. Even bear behavior experts cannot suggest one all-purpose defense technique. Many people who've survived a mauling had a brave companion beating on the bear. But we agree with the specialists who think victims might have lived or been less brutalized if they'd been passive. Read Steve Herrero's *Bear Attacks: Their Causes and Avoidance*. Then, if you encounter a bear, you'll have a better idea what to do.

Consider bringing a spray canister of oleoresin-capsicum, as a last line of defense. Cayenne pepper, highly irritating to a bear's sensitive nose, is the active ingredient. It's been successfully used in many cases to turn back a charging bear. Without causing permanent injury, it disables the bear for about an hour—long enough to let you escape. But remember: vigilance is your best defense. Spray only if you really think your life is at risk. Before you need to, visualize yourself calmly pointing and spraying, so you'll be able to do it effectively under threat. You can buy bear spray—possibly labeled Bearguard, Counter Assault, OC-10, or Phazer—at backpacking stores.

Merrily disregarding bears is foolish and unsafe. Worrying about them is miserable and unnecessary. Everyone occasionally feels afraid when venturing deep into the mountains, but fear of bears can be restrained by knowledge and awareness. Just take the necessary precautions and don't let your guard down. Experiencing the grandeur of the Coast Mountains is certainly worth risking the remote possibility of a bear encounter.

Lightning

Many of our recommendations take you to high ridges, open meadows and mountain peaks where, during a storm, you could be exposed to lightning. Your best protection is, of course, not being there. But it's difficult to always avoid hiking in threatening weather. Even if you start under a cloudless, blue sky, you might see ominous, black thunderheads marching toward you a few hours later. Upon reaching a high, thrilling vantage, you could be forced by an approaching storm to decide if and when you should retreat to safer ground. Try to reach high passes early in the day. Rain and lightning storms tend to develop in the afternoon.

The power of nature that makes wilderness so alluring often presents threats to your safety. The following is a summary of lightning precautions recommended by experts. These are not guaranteed solutions. We offer them merely as suggestions to help you make a wiser decision on your own and reduce your chance of injury.

A direct lightning strike can kill you. It can cause brain damage, heart failure or third-degree burns. Ground current, from a nearby strike, can severely injure you, causing deep burns and tissue damage. Direct strikes are worse but far less common than ground-current contact.

To avoid a direct strike, get off exposed ridges and peaks. Even a few meters off a ridge is better than right on top. Avoid isolated, tall trees. A clump of small trees or an opening in the trees is safer.

To avoid ground current, stay off crevices, lichen patches, or wet, solid rock surfaces, and away from gullies with streams in them. Loose rock, like talus, is safer.

Crouch near a high point at least 10 meters (33 feet) higher than you. Sit in the low-risk area: near the base of the high point, at least 1.5 meters (5 feet) from cliffs or walls.

If your hair is standing on end, there's electricity in the air around you. Get outa there! That's usually down the mountain, but if there's too much open expanse to traverse, look for closer protection.

Once you chose a place to wait it out, squat with your feet close together. To prevent brain or heart damage, you must stop the charge from flowing through your whole body. It helps to keep your hands and arms away from rocks. Several books say to insulate yourself by crouching on a dry sleeping pad, but we wonder, how do you do this if it's raining and you're not in a tent or cave?

Stay at least 10 meters (33 feet) from your companions, so if one is hit, another can give cardiopulmonary resuscitation.

Deep caves offer protection, but stay out of shallow or small caves because ground current can jump across openings. Crouch away from the opening, at least 1.5 meters (5 feet) from the walls. Also avoid rock overhangs. You're safer in the low-risk area below a high point.

Hypothermia

Many deaths outdoors involve no obvious injury. "Exposure" is usually cited as the killer, but that's a misleading term. It vaguely refers to conditions that contributed to the death. The actual cause is hypothermia: excessive loss of body heat. It can happen with startling speed, in surprisingly mild weather—often between 0 and 10° C (32 and 50°F). Guard against it vigilantly.

Cool temperatures, wetness (perspiration or rain), wind, or fatigue, usually a combination, sap the body of vital warmth. Hypothermia results when heat loss continues to exceed heat gain. Initial symptoms include chills and shivering. Poor coordination, slurred speech, sluggish thinking, and memory loss are next. Intense shivering then decreases while muscular rigidity increases, accompanied by irrationality, incoherence, even hallucinations. Stupor, blue skin, slowed pulse and respiration, and unconsciousness follow. The heartbeat finally becomes erratic until the victim dies.

Avoid becoming hypothermic by wearing synthetic clothing that wicks moisture away from your skin and insulates when wet. In case of emergency, pack extra layers in a plastic bag: fleece gloves and hat, synthetic socks and underwear (top and bottom). A windproof, waterproof shell (jacket) and pants are mandatory. So are a lighter and fire starters. Food fuels your internal fire, so bring several energy bars for emergencies only. On dayhikes, also carry a heat reflecting "space" bag, or at least a couple big garbage bags, in case you're forced to bivouac.

If you can't stay warm and dry, you must escape the wind and rain. Turn back. Keep moving. Eat snacks. Seek shelter. Do it while you're still mentally and physically capable. Watch others in your party for signs of hypothermia. Victims might resist help at first. Trust the symptoms, not the person. Be insistent. Act immediately.

Create the best possible shelter for the victim. Take off his wet clothes and replace them with dry ones. Insulate him from the ground. Provide warmth. A prewarmed sleeping bag inside a tent is ideal. If necessary, add more warmth by taking off your clothes and crawling into the bag with the victim. Build a fire. Keep the victim conscious. Feed him sweets. Carbohydrates quickly convert to heat and energy. In advanced cases, victims should not drink hot liquids.

Atop Flute Summit (Trip 2), high above Cheakamus Lake

DAYHIKES

Trip 1
Brandywine Meadows

Location	Whistler
Round trip	13.6 km (8.4 mi)
Elevation gain	600 m (1970 ft)
Time required	3 to 4 hours
Available	mid-July through October
Maps	ITM Whistler & Region; Brandywine 92 J/3

OPINION

The scenery is 100 proof, yet it's the most easily accessible alpine destination in this book. The intoxicants: a gurgling stream meandering through a lengthy meadow beneath towering cliffs, and, if you hit it right, a lollapalooza wildflower show. Easy-to-scramble talus slopes at the valley headwall tempt you to get even higher.

When you've maxed-out on North Shore sameness, make this your first summer blitz deeper into the mountains. In 1¼ hours, fit hikers will bound into the expansive alpine bowl containing Brandywine Meadows. There, you can wander, rock romp, or get tranquilized by the beauty. It's possible to find solitude here, regardless of how many others show up.

To see the meadow blush in multiple shades of wine and champagne, wait until early August. But that's also when flies and mosquitoes are likely to exasperate you. Escape the buggers by bolting up the headwall or the western ridge.

FACT

By Car

From Vancouver, drive Highway 99 north to Squamish. From the first traffic light in Squamish, by McDonald's, continue 41.5 km (25.7 mi) north to Brandywine Falls Provincial Park. From the park entrance, drive another 2.7 km (1.7 mi) north, then turn left (west) onto the signed Brandywine Forest Service Road.

From Village Gate Blvd. in Whistler, at the large, brown sign WELCOME TO WHISTLER, drive 14.8 km (9.2 mi) south, then turn right

Looking southeast over Brandywine Meadows in early July

(west) onto the signed Brandywine Forest Service Road.

At the start of the FS Road, set your trip odometer to 0. At 1.3 km (0.8 mi) ignore the looping side roads; stay straight on the main road. At 3.6 km (2.2 mi) proceed through what should be an open gate. If it's locked, park here and walk up the road. Continue straight at 3.9 km (2.4 mi). If you're afraid you'll trash your car if you keep driving, park on the left at 4.4 km (2.7 mi). About 100 meters farther, stay straight, ignoring a hard right fork. After a deep ditch at 4.7 km (2.9 mi), pass a sign guiding you straight ahead. At 5.9 km (3.7 mi) park in the pullout on the left. The elevation here is 850 m (2786 ft). Low-clearance, 4WD vehicles can make it this far. So can many cars. Just beyond, a pipe in a deep ditch will deter all but the studliest 4WDs. There's no reason to drive farther anyway; the trail is a mere 15-minute walk up the road. Besides, on foot you can thoroughly enjoy the view of Mount Fee, straight ahead.

On Foot

Walk up the road, covering 0.8 km (0.5 mi) and gaining 100 m (330 ft) in about 15 minutes. The slopes are clearcut. Pass through a band of trees, then another clearcut. At the second band of trees, reach a healthy stream roaring down the mountainside. It's bridged by logs. The dirt road continues northwest, but you shouldn't. Immediately before the stream, look to your right for the trail heading north. It's signed

BRANDYWINE MEADOWS TRAIL, 6 KM, ELEV GAIN 500 M. The elevation here is 950 m (3116 ft).

Ascend steeply northeast through big timber, within earshot of the stream. The understory is lush. The trail stays in the trees but soon skirts the edge of a clearcut. Boardwalks and ladders assist you through bogs and over awkward areas. The creek is now visible. About 1 hour of hard hiking will grant you the upper valley, near 1300 m (4264 ft). That's a gain of 350 m (1148 ft) from where the trail departed the road. The forest opens up now and the ascent eases for about 10 minutes as the trail heads northwest.

Climb moderately for about 20 minutes before the trail finally levels out in the heather of Brandywine Meadows, at 1450 m (4756 ft). You've hiked 6.8 km (4.2 mi) to this point. Huge boulders invite you to sprawl and savour the view of Brandywine Creek and the surrounding valley. Allow at least 1 hour to descend from the meadow to the road.

On the east side of the creek, a path continues northwest about 1 km (0.6 mi) through the meadow to the headwall, where talus slopes and cliffs encircle you. Scrambling part way up the headwall presents no serious difficulties. Pick your own route. Staying left (initially angling northwest) is easiest. It's another 730 m (2400 ft) to the top of 2230-m (7314-ft) Brandywine Mountain.

Trip 2
Musical Bumps

Location	Whistler, Garibaldi Provincial Park
Round trip	19 km (11.8 mi) to Singing Pass
Shuttle trip	22 km (13.6 mi) out Fitzsimmons
Elevation gain	727 m (2385 ft) for Singing Pass; 575 m (1885 ft) one way; both gains include the 345-m (1135-ft) ascent of Whistler Mtn.
Time Required	7 to 8 hours for either option
Available	late July through early October
Maps	ITM Whistler and Region; Whistler Hiking brochure; Whistler 92 J/2

OPINION

It really hits people up here. They're smiling. Giddy. Carefree. Blissed out. 65-year olds romping around like kids. Children staring, enraptured, like wise sages. It's as if they're all on magic mushrooms. And if you're with them, you'll be feeling euphoric too. That's the power of the supernatural mountain scenery on this sustained, high-altitude ridgewalk.

The ski-area gondola whisks you above treeline—a 1136-m (3725-ft) ascent that would normally take hardened hikers three sweat-drenched hours. A spurt of energy then propels you to the ridgecrest, where the 360° peak-and-glacier panorama will consume you. Bring at least one full roll of film. You'll be snapping photos furiously. The Cheakamus Glacier flooding off Castle Towers Mountain and Mt. Davidson is just one of the heart-stopping sights. Another is immense, intense turquoise Cheakamus Lake, far below. Keep walking (floating is what it feels like in this airy environment) southeast, and the rock-lined path leads you to vast alpine meadows like the ones that inspired Maria in *The Sound of Music*. Maybe that's the source of the fanciful names: Piccolo, Flute and Oboe Summits (nicknamed the Musical Bumps), and Singing Pass.

This combination of effortless access and surpassing beauty ensures you won't be alone. Coming mid-week helps, but not as much as it does on more remote trails; tourists flock to Whistler all summer. Don't worry about it. What would be a bothersome crowd elsewhere is

Oboe Summit wildflower gardens

tolerable here, even enjoyable. Everyone's ecstatic. Tripping out, just like you. Besides, they tend to disperse past Harmony Meadows.

Of course, if the weather gets nasty, this could quickly turn into a bad trip. You'll be totally exposed to whatever the sky throws at you. Wind. Rain. Hail. Lightning. Pack all the gear you think you won't need. See our *Preparation* section. And try to save this hike for a gorgeous day when the only protection necessary is sunblock, and when you won't be sorry you spent all that money on the gondola.

Although it means walking the service road, first go to the summit of Whistler Mountain for a sensational view of nearby Brandywine Mountain, the glacier-globbed Tantalus Range, and the distant, sprawling Pemberton Icefield.

On the way back from Whistler Mountain, proceed down the Burnt Stew trail described below. Although most people reach the Musical Bumps via Harmony Lakes, our recommended higher route lets you experience a wilder side of Whistler but lengthens the time to Singing Pass by no more than an hour.

Ideally, make this a one-way shuttle trip over the Musical Bumps to Singing Pass, then out Fitzsimmons Creek valley (see Trip 12). In mid-summer, you'll have a luxurious 10 hours of daylight to pull it off. If you motor, you can even squeak in a side trip to Russet Lake. Most people turn around on or before Flute Summit. But farther, on the east slope of Oboe Summit, the meadows are lusher and the lupine more prolific.

To give yourself maximum time on high, be at the gondola before they fire it up—probably 10 A.M. Check the hours of operation by calling 604-932-3434, or 664-5614 toll-free from Vancouver. Moderate-paced hikers should be able to reach Flute Summit and return to the gondola in time to catch the last ride down—probably 5 P.M. Even swift hikers would be pressed to reach Oboe Summit, glimpse Singing Pass, and be back to the gondola before it stops running.

FACT

By Car

In Whistler, turn east off Highway 99, onto Village Gate Blvd. There's a traffic light here, and a large brown sign WELCOME TO WHISTLER. Continue straight through the next light at Whistler Way. Reach a T-intersection in 0.4 km (0.25 mi) and go left on Blackcomb Way. Then immediately turn right into the long dirt parking lot. Park as close as you can to the far (southwest) end. The gondola is a few minutes from there, across Blackcomb Way. Nearby is the dirt road that accesses the Fitzsimmons Creek trailhead you'd end at if you do a shuttle-trip. Before hiking the Musical Bumps one-way, read Trip 12.

On Foot

Carry all the water you'll need. The entire ridge is dry.

The gondola unloads at Roundhouse Lookout. Elevation: 1837 m (6025 ft). Beyond, the trail junctions are clearly signed. Walk straight from the gondola to a signpost.

Hike the Harmony Lakes trail only if you want to avoid the 345-m (1135-ft) ascent to Whistler Mountain. For Harmony, go straight toward the green chairlift, then left at its top and down into the bowl. In 3.9 km (2.4 mi) the Harmony Lakes trail is joined by the Burnt Stew trail, which is what you'll descend if you follow our recommendation and first ascend Whistler Mountain. It's 4.5 km (2.8 mi) to the Burnt Stew / Harmony junction if you go over Whistler Mountain. The added distance and elevation-gain will increase your hiking time to Singing Pass by one hour, possibly less.

If you choose to start left (southeast) on the Harmony Lakes trail, take either branch at the upcoming junction. The left fork loses about 50 m (165 ft), which you'll have to regain. Either way, you'll ascend gently around the east shoulder of Whistler Mountain before descending to the junction with the Burnt Stew trail. From there, proceed southeast toward the Musical Bumps.

If you follow our recommendation and first ascend Whistler Mountain, walk straight from Roundhouse Lookout toward the Ridge Lookout. Ignore the trail to Whistler Glacier. Looking south from Round-house, you can see Little Whistler Peak above the top of the Harmony Express chairlift; that's where you're headed. Walk the service road, ascending steeply. Below to your left are the Harmony Lakes. The Spearhead Range is east across the Fitzsimmons Creek valley.

Reach 2115-m (6937-ft) Little Whistler Peak 1.9 km (1.2 mi) from Roundhouse. This is an especially fascinating viewpoint if you've hiked in Garibaldi Park. The Black Tusk, visible southwest, is a striking landmark. Below and east of the Tusk is Helm Lake. Panorama Ridge (Trip 27) rises southeast of it.

Proceed west on the gravel service road. Pass the top station chair-lift. About 15-20 minutes from Little Whistler Peak, reach 2187-m (7173-ft) Whistler Mountain. Turn around and walk back on the service road. Before you pass the top station chairlift again, turn right (east) and descend the Burnt Stew ski trail into a gully. The upper end of the gully can be snow-covered through August, but the grade is gentle, and you can take giant, sliding steps. Initially there might be no sign or marked route, but where the ground is bare you'll find a meter-wide path lined with stones. That's the way to the Musical Bumps. Gradually curve southeast, descending to a signed trail.

At the sign for the Crescendo ski run, curve left around the rock clump. The trail to the Musical Bumps is 0.5 km (0.3 mi) farther. In the meadowy pass below you is Burnt Stew Lake (a pond) near 1815 m (5950 ft). The Harmony Lakes trail is northeast. Piccolo Summit is above to your right (south) as you descend east. Soon reach a signed junction with the Harmony Lakes trail. Turn right and proceed south-east to the Musical Bumps. Singing Pass is 5.6 km (3.5 mi) farther.

The trail ascends the east slope of Piccolo, but doesn't go over the top. After a minor descent to a pass, enter Garibaldi Park and ascend to 1982-m (6500-ft) Flute Summit. Visible south, 1160 m (3805 ft) below, is Cheakamus Lake (Trip 51). The Castle Towers Mountains and Cheaka-mus Glacier on Mt. Davidson are across and above the lake canyon.

Descending southeast to the pass between Flute and Oboe sum-mits, the trail is marked with cairns where it becomes faint across rocky, grassy terrain. Looking east from Oboe, you can see the trail to Russet Lake switchbacking up emerald slopes. The meadows are lusher on the far (east) side of Oboe Summit, where you descend steeply through flowers to 1640-m (5380-ft) Singing Pass. At the pass, intersect the trail that ascends Fitzsimmons Creek valley (Trip 12). Left descends toward Whistler. Right ascends 2 km (1.2 mi) in 45-60 minutes to Russet Lake.

Trip 3
Blackcomb Peak

Location	Whistler, Garibaldi Provincial Park
Round trip	9 km (5.6 mi) to Overlord Lookout
Elevation gain	355 m (1164 ft)
Time required	4 hours
Available	July through early October
Maps	ITM Whistler and Region; Blackcomb Alpine Hiking brochure; Whistler 92 J/2

OPINION

Urban life has distanced most of us from the natural world. The catastrophic results are now widely recognized. But there's a humourous side to it. When you get off the Solar Coaster chairlift on Blackcomb Peak, notice people's hiking attire. Venturing into this cold, hard, unforgiving wilderness, we've seen women wearing dresses and Keds. Men in slacks and wing tips. And foreign tourists sporting top-of-the-line expedition gear, obviously for the first time, in an attempt to be fashionable. You gotta laugh.

What's great is that they're here, appreciating nature in one of her boldest incarnations. This trip, like the Musical Bumps (Trip 2), enables almost anyone to enjoy hiking. Everyone comes away more respectful of the natural world. Even hardened hikers should splurge on the chairlift ride and save themselves the 1174-m (3850-ft) climb. By taking advantage of this rare opportunity to start hiking near treeline, they can quickly outdistance the crowds and scramble higher, closer to the gods.

If you want only a short hike of 7 to 9 km (4.5 to 5.5 mi), skip Whistler Mountain (Trip 2). You'll encounter fewer people on the initial trail system at Blackcomb. There's a more satisfying loop hike here. You'll more quickly escape chairlifts and ski runs. And the scenery is equally impressive.

Within 15 minutes, the prodigious Overlord and Cheakamus glaciers will dominate your field of vision. You'll hike through fields of subalpine fir and heather, brightened by wildflowers. If you lack time or energy to visit both, the frolicking creek at Decker tarn is a more appealing lunch spot than Blackcomb Lake.

Overlord Glacier from Blackcomb Peak

Established trail ends at Decker tarn, but that's where the adventure begins for experienced scramblers. It's possible to continue ascending alpine slopes to 2134 m (7000 ft). Climbing a mere 75 m (246 ft) above the tarn provides a more complete view of Russet Lake and the Overlord Glacier cirque. But if you want to explore more of the Spearhead Range southeast of Blackcomb Peak, then make this an overnight backpack trip. After being whisked up to these intriguing heather-and-talus slopes, anyone with a head for heights and wanderlust in their heart won't want to be fettered. Trek toward Decker Mountain. Set your sights on the ridgecrest and the Decker Glacier. The sky is yours.

FACT

By Car

See Trip 2 for directions to the dirt parking lot in Whistler Village. Park as close as you can to the division between the middle and far (southwest) sections.

The chairlift typically runs 8 A.M. to 4 P.M., June 15 through August 5; 9:30 A.M. to 5 P.M., August 6 through Sept. 2. Check the hours of operation and ticket prices by calling 604-938-7747, or 604-687-1032 toll-free from Vancouver.

On Foot

To reach the chairlift, walk the Fitzsimmons trail—a paved path starting in trees between the middle and far sections of the parking lot. Follow signs for Blackcomb Peak. Watch for the posted chairlift icon. Continue straight over a bridge, pass Fitzsimmons Creek Park on your left, then cross the creek on a covered bridge. Stay right to go through the underpass. Walk up the steps and turn left at Merlin's Restaurant. Just beyond is the ticket office. Ride the Wizard Express and the Solar Coaster chairlifts up to Rendezvous Lodge at 1860 m (6102 ft).

When you get off the chairlift, follow the rock-lined path straight ahead. You'll see a sign directing you left to all hiking trails. The well-constructed path leads you on an easy tour through subalpine trees and meadows dotted with pink heather, Arctic lupine, fleabane, Sitka valerian, arnica, and Indian paintbrush. At 0.5 km (0.3 mi) reach Fitzsimmons Lookout, where you can see Whistler Mountain (southwest), and the Musical Bumps (south) with Cheakamus Glacier beyond.

At 2 km (1.2 mi) reach a signed junction. The upper Lakeside trail is left, the lower Lakeside trail right. They eventually rejoin, so you can go either way, but left ascends more and takes a bit longer to reach the premier scenery. Go right on the lower trail through subalpine fir.

In another 15 minutes, where the upper and lower Lakeside trails rejoin, stay right for the Overlord and Outback trails. Enter Garibaldi Park. About 5 minutes farther reach the next junction at 1770 m (5806 ft). The Outback trail, the easier way to Decker tarn, ascends right. Go left on the Overlord Summit trail, ascending 250 m (820 ft) to a viewpoint at 2012 m (6600 ft). It's technically not a summit, but you can clearly see the Overlord Glacier southeast, behind Fissile Peak. From there descend to Decker tarn at 1880 m (6166 ft). Giant boulders over and beside the outlet stream provide seating.

If you don't want to scramble higher, descend right on the Outback trail. Pass the junction where you ascended the Overlord Summit trail. At the next junction, where the upper and lower Lakeside trails split, you can vary your return route by going right on the upper trail. You'll climb an extra 90 m (295 ft) that way, but you'll see Blackcomb Lake before descending to the chairlift.

From Decker tarn, experienced scramblers can continue southeast up the ridge. To get to the ridge, head east at about the same elevation as the last directional sign before the trail crosses the outlet stream and loops back. On the ridge, ascend through boulders and krummholz. Within 30 minutes of leaving the tarn, reach an open area of heather and grass. If you're capable, you'll have no trouble choosing your own route steeply up the ridge to ever expanding views.

Trip 4
Wedgemount Lake

Location	Whistler, Garibaldi Provincial Park
Round trip	14 km (8.7 mi)
Elevation gain	1160 m (3805 ft)
Time required	5 to 7 hours
Available	mid-July through October
Maps	ITM Whistler and Region; BC Parks brochure; Whistler 92 J/2

OPINION

Not all violence is ugly and destructive. When nature turns violent, it can be a beautiful act of creativity resulting in a magnum opus like the glacier-gouged Wedgemount Lake cirque. Here, long ago, great masses of rock heaved so dramatically, you can still feel the impact today—with your heart. It's as moving as any trail-accessible sight in the Coast Mountains; as awesome as the scenery prevalent in the Canadian Rockies.

You might have heard rabid descriptions of the ascent to Wedgemount Lake. It is severe. But it's not insane, or dangerous. If your workouts are limited to hanging on in a moving bus, Wedgemount could be your heart-attack hill. But even occasional hikers survive it and merely wake up sore the next morning. Wedgemount requires you to climb only 300 m (1000 ft) more than the Grouse Grind (Trip 66), which many Vancouverites hike regularly. And, unlike the Grind, what you'll see on the way up Wedgemount is inspiring. Compared to Lake Lovely Water (Trip 26), a setting of comparable beauty, Wedgemount is less demanding, especially when backpacking. You'll gain 1100 m (3600 ft) in 6 km (3.7 mi). If you're tempted by cheesey television ads for exercise gizmos, figure about 4 hours one way. Shoot for 2¼ hours if you have buns of steel.

Climbing through forest, the trail sidles up to rowdy Wedgemount Creek—a welcome diversion. The grade eases at times, granting you a reprieve. Crossing a rockslide adds variety. Then Wedgemount Creek lifts its skirt, revealing a 300-m (980-ft) waterfall. This and Place Falls (Trip 63) are among the more impressive cascades in the Coast Range.

Wedgemount Lake

Even on a dayhike, bring warm clothing, so you can hang out in the lake basin a couple hours and gawk at the phenomenal surroundings. It's a waste to hike all the way up here, then have to leave in 15 minutes when you start shivering. Wedgemount can get cold, even on a nice day. Camping in the basin will ensure you have time to explore the area. Bring your tent. There's a hut near the lake, but it's a pit. Competent scramblers hungry for more height can pick any of several routes. Attain open views north by continuing 2 hours up the talused ridge on your left when facing the lake from the cirque lip.

Trekking poles will ease your ascent. This is your opportunity to discover what a difference they make. On the descent, poles will do more than protect your knees, they'll keep you from imitating that crazed bus in the movie *Speed*. Competent pole-wielding hikers can schuss down the rocks and roots in 2 hours. Anyone less agile, or empty handed, will be waddling safely like a porcupine and take at least 3 hours.

FACT

By Car

From the Whistler Village turnoff at Village Gate Blvd., near the sign WELCOME TO WHISTLER, drive north 11.8 km (7.3 mi) on Highway 99. Or, from the 3-way junction just outside Pemberton, drive southwest 20.6 km (12.8 mi) on Highway 99. From either approach, turn east at the sign (GARIBALDI) WEDGEMOUNT LAKE. Cross railroad tracks and the Green River. Hit a a T-junction in 100 meters. Go left on Wedge Creek FS Road. At 0.4 km (0.25 mi) curve right at a signed fork, then left at the next. Reach the parking lot at 1.9 km (1.2 mi). The elevation here is 760 m (2493 ft).

On Foot

The trail starts at the far corner of the parking lot. It ascends moderately through a brushy area. In 15 minutes cross large planks over plummeting Wedgemount Creek. Enter big timber. Head generally southeast. Soon, at a break in the forest, look west to glacier-topped Rainbow Mountain and north up the Green River valley. After ascending 440 m (1443 ft), the grade relaxes for 10 minutes.

The trail is rooty—typical for these mountains—but the roots are not major obstacles. With the roaring creek on your right, climb 215 m (705 ft) higher, then enjoy another reprieve. Strong hikers will be here in about 1¼ hours. Then cross the base of a boulder field. Near 1524 m (5000 ft), you can see Wedgemount Creek plunging down the cliffs of Rethel Mountain. Near 1723 m (5650 ft), cross a creeklet, just before emerging onto alpine slopes. By filling water bottles here, day-hikers can later forego the 70-m (230-ft) descent to the lake for water.

The final pitch through rocks and heather is rugged, but you'll find good footholds as the route ascends. Views west and northwest over the Coast Range are tremendous. At 1950 m (6400 ft), reach the lip of the Wedgemount Lake cirque and enter the mountain sanctum.

Wedgemount Glacier tests its toe in the turquoise lake. 2905-m (9527-ft) Wedge Mountain, the highest peak in Garibaldi Park, rises to the southeast, its snowfields extending to the Weart Glacier higher above. Mt. Weart is northeast.

The best view of the lake is from the knoll to the right (north) as you enter the basin. Look for a boot-beaten path on your right as you cross the cirque lip. It climbs 10 m (33 ft) through heather and lichen-splotched rocks. On top of the knoll, you'll be just across the lake from the spires of Rethel Mountain.

From the cirque lip, the trail leads straight to the red B.C. Mountaineering Club hut and a smaller toilet hut. There are campsites sheltered among boulders, left (north) of the hut, and more sites on rock slabs higher up the heather slopes. Beyond the hut, north and a bit east, a path wanders 10 minutes to a cascade at the edge of heather. This is where competent scramblers will likely begin ascending the northerly ridge.

Trip 5
Joffre Lakes

Location	Duffey Lake Road
Round trip	11 km (6.8 mi)
Elevation gain	370 m (1214 ft)
Time required	4 to 5 hours
Available	early July through mid-October
Map	ITM Garibaldi Region; Duffey Lake 92 J/8

OPINION

The Joffre Lakes are to the Coast Mountains what Robson Street is to shopping in Vancouver. All the treasures are grandly displayed within tempting reach: three teal lakes in an achingly perfect mountain setting that includes a daunting glacier and striking cliffs. It's enough to entice shopaholics out of the city. Which is why you'll see people on the trail who've never carried much more than a Gucci bag. Though you'll probably leave them behind at the first lake, you still won't be alone. The high price you'll pay here is having to tolerate a crowd. On weekends, expect to see three dozen cars at the trailhead. On a long weekend, expect 50 cars. The beauty and accessibility is exceptional, but not worth suffering a Robson Street mob. Try to come midweek, or after Labor Day.

The trailhead starts high, at Cayoosh Pass, so the scenery is immediately lavish. The first lake would be worth hiking hours to see, but it's so close you could push a shopping cart to it in 10 minutes. The Matier Glacier, visible beyond, doesn't just hint of what's to come, it screams. Fledgling hikers will get turned on to the sport here. Veterans will appreciate the reprieve from stiff ascents and long, unscenic approaches. Fit dayhikers can reach Upper Joffre Lake in 1½ hours.

Though the trail is easier than most in the range, the boulder field 30-45 minutes in can be challenging to kids and anyone accustomed to groomed paths.

Cold-blooded swimmers will love the plunge-hole where Joffre Creek flows into a deep, sandy bowl at the northwest end of Upper Joffre Lake, near the bridged crossing.

FACT

By Car

From the 3-way intersection at the Petro Canada station on the edge of Pemberton, drive Highway 99 northeast 30.5 km (18.9 mi) to the Joffre Lakes Recreation Area pullout. From Lillooet, at the junction of Highways 99 and 12, drive Highway 99 southwest 69 km (42.8 mi) to the pullout, at 1220 m (4002 ft).

On Foot

At the end of the dirt parking lot, walk the pleasant, gravel path through forest. Reach the north end of Lower Joffre Lake in about 5 minutes. Go right to continue to Middle and Upper Joffre lakes. Soon cross bridged Joffre Creek, then ascend gently through beautiful trees. Devil's club and ferns thrive here. You'll soon lose sight of the first lake as you climb above its west side. Ignore older, secondary trails branching right. Stay left on the main trail. Follow the orange blazes.

In about 20 minutes, descend left. Reach a boulder field and, soon after, traverse a brushy area where a stream is audible. Follow the pink flagging. Watch out for deep gaps between the boulders. Behind you (north) are Cayoosh Mountain and Mt. Marriott. After negotiating boulders for about 10 minutes, you'll be back on a rooty trail through forest. Descend 20 m (66 ft) to cross Joffre Creek.

About 1 hour after setting out, reach Middle Joffre Lake at 1540 m (5050 ft). There are good tent sites at the north end, where you arrive. No fires allowed. The trail continues on the east (left) side of the lake. At the south end, cross Joffre Creek again on two log bridges. After ascending a small rockslide, ignore a blazed path descending right, back to Middle Lake. Bear left toward Upper Lake and views of Matier Glacier.

At 5.5 km (3.4 mi), elevation 1590 m (5215 ft), about 20 minutes beyond Middle Lake, reach the north end of Upper Joffre Lake. You're entering the cirque created by 2713-m (8900-ft) Joffre Peak and glacier-draped 2774-m (9100-ft) Mt. Matier (both southeast) and Slalok Mountain (south). The trail stays above the rocky shore, soon reaching high-traffic campsites next to the bridged inlet stream.

Most hikers turn left (east) here, cross the creek, and pick up one of two faint, rough routes leading to desirable picnic spots and tent sites on a sandbar at the south end of the lake, near the booming waterfall.

The lake level determines how many tents can fit on the beach.

At the bridged inlet stream, your other choice is to stay on the west (right) side and proceed south. The trail soon dwindles to a cairned, blazed route. Cross a boulder field and ascend to a forested saddle. The route then angles southeast, crosses the stream at a higher point, and ends below the snout of the glacier.

Upper Joffre Lake and the Matier Glacier

Trip 6
Rohr Lake / Marriott Basin

Location	Duffey Lake Road
Round trip	9 km (5.6 mi) to Rohr Lake; 16 km (10 mi) to the lake in Marriott Basin
Elevation gain	430 m (1410 ft) to Rohr Lake; 370 m (1210 ft) to Marriott Basin
Time required	5 hours for Rohr, 8 for Marriott, up to several days for either
Available	mid-July through mid-October
Map	Duffey Lake 92 J/8

OPINION

Mountaineers get all the glory in outdoor-gear ads and catalogs. Yet hikers do most of the buying. Seems wrong. Until you realize that alpinists are hikers too. They just don't turn around at the end of the trail. They keep going. And often they're the pathbreakers. They crash into the bush, creating routes with their boots. The rest of us blithely follow—to Rohr Lake, for example, and into Marriott Basin.

Thanks to the B.C. Mountaineering Club, who pioneered this route so members could climb in the area, you can easily hike to Rohr Lake in 2 hours. There, if the resident bug population allows, you can sit and stare into the amethyst depths beneath a towering cliff of Mt. Rohr. Or you can scramble up the nearby kiwi-green slopes. Or venture deep into the basin, perhaps aiming for the summit of Mt. Rohr. If you start early, you can bag Rohr and return in a day. But once you see this Xanadu, you'll want to camp overnight.

Where the trail forks right to Rohr Lake, left proceeds to Marriott Basin in 1½ to 2 hours. A googolplex of options for camping and alpine exploring will inflame your mind with plans for the next visit, before this one's over. Light out for whatever ridge tugs at your imagination.

Though short, both destinations are for experienced backpackers only. The paths are rough, narrow, and sometimes steep, requiring stability and perseverance. The B.C. Mountaineers did a great job clear-

Rohr Lake and Mt. Rohr

ing the trail to Rohr Lake and Marriott Basin, but a lot of it's in a boggy drainage. The unstabilized path erodes easily. Just below Rohr Lake, is an untrammeled, pristine meadow. It looked as if we were the first ones to walk there. Nobody had gouged the tall, waving grass. Nobody had sullied the clear streams threading the natural garden. If you enter this sacred place, walk on rocks, around the edge of the meadow. Avoid impressing the soil. This will take you a few more minutes, but it will preserve the meadow. Don't even consider camping here. There are so many hikers these days, we all have to be conscious conservationists.

FACT

By Car
From the Joffre Lakes Recreation Area parking lot on Highway 99, drive northeast. Cross Cayoosh Creek in 3.3 km (2.0 mi), then slow down. Mt. Rohr is the high, gentle ridge on your left (northeast). At 3.7 km (2.25 mi), turn left (north) on deactivated Cayoosh Creek FS road. Drive in just short of 1 km (0.6 mi). Park on the left, in a pullout, before a fork. The elevation here is 1384 m (4540 ft).

On Foot
To your left (west), across the creek valley, is impressive Cayoosh Mountain. Joffre Peak is south. Walk the left (lower) fork of the old logging road north. (The upper fork ends within 10 minutes.) Across, to

the left, is an avalanche slope. In about 15 minutes, notice the waterfall on the forested slope to your right; it's pouring out of Rohr Lake. The road ends within 20 minutes. Proceed on the rough trail.

Walk through the lush berry bushes and cow parsnip that obscure the trail. A few well-placed logs help you over muddy spots. Soon pass an orange blaze on a small tree. Enter forest. After 40 minutes from your vehicle, hop across braided creeklets. Then cross a wider stream, but stay on the east side of the much bigger creek, roaring below to your left. Ascend steeply on decent trail. Having gained 140 m (460 ft) within 1 hour, reach a signed junction. Rohr is right. Aspen (Marriott) is left. Both trails are blazed.

Heading to Rohr, the trail soon grants views northwest into Marriott Basin. In 1¼ hours, at about 1600 m (5250 ft), reach the pristine meadow full of fleabane, laced with gurgling streams, ringed by sub-alpine fir and blue spruce. Preserve the meadow by tiptoeing on rocks, well back from the edge, around the south and east sides. Head northeast toward the boulder chute. Jump across the brook at the base of the chute. Look for a small cairn. Your goal is the top of the boulder chute.

Scramble through corn lilies and over boulders. Follow flagging on bushes and heather, and an occasional cairn. Reach the top of the chute at 1814 m (5950 ft), about 4.5 km (2.8 mi) from the trailhead. Total hiking time: 2 hours. A few minutes farther southeast, the lake is visible 20 m (70 ft) below. You'll find possible campsites here, above the lake, with a view northwest into Marriott Basin. Nequatque Mountain is the pyramidal peak behind the humped ridge of Mt. Marriott. Look west to Cayoosh Creek basin and 2591-m (8500-ft) Cayoosh Mountain. Beneath the high, meadowy slopes to the east, a talus bowl leads southeast to 2440-m (8000-ft) Mt. Rohr.

Back at the Rohr/Marriott junction, left on the trail signed ASPEN leads to Marriott Basin. Ascend steeply for 5 minutes, then cross the creek on a heap of deadfall. It seems you're heading northeast toward the other trail, but then the path turns generally north to ascend more gently through pocket meadows and forest. Be prepared to mush through boggy stretches. Reach the subalpine basin about 1½ to 2 hours from the junction. There's a lake at 1753 m (5750 ft.)

Trip 7
Cerise Creek

Location	Duffey Lake Road
Round trip	8.0 km (5.0 mi)
Elevation gain	305 m (1000 ft)
Time required	3 ½ hours
Available	mid-July through October
Map	Duffey Lake 92 J/8

OPINION

Standing on the moraine above Cerise Creek, you'll peer wide-eyed at the Anniversary and Matier glaciers—massive swaths of ice swooping down from the striking peaks. You might feel your heart quicken as you imagine, or perhaps see, bold mountaineers climbing into the unknown. They haven't departed the planet, but they've entered a different world. It's as awesome as watching a space shuttle launch. It even sparks the same questions, like how does it feel to leave the mundane so far behind? The vicarious experience on the moraine will satisfy most people's curiosity. Just being in this powerful place is deeply affecting.

The hike is shamefully short. So, although it's in forest the whole way, with only one viewpoint en route, nobody can complain. The trail isn't even steep, except for a short stretch at the end before bursting out of the trees at Cerise Creek hut. Just beyond, within view, is the moraine.

The hut was meticulously crafted by the family and friends of a 22-year-old climber killed in an avalanche on Mt. Logan in 1986. They considered it a memorial to the young man they loved, and a gift to all who cherish the mountains. The hut is also a solemn reminder that whatever mountaineers feel, it must be rapturous, but they risk everything for it.

Treat the hut and the builders' mementos with respect. It's not intended for commercial use. There is no specified charge for sleeping in the hut, but you should pay for firewood, which is flown in, and maintenance. Send your donation to Flavelle Memorial Hut Fund, P.O. Box 1518, Squamish, BC V0N 3G0.

Anniversary Glacier

FACT

By Car

If you're heading northeast on Highway 99 from Mt. Currie, drive 11.4 km (7.1 mi) past the Joffre Lakes Recreation Area parking lot, cross Cayoosh Creek, and slow down. At 12.5 km (7.75 mi) there's a sign CERISE CREEK MAIN, NO THRU ROAD. Turn right (southwest) here, west of the bridge over Van Horlick Creek.

If you're heading southwest on Highway 99 from Lillooet, drive 51 km (32.2 mi) past the turnoff to Seton Lake. Slow down. From Van Horlick Main, on the east side of Van Horlick Creek, continue 0.8 km (0.5 mi) and turn left (southwest) onto Cerise Creek Main.

From either approach, set your trip odometer to 0 again as you start on Cerise Creek Main. Cross Caspar Creek at 2.3 km (1.4 mi). Immediately after, ignore a right turn. Continue straight, on the higher road. At 5.7 km (3.5 mi) get a view of Mt. Matier and Joffre Peak. At 5.9 km (3.6 mi) there's a pullout before the bridge over Cerise Creek. A trail that's used mostly by skiers begins here. Hikers should proceed, either on foot or in a tough vehicle, a short distance to the higher, newer trailhead. Cross the bridge to the west side of the creek and immediately fork left (south) up the rough, spur road. Don't continue right. Go about 350 meters (6-8 minutes on foot) into the parking area at the end of the spur road. The trail starts on the far southeast corner, at 1372 m (4500 ft).

On Foot

The trail is initially flagged, but unsigned. It heads south at the edge of the slash and soon enters forest. Within 5 minutes reach a fork. Stay straight (level). Within 10 minutes, the trail is high on a slope above Cerise Creek.

Skirt a small meadow in about 20 minutes. Curve southwest and within another 5 minutes attain a view of nearby Joffre Peak and glacier. Cross a creek on logs and angle southeast. After hiking 35 minutes and gaining 85 m (280 ft), reach a signed junction. The route to the glacier is left. Go right, toward the hut, and ascend south.

Within 1 hour of the trailhead, after gaining 200 m (656 ft), angle left (southeast) across a boulder field. Look for flagging—on a bush in the middle, and on trees at the far side. Then continue steeply over embedded rocks and exposed dirt—slippery when wet. A fixed rope will assist you. The trail then resumes at a more moderate grade.

About 15-20 minutes above the boulder field, reach a small, murky pond at 1690 m (5540 ft). The glaciers on Mt. Matier and Joffre Peak (southwest) are visible here. Vantage Peak is southeast. The ridge of Mt. Chief Pascall runs off Joffre Peak on your right (northwest). A few minutes beyond the murky pond, arrive at the hut. The front porch faces the peaks and glaciers. Just ahead is a small lake. Avoid drinking the lake water, which is said to harbour giardia. Fill up at the spring, about half way around the right side of the lake, 15 meters northwest of the shore.

The optimal viewpoint is on the other side of the lake, on top of the moraine. From the hut, it's about a 10-minute hike gaining 60 m (197 ft). Follow the trail around the right side of the lake. A boot-beaten path continues upward among trees and heather. Crash through krummholz, then pick your way up the cement-like side of the moraine to look down on Anniversary Glacier.

If you're backpacking, and you prefer your tent to the hut, campsites with great views are past the southeast end of the lake.

Trip 8

Mt. Strachan ✓

Location	Cypress Provincial Park
Round trip	10 km (6.2 mi)
Elevation gain	534 m (1752 ft)
Time required	4½ to 5 hours
Available	early July through mid-November
Maps	BC Parks brochure; ITM Vancouver's Northshore; North Vancouver 92 G/6

OPINION

Mountains, like people, have personalities. Mt. Strachan, for example, has a friendly countenance that belies a mean streak. The Howe Sound Crest Trail (HSCT) breezes into magnificent cedar and hemlock forest, leading you gently around the southwest shoulder. There you must grapple with Strachan's dark side if you want to reach the top.

The rough route up the back plows through tight, gnarled krummholz, on the edge of a steep gorge, to the narrow cleft between Strachan's twin peaks. But it's a relatively short hike granting look-at-that! views: Howe Sound is west, the Lions are north, Crown Mountain is east, and beneath you on three sides of the north summit are steep, I-better-sit-down cliffs that plunge into forest. Though Hollyburn Mountain (nearby, southeast) is also a terrific viewpoint, Mt. Strachan is superior. Here nothing obstructs your view of the Lions, whereas Hollyburn's panorama is interrupted by Strachan.

The ascent route we describe is likely to hold snow until mid-July. If you're uncomfortable on steep snow, wait until mid-summer. Also, keep Strachan Meadows in mind as a possible destination for an easy, couple-hour hike. It's at the base of the ascent route. If you don't want to continue climbing, you can enjoy the meadow and (in early summer) the nearby cascades, then return the way you came.

Descending Strachan's south side presents no serious difficulties, but it's not the cake walk you might expect on slopes that in winter serve as Cypress ski runs. The steep trail requires giant lunging steps. If you're here before mid-July, expect to hike in snowmelt streaming down shallow trenches in the eroded trail. The last leg of the trip is

Mt. Strachan

through beautiful ancient forest.

Of course you could reverse the trip, but Strachan's mean streak is harder to handle on the descent. Following our recommended loop, you can enjoy getting acquainted with all sides of the mountain. Despite the ski lifts and human detritus, it's a stimulating mini-adventure, worth repeating.

FACT

By Car

Driving Highway 1 through West Vancouver, turn off at Cypress Bowl, Exit 8. Continue 16 km (10 mi) up the Cypress Parkway to the ski area. Near the end of the road, just before it curves south into a huge parking lot, on your right is a big map of the ski area. That's the trailhead, at 920 m (3018 ft).

On Foot

Starting in late spring, black bears roam Cypress Bowl, feasting on the lush grass that grows on the ski runs. If you see a sign CAUTION: BEAR IN AREA, walk slowly, be observant, and make noise. For details, read our *Bears* section. Some summers, BC Parks closes all trails in the area, except the one to Hollyburn Mountain, which heads into the trees, away from the meadows that bears frequent. If the area is closed to hikers when you arrive, obey the signs. Otherwise, you endanger yourself and the bears. A bear that attacks someone—regardless that it does so instinctively, motivated by self-preservation—will probably be destroyed.

From the north end of the parking lot, walk past the gate onto the gravel road. Head straight past the administration buildings. In 20 meters, angle left on the wide, gravel path signed YEW LAKE TRAIL and HOWE SOUND CREST TRAIL (HSCT). Stay on the HSCT until you reach Strachan Meadows in about one hour. The HSCT is well-signed through this initial confusing area of intersecting trails and roads. But here are the specifics. About 100 meters from the parking lot, the trail crosses the road. Go right, following the signed HSCT. Cross a small bridge. In a few more minutes, branch right. When you're back at the gravel road in about 75 meters, continue up left. In another 3-4 minutes, go up right onto the HSCT where a sign directs you to the Lions. Ascend moderately through pretty forest for 10 minutes. Then reach the road again where a stream passes under it. Go left. In a few minutes the gravel road narrows to a path. This is the HSCT. Continue north.

About 30 minutes from the parking lot, go left 75 meters to a viewpoint on the signed Bowen Island Lookout spur trail. Campsites in tall timber are ideal. About 20 meters farther north from this junction, the Lions are visible to the north. Cross a creek 10 minutes after the Lions Lookout, then come to a view of the ocean and Sechelt Peninsula. About 50 minutes from the parking lot, cross a stream on a wood bridge. Immediately after, when you're between two small bridges on the HSCT, turn right (east) into Strachan Meadows, at 1070 m (3510 ft).

Mt. Strachan is directly east.

The meadow is a motley mix of grass, Indian hellebore (corn lily), mud, and rocks. Work your way up the left side of the creek gorge, gaining about 35 m (115 ft), until grass and heather end and you're at a rock bluff. Look for flagging at the edge of the krummholz (short, tight, windblown trees). The flagged route ascends at a 30° angle. A fixed rope offers some security. Burrow through the trees for 15 minutes, then clamber over rock to the cleft beneath the two summits of Strachan.

The north summit offers the best view. That's your goal. Head left, following paint on rock. You'll top out at 1454 m (4769 ft). Total hiking time: about 1¾ hours. Total distance: roughly 5 km (3.1 mi). You can survey the Howe Sound Crest to the north, and its two most famous bumps—the Lions. Crown and Goat mountains are east, at the edge of Lynn Headwaters Regional Park.

After dropping back into the cleft, ascend south, dead-center up the slope of the south summit. On top, you'll be greeted by ski lifts, pylons, fences, meteorological gizmos, and garbage left by thoughtless skiers. On the rocky summit (snow-covered, if you're here before July), walk south. Watch for a cairn, and orange paint on rocks. You'll see a marker on the left at the forest edge. After 45 meters, an orange-painted rock marks where the trail shoots left in the direction of Vancouver. About 120 meters beyond the orange-painted rock, still with the chairlift in sight on your right, head left (east) into trees and slightly downhill.

About ½ hour below the south summit, reach the debris from a 1963 plane crash. Next, circle the southeast side of a pond. Soon descend more steeply, into a basin. Blazes on a giant Douglas fir help keep you on track. Then the route turns southeast. It gets very rooty. In early summer, snowmelt courses down the path, further eroding it.

Where the trail heads up to a low rock bluff in an open area, go left over the bluff to parallel the ski run; otherwise you'll end up on the ski run. On your left, pass a hanging sign DANGER STEEP CLIFFS. At a metal sign, where the trail is immediately beside the ski run, and there are logs and big roots on your right, proceed toward Hollyburn. In about 50 meters, the trail dumps you in a narrow pass between Strachan and Hollyburn. Go right, down the gully. Just south, pass a small lake in a meadow. About 5 minutes farther, blazes are frequent. The trail now meanders through beautiful forest and beside a pretty creek gorge. About 30 minutes below the Strachan/Hollyburn pass, go right at a fork. In another 10 minutes, intersect the Baden Powell Trail. Go right, cross a creek, and in about 15 minutes arrive at the trailhead.

Trip 9
Mt. Seymour ✓

Location	North Shore, Mt. Seymour Park
Round trip	9 km (5.6 mi)
Elevation gain	440 m (1443 ft)
Time required	5 hours
Available	mid-July through October
Maps	ITM Vancouver's Northshore; Coquitlam 92 G/7

OPINION

New Age thinking asserts we should expect abundance. That we shouldn't have to struggle to achieve. And there's a mountain of evidence supporting this view. It's called Mt. Seymour. Rarely, especially in this forbidding range of surly peaks, are summit panoramas so effortlessly attained.

Perched on Mt. Seymour, you can see it all: Vancouver, the Fraser Valley, the Gulf Islands, Vancouver Island, Howe Sound Crest, Crown and Coliseum mountains (west), the 900-m (2950-ft) wall of Cathedral Mountain (northwest), peaks and glaciers in Garibaldi Provincial Park (north), even Mounts Robie Reid and Judge Howay (northeast) in Golden Ears Provincial Park.

Though it begins in a paved parking lot, on the edge of the city, this hike isn't a cinch. The trail is often merely a blazed route over rock. In places, the choice of routes is confusing. If you don't know the area, watch vigilantly for the blazes and signposts that'll keep you on track. Ascending the three Pumps, as the peaks are called, be careful you don't take a quick exit down the mountain and into oblivion. And when inclement weather blows in, Seymour can be a dangerous place. Be prepared.

Why are the peaks called Pumps? On top of the first one, there used to be a stump with a protruding branch. It looked like a pump. The goof who thought this was significant further compounded the weirdness by also calling the other peaks Pumps. It caught on.

After gently ascending through subalpine forest, the trail bucks over and around rock outcroppings. If you have kids in tow, or you

Mt. Seymour

lack scrambling experience, consider stopping on Second Pump Peak. The views are superb there too.

Seymour can be doable earlier, but after a winter of heavy snowfall wait until August, when the route is more discernible and the hiking more pleasant. The east-facing gullies between Brockton Point and the Elsay Lake junction hold a lot of snow, and meltwater streams can crisscross the route through July.

It's possible to extend this trip, to Mt. Elsay. The route loses 300 m (984 ft) as it jettisons off Seymour and scampers over forested ridges. It's an ordeal—more difficult than rewarding. The summit scenery is similar to Seymour's. Yes, you you can see Elsay Lake, and you can look back at Seymour, but so what? Mt. Elsay is for hard-core hikers who want a challenge but can't or won't drive farther north in the range for an excellent adventure.

FACT

By Car

From Mount Seymour Parkway in North Vancouver, drive up Mount Seymour Road to the end. Park in the upper lot near the chairlift, at 1015 m (3329 ft).

On Foot

The main trail to Mt. Seymour is initially a gravel road. It starts at the north end of the upper parking lot, left of the chairlift. Ignore the trail veering left to Dog Mountain. Proceed straight (slightly left) for Mt. Seymour. Also ignore the road leading right toward Mystery Lake. Then pass spur trails, to First Lake and the Dinkey Peak Loop, both on your left. Where the Mt. Seymour trail takes you toward a bedrock road at the top of a rise, stay straight on the gravel road. Don't ascend the steep bedrock road to the right, or the less steep one cutting back right. In 50 meters, follow the trail down to a pond, cross a small creek, then rise steeply. The road you were on continues right.

About 35 minutes up, Second Pump Peak is visible north. Looking east, you can see Golden Ears in the distance, and Eagle Ridge in the foreground rising above the east shore of Indian Arm. Mounts Cheam, Shuksan and Baker are southeast.

After following a sign directing you right on the main trail, stay right again at the flagging, ignoring a little-used route up First Pump Peak. In early summer, snow lingers through here. Follow orange paint on rocks. Skirting First Pump on its southeast side, the main trail zigzags through trees and boulders, up and down bluffs and gullies.

At 3.0 km (1.9 mi) reach a signed junction with the Elsay Lake trail. Elevation: 1180 m (3870 ft). Hiking time to this point: about 1 hour. Go left. The trail now rises steeply. After ascending about 50 meters, pass a rock with "3.0 KM" painted on it. That was the distance to the junction. Soon, from a saddle, you can look west to forested Lynn Peak, northwest to Cathedral Mountain, and north to the glaciers of enormous Mt. Garibaldi. From the rocky saddle between First and Second pumps, the route climbs a steep gully up Second Pump Peak.

Reach the summit of Second Pump in about 2 hours total. In early summer, you might have to ascend a snow chute to get there. To continue to nearby Mt. Seymour, ease carefully down the steep northwest side of Second Pump, then turn right toward the gully below Mt. Seymour. Ascend the short, steep, rocky gully to the 1455-m (4772-ft) summit.

The forested mounds you see nearby in the north are: 1422-m (4664-ft) Mt. Elsay sneaking out from behind 1453-m (4766-ft) Runner Peak, and 1507-m (4943-ft) Mt. Bishop farther behind them. To descend Second Pump, go west off the ridge, then north following orange paint dots to a low point where there's a rock with "4 KM" painted on it.

From the gully between Second Pump Peak and Mt. Seymour, a route leads to Mt. Elsay. It starts at the low point of the notch, not straight down the steep escarpment below Second Pump. Flagged trees to the right of the gully on the side of Mt. Seymour mark the exit. The route heads northwest to outlying ridges, then northeast to reach Mt. Elsay in roughly 2½ more hours.

Trip 10
The Lions

Location	Howe Sound
Round trip	15 km (9.3 mi)
Elevation gain	1525 m (5002 ft)
Time required	7 hours
Available	July through October
Maps	ITM Vancouver's Northshore; North Vancouver 92 G/6

OPINION

They don't look like lions, but that's what these two companion peaks are called. They're a Vancouver landmark—someone's strange imagining set in stone. People who know nothing of the mountains can look up from downtown and point to the Lions.

The route is steep and begins on a road, but after 45 minutes the forest is nicely overgrown. Much of the way is through big timber. And just 2 ½ hours up is a wondrous heather-and-rock slope with a fantastic view of Howe Sound, Gambier Island, Sechelt Peninsula, Georgia Strait, Vancouver Island and, directly below, the village of Lions Bay. Continuing the ascent to the base of the Lions will grant you views eastward, but is not essential to enjoy the trip.

What's critical is that you not turn around at the first viewpoint, above Harvey Creek drainage. In just a few minutes, the scenery vastly improves on the slope described above.

If you reach the base of the Lions, you might see others scaling the West Lion. Don't be duped into following them. Try it only if you're an experienced climber. The route is dangerously exposed. People die here every year. The West Lion summit-view is little better than what you can see by safely scrambling down and across to the gap between the Lions. There you can look north along the Howe Sound Crest.

FACT

By Car

From the turnoff to Horseshoe Bay, just outside West Vancouver, drive 11.5 km (7.1 mi) north on Highway 99 to Lions Bay. Or, if you're

Lions Bay and Howe Sound

driving south on Highway 99, Lions Bay is 4.2 km (2.6 mi) past Murrin Provincial Park. From either approach, turn east onto Oceanview Road and set your trip odometer to 0.

In 200 meters, go left on Cross Creek Road, then right on Centre Road. At 0.4 km (0.25 mi) go left on Bayview Road. At 1.5 km (0.9 mi) go left on Mountain Drive. At 1.8 km (1.1 mi) go left on Sunset Drive. Park in the lot before the gate. The elevation here is 207 m (680 ft). If this parking lot is full, drive downhill 1 km (0.6 mi) to the school on Mountain Drive.

On Foot

Start on the old logging road. Ascend about 370 m (1214 ft) to a junction. Strong hikers can do it in 30 minutes, others might take an hour. Curve right on the main road. A nearby tree, slightly off the road, is blazed. Don't go left (straight) on the faint road. The steep ascent eases. Soon reach another junction. Go right (southeast), ignoring an obscure road forking left. The road then contours Harvey Mountain. After an open area where Howe Sound is visible, stay on the main road.

Come to a rocky bluff and a view south to Horseshoe Bay. Pass a small cascade where you can fill water bottles. The road narrows to trail. After contouring for 15 minutes, ascend a rocky stretch, then drop right on an obvious trail. (Don't climb left, up the rocky course.) About 1 ¼ hours up, at 740 m (2427 ft), rockhop across Harvey Creek. You're now in big timber with occasional glimpses of sea and sky. An open area provides a view of your goal: the Howe Sound Crest (HSC).

After 2 ½ hours, at 1220 m (4000 ft), reach a viewpoint across from the clearcut slopes of Mt. Harvey. (On the Northshore map this spot is marked with a camera.) The West Lion is east (right). David Peak is northeast. Rock slabs provide seating. Bare spots accommodate tents. But if you proceed right (southeast), you'll soon be out of the trees, on a heather-and-rock slope. The HSC is 215 m (700 ft) above—another 20-30 minutes of hiking, with an ocean view the whole way. Follow dots of orange paint and a few cairns. The West Lion is east (left) above you. Unnecessary Mountain is south.

Intersect the Howe Sound Crest Trail (HSCT) at 1433 m (4700 ft). To reach the Lions, go left (northeast) on the HSCT. Ascend 10 minutes over an outcropping—the high point of the trip, at 1530 m (5018 ft). After dropping into a defile, climb another 5 minutes to the base of the West Lion.

People congregate at the base of the West Lion to watch rock climbers (and usually a few idiots) clamber up to the 1646-m (5400-ft) summit. But there's another, safer way to expand your view. Descend right on the HSCT. It's a rough, narrow route here, marked with blazes and a yellow BC Parks sign. After dropping about 23 m (75 ft), contour northeast across a rock face to the gap between the Lions. Or follow the route farther down the gully, where crossing to the gap is less steep.

From the gap between the Lions, continue one minute up the rocky knob for unobscured views. Southeast is Capilano Lake. Vancouver is beyond. South are Mt. Strachan, Hollyburn Mtn. and ski runs on Black Mountain, in Cypress Provincial Park. Southeast are Crown, Goat and Grouse mountains. The more impressive Coliseum and Cathedral mountains are farther east and a bit south.

The HSCT is visible to the north, linking Thomas and David peaks. Hanging Lake is visible just east of the crest, way below David. The Coast Mountains march north to Garibaldi Park and beyond.

From the base of the West Lion, surefooted hikers can descend to the Sunset Drive parking lot in 2 hours. From the viewpoint at 1220 m (4000 ft), above Harvey Creek drainage, follow pink flagging where the trail drops into forest.

If you arranged a vehicle shuttle allowing a one-way trip to Cypress Bowl, stay on the HSCT when returning from the Lions. Proceed to the base of Unnecessary Mountain, scramble 100 m (330 ft) up its ragged north side, then follow the HSCT generally south (Trip 15).

Trip 11

Brew Lake

Location	Whistler
Round trip	13 km (8 mi)
Elevation gain	963 m (3160 ft)
Time required	6 ½ to 11 hours
Available	July through mid-October
Maps	ITM Whistler and Region; Brandywine 92 J/3

OPINION

You wouldn't sit through the previews and credits, then leave the theatre when the movie starts. But that's how it feels to reach Brew Lake then turn around. Worse, because the price of admission here is a bucket of sweat.

So don't plan on plopping down for a languorous picnic at the lake. Start early and keep going. Above Brew are alpine slopes—superb wandering country where the scenery is exhilarating. An obvious, worthy goal is Mt. Brew, north of the lake and about 320 m (1050 ft) higher. Or be creative. Explore. High on the ridges dividing the Cheakamus and Squamish valleys, you can attain views of Tricouni Peak (southwest), Cypress Peak (west), Mt. Fee (northwest), and Brandywine Mountain and Metal Dome (north). More distant are the fantastic ranges of Garibaldi Park (east).

Get cracking by 8 A.M. to fully enjoy the area on a dayhike. Strong hikers need 6½ hours round trip just for Brew Lake. Allow 10 to 11 hours to include a satisfying ridge tour or an ascent of Mt. Brew, but wait until early August, unless you're willing to combat snow.

If you can't or won't hike at a fiendish pace, make this an overnight trip. The Brew Lake basin is an excellent site for a basecamp. Of course, that means hauling a full pack up to the lake—ugh! The trail is rough and steep, through a rumpled, tufted landscape. Some stretches feel more like a scramble than a hike. You'll run the full gauntlet: trees, boulders, brush, muck. Views are minimal until just before the lake, though you will see extensive clearcuts. Try to enjoy your

Looking toward Brew Mountain, from Whistler Mtn. (Trip 3)

immediate surroundings: a charming, sylvan forest, brightened with glowing moss.

FACT

By Car

From Vancouver, drive Highway 99 north to Squamish. From the first traffic light (by McDonald's) in Squamish, continue north 41.5 km (25.7 mi) to Brandywine Falls Provincial Park. Or, if you're coming from Whistler, from the large, brown sign WELCOME TO WHISTLER on Highway 99, drive south 17.5 km (10.9 mi) to Brandywine Falls Provincial Park. Leave your car in the visitor lot, straight ahead after you turn in. The elevation here is 457 m (1500 ft).

On Foot

To access the trail, you have to walk 30 minutes on railroad track. From the provincial park, go to the highway and turn left (south). In a couple minutes, go right (southwest) onto the track. Be extremely wary of approaching trains. You'll see a white sign 65.5 [km]. The track curves right (west) at the sign 64.5. About 15 meters after crossing high above a creek, look for the trail on your right. It's flagged 4 meters above the track. There's also a post with an orange blaze, and a sign ADOPT A TRAIL.

Silver and orange blazes continue to mark the trail. It rises onto a rocky, mossy bluff in about 10 minutes, then climbs steeply through mixed forest with pretty undergrowth.

After 1 ½ hours, the trail leads you over a rocky ridge. Ten minutes later, wind through an attractive hollow adorned with skunk cabbage. Glimpses east over the Cheakamus valley reveal colossal clearcuts. The Black Tusk is visible southeast. Notice how high the trees are on the distant mountainsides—a mirror image of the forested slope you're ascending to reach the Brew Lake alpine basin.

Approach a major rock slide at 1037 m (3400 ft), after about 2 ⅓ hours of hiking. The trail skirts it to the right, then crosses its north edge, ascending 65 m (213 ft) in the process. Follow the flagging. Daisy Lake is visible southeast. Near the top of the slide, angle left toward tall trees and bushes with flagging. Whistler soon comes into view northeast.

About 2 ¾ hours will bring you to a wickedly steep section requiring use of hands as you proceed west. Then head south (slightly left). Step onto a boulder, with other large boulders to your right. There might still be a hard-to-see orange flag on a low willowy bush, and another flag ahead. Expect to plow through brush and blueberries for a while. Cross a creek. After about 3 ¼ hours, reach a rock slab suitable for camping, with views east over the valley to the Black Tusk. Continue through marshy meadows, which should be drier in late summer. Ascend through hemlocks and over heathery slopes.

Arrive at the southeast shore of Brew Lake about 3 ½ hours after leaving the highway. The elevation here is 1420 m (4658 ft). To proceed to the summit of 1740-m (5707-ft) Mt. Brew, rockhop over the outlet stream, round the west side of the lake, ascend the open, gentle slope, and head north. If you're capable, you'll find a suitable route. For views east across the valley, climb the ridge left of where you first saw the lake view.

Allow about 2 ½ hours to descend from the lake to the railroad track. It takes nearly as along as the ascent because sections require caution.

Trip 12

Fitzsimmons Creek / Russet Lake

Location	Whistler, Garibaldi Provincial Park
Round trip	19 km (11.8 mi)
Elevation gain	945 m (3100 ft)
Time required	7 hours
Available	late July through October
Maps	ITM Whistler and Region; BC Parks brochure; Whistler 92 J/2

OPINION

Hiking to Russet Lake, you can begin to fathom the icy vastness of southwest B.C. Just above the lake, on an easily-attained ridge, is the quintessential trailside vantage for witnessing the raw resplendence of Coast Mountain glaciers.

The Cheakamus Glacier, between Castle Towers Mountain and Mt. Davidson, is a jolting sight—as spellbinding as the Athabasca Glacier in Jasper National Park. The appropriately named Overlord Glacier licks the earth from behind reddish Fissile Peak. All the east-facing glaciers on the immediate coastal mountains are visible as well. So is the enormous Pemberton Icefield. The neck-craning view from far below in Whistler only hints at these tidal waves of ice. Not even the Tantalus Range glaciers near Squamish are as magnificent.

But not all the marvels of this journey are frozen. You'll walk through hugely inviting flower-knit meadows for nearly 2 km (1.2 mi), from Singing Pass to the ridge above Russet Lake. Even if the tumbling ice weren't visible, and the trail ended here, it would still be a worthwhile trip. Beneath the ridge is dazzling turquoise Cheakamus Lake, a child of the glaciers. Then there's Russet Lake, in a stark, dramatic setting, lapping at the toe of Fissile Peak. You can enjoy staring at it without having to proceed from the ridge down to the shore.

Before you commit to hiking up the Fitzsimmons Creek valley, read Trip 2. If you can afford the expensive gondola ride up Whistler Mountain, then it's best to descend Fitzsimmons as the final leg of a one-way Musical Bumps traverse. Keep in mind, that trip requires you to hitchhike down to Whistler (no problem on summer weekends) or

The Spearhead Range, from the ridge above Russet Lake

pre-arrange a shuttle. If you'd rather pay for alpine grandeur with sweat instead of money, hiking up Fitzsimmons through pretty forest is remarkably pleasant. The trail is wide, smooth, free of roots and mud, easy to follow, and climbs at a comfortable grade. Compared to the typical Coast Mountain route ascending to treeline, this is the Yellow Brick Road.

Though you can usually hike to Singing Pass by the end of June, wait until late July if you want to see the meadows in full bloom. By then, the trail continuing to Russet Lake should also be hikeable.

FACT

By Car

In Whistler, turn east off Highway 99, onto Village Gate Blvd. There's a traffic light here, and a large brown sign WELCOME TO WHISTLER. Continue straight through the next light at Whistler Way. Reach a T-intersection in 0.4 km (0.25 mi) and go right on Blackcomb Way. Continue through the light at Sundial Crescent. Look right for the sign FITZSIMMONS CREEK BUS LOOP, SINGING PASS. At 0.7 km (0.4 mi), fork right through the bus stop area. 100 meters after the sign SINGING PASS TRAILHEAD (GARIBALDI PROVINCIAL PARK), turn right onto dirt and head uphill on the main dirt road. It's rough, but passable in 2WD. Acrophobes won't enjoy looking over the edge. Continue 5 km (3.1 mi) up the valley to the trailhead parking lot at 1037 m (3400 ft).

On Foot

Head southeast on the old road through regrowing forest. Looking east, across Fitzsimmons Creek, you can see the austere, grey peaks of the Spearhead Range. Soon pass an abandoned mine shaft and ore-car tracks. Near 2.5 km (1.6 mi) reach the Garibaldi Park boundary. Mountain bikes are prohibited in the park. Stay left, proceeding generally southeast into substantial forest. Cross Harmony, Flute (with a cascade in the gorge), and Oboe creeks. All are bridged. The trail then turns southward into the Melody Creek drainage at 1500 m (4920 ft). The trees diminish and meadows appear as you enter the subalpine zone.

At 7.5 km (4.7 mi), 1640 m (5380 ft), reach the vast Singing Pass meadows. Just out of the trees, the trail to Oboe Summit and the Musical Bumps forks right (west). This junction was not signed in 1996. To continue to Russet Lake, stay straight (left). The moderate, switchbacking ascent from the junction, southeast to the ridge above Russet Lake, takes 40-60 minutes. After climbing 340 m (1115 ft) above the junction, you're 1928 m (6500 ft) high on the open slopes of the Fitzsimmons Range, with broad views of glaciers near and far. The dominant one, Cheakamus Glacier, is south. The Pemberton Icefield is northwest, beyond the Musical Bumps ridge and Whistler Mountain. Cheakamus Lake is visible southwest, 1100 m (2821 ft) below.

As you round the ridge and head east, Russet Lake appears beneath the reddish slopes of Fissile Peak. The Overlord Glacier peeks out from behind the peak's north face. It's an 80-m (262-ft) descent to the shore of Russet Lake, 9.5 km (5.9 mi) from the trailhead. Campsites are near the lake's northwest corner, near a hut built by the B.C. Mountaineering Club.

If you don't want to drop to the lake, but need to refill water bottles for the return trip, you'll find deep-enough dribbles crossing the trail 10 minutes back down from the ridge. Or wait until Oboe Creek, 40 minutes down.

Trip 13

Cougar Mountain Cedar Grove

Location	Whistler / Pemberton
Round trip	5 km (3 mi)
Elevation gain	150 m (492 ft)
Time required	3 hours
Available	late June through October
Maps	ITM Whistler and Region; Whistler 92 J/2

OPINION

A touching walk among the grandest of Gaia's trees gives balance and depth to the panoramic high ridges and austere glacial cirques that hikers primarily seek.

Here you'll encounter ancient cedars, 3 meters (9 feet) in diameter, like those that prevailed in southwest B.C. before logging began. You'll feel profound peace, perhaps even reverence, in this sanctuary. Devout hikers and mall-storming tourists alike should pay homage to the cedars. No one will be unmoved.

The grove is an idyllic place to sit and listen to coastal forest sounds: chattering red squirrels, splashing water, buzzing insects, singing birds, cedar boughs raking the breeze, and on a stormy day, the great cedar trunks creaking where they lean together. Appreciate the giants with your other senses as well. Run your fingers along their soft, flakey bark. Press your nose into them and inhale the trees' essence. They are, after all, living beings. Get to know them intimately.

Frenetic Whistler is meaningless compared to these hallowed cedars that have survived nearly a thousand summers and winters. Yet at the height of the summer tourist season, which is also when hikers are out full force, we met only three people near the cedar grove in a five-hour period. It's wonderful to experience the grove alone, but more people need to meet these noble beings so they can understand their significance. Ancient trees will survive the threats of ravenous logging companies when enough of us demand they be saved from the saw.

Logging has mangled the slopes beneath the cedars, so the nearly

Cougar Mountain Cedar Grove

one-hour road-walk to the grove is not pleasant. But the trees will help you forget the approach.

FACT

By Car

From the north end of Whistler, at Alpine Way, drive northeast 4.8 km (3.0 mi) on Highway 99. Immediately after you lose sight of Green Lake, when the highway curves sharply left around a ridge, turn left (west) onto the dirt road signed COUGAR MTN ANCIENT CEDAR TRAIL, SHOWH LAKES 5 KM. Or, from the edge of Pemberton, at the 3-way junction by Petro Canada, drive Highway 99 southwest 23.6 km (14.6 mi), then turn (west). From either approach, set your trip odometer to 0 again as you start up the dirt road.

At 2.1 km (1.3 mi) cross to the east side of Sixteen-mile Creek and head northwest. At 4.5 km (2.8 mi) fork right at the sign. The road is rougher and steeper now. At 4.9 km (3.0 mi), just before a fork, pull off on the left. The elevation here is 915 m (3000 ft). 4WD vehicles can proceed a bit farther, following the directions below. The left fork continues to Showh Lakes Recreation Site.

On Foot

Just beyond where 2WD cars should park, take the right fork. Hike up the steep, rough road. Look for a roadside sign COUGAR MTN

ANCIENT CEDARS, 4 KM RETURN, VERTICAL RISE 150 M. The ascent moderates within 8-10 minutes. Near 1.5 km (0.9 mi) a sign on the left indicates a trail descending to Showh Lakes. Another sign directs you right, on the main road, heading generally east. Bedrock is exposed where the road steepens again.

Pass a sign on the left stating the same statistics as the previous sign, 20 minutes below. You've obviously made progress, so one of the signs is incorrect. You're walking past stumps, short regrowth, and fireweed. Just before the road curves sharply left, at about 1037 m (3400 ft), there's a lily pond below to the right. Finally, enter forest and continue on trail.

The forest is initially a mix of trees other than cedars. About 5-8 minutes along the trail, a spur forks left to a viewpoint overlooking tiny Showh and Cougar lakes and the valley's clearcuts. Back on the trail, just downhill from the spur, arrive at the Cedar Loop. Hiking time to this point is about 1 hour.

Near a bridge over the little creek, go right. The loop builds to a climax that way. Medium-size cedars thrust out of a lush bed of ferns and skunk cabbage. Farther along are colossal cedars with long, tendril branches. Just before a bridge, where the loop curves left, you'll see a huge Douglas fir (branches high on the trunk) and an enormous, lone, western hemlock (branches lower on the trunk). Meter-wide devil's club leaves float on the gentle air in the dim light.

It takes only 15 minutes to walk the loop without pausing, but expect to spend an hour or more.

Trip 14
Black Mountain ✓

Location	Cypress Provincial Park
Round trip	7.5 km (4.7 mi) to 10.9 km (6.8 mi)
Elevation gain	297 m (974 ft)
Time required	3 hours, plus time for swimming
Available	mid-June through mid-October
Maps	BC Parks brochure; ITM Vancouver's Northshore; North Vancouver 92 G/6

OPINION

It's not the hiking that makes Black Mountain worthwhile. It's the swimming. Cabin Lake is the perfect plunge—warm enough to stay in and enjoy. You can swim laps. Float on your back. Other nearby lakes are shallow, murky, muddy, reedy. But Cabin is deep and clear, ringed by rocky perches ideal for mermaids and manmaids.

Cypress Parkway enables you to drive most of the way up Black Mountain. Then it's a miserable road-walk, made tolerable only because it's short and offers one striking view of Georgia Strait and the Vancouver metropolis.

Many of the trail junctions, and most of the lakes in the area, are not signed. Paths fork every which way. Just stay aware of your general direction. To enjoy wandering among the lakes and ultimately get where you want to go, it helps to have the BC Parks Cypress Park map in hand.

Come mid-week and you might find the lake is yours alone. The best swimming is obviously on clear days—when the approach road is wiltingly hot. Descend the road after 5 P.M., when you'll have shade.

FACT

By Car

Driving Highway 1 through West Vancouver, turn off at Cypress Bowl, Exit 8. Continue 16 km (10 mi) up the Cypress Parkway to the ski area. Near the end of the road, just before it curves south into a huge parking lot, on your right is a yellow gate. Left of it is the signed Baden Powell trail (BPT), at 920 m (3018 ft).

Cabin Lake

On Foot

Set out west (left) on the BPT, which quickly curves south (left) and becomes a road. Ignore the blazed trail forking right. Continue ascending the ankle-eating, rocky road to a hairpin turn. From there you can look south at Point Grey and the Fraser River estuary.

About 10 minutes beyond the hairpin, the road joins a broad ski trail. Stay on the rocky road, curving sharply left (south). About 5 minutes later, reach another bend in the road. If you want to leave the road and complete the ascent by trail, look for a blazed path departing left, beside a gully. It briefly descends into forest and soon becomes clearer, heading southwest, then northwest. About 800 m (0.5 mi) after leaving the road, it joins the Black Mountain Loop trail (BMLT), where you go left.

If you stay on the road, you'll reach the top of the Black Chairlift about 45 minutes from the carpark. (To orient yourself, see the map near the chairlift structure.) Follow the trail marked with orange blazes on trees. It descends to a junction in 5 minutes. Stay left, toward Sam Lake, on the BMLT. You'll return to this junction, via the right fork (BPT), after touring the lakes. Immediately after you turn left, pass an unmarked trail on the left (ascending from the road below) joining the BMLT. Stay right (straight). You're in subalpine country now, among hemlocks and heather. The BMLT distance is 2.5 km (1.6 mi), with a total gain of only 100 m (330 ft).

From either approach, continue southwest, passing between Sam and Theagill lakes. Then curve north again, ascending to Owen Lake, about 10 minutes from the last junction. On the northeast side of Owen, the BPT goes right (north) to Cabin Lake. To extend your hike, proceed 1.7 km (1.0 mi) left (southwest) on the BPT to Eagle Bluff. Within 15 minutes, you'll descend gently past the Cougar Lakes, then a couple ponds. Eagle Bluff is high above Howe Sound and Horseshoe Bay, offering a clear view of the Gulf Islands. The BPT drops steeply beyond Eagle Bluff (Trip 52).

From Owen Lake, head right (north) about 10 minutes, passing a pond on the right. Follow arrows as the trail ascends left, over the 1217-m (3992-ft) south summit of Black Mountain. In a few more minutes, a spur trail forks left to Cabin Lake. To complete the loop, go right, then immediately right again on the well-signed BPT. It leads southeast, back to the junction north of Sam Lake, where you have a choice of return routes: left to the Black chairlift; or right briefly, then left descending via trail.

After leaving Cabin Lake, before you turn right on the BPT to complete the loop, a few minutes straight ahead is the Yew Lake lookout. Yew Lake itself is barely visible, but you can see Howe Sound, the Lions, and the Tantalus Range.

Trip 15
Unnecessary Mountain from Cypress Ski Area

Location	Cypress Provincial Park
Round trip	18 km (11.2 mi)
Elevation gain	844 m (2770 ft),
	plus 230 m (755 ft) on the return
Time required	7 hours
Available	early July through mid-November
Maps	BC Parks brochure; ITM Vancouver's
	Northshore; North Vancouver 92 G/6

OPINION

Too many mountains have boring names. Take Brunswick Mountain, for example, on the Howe Sound Crest. It was named after a British naval officer's ship. Who cares? But Unnecessary Mountain—now there's a bold, colourful statement. Trudging up from West Vancouver, gunning for the Lions, climbers used to curse this summit. To them it was just an obstacle. The name echoes their frustration. Today, voting with their boots, hikers have elected Unnecessary a favourite North Shore destination, giving the name an ironic twist.

Unnecessary is a gnarly, dual-peaked mountain offering a head-swiveling panorama of Howe Sound. But other Crest vantage points afford similar views. And Unnecessary isn't easy to surmount. The descent from St. Marks to the col beneath Unnecessary is an exasperating loss of 180 m (590 ft) that becomes downright maddening when you have to regain all of it and more: 354 m (1161 ft). On the return you must repeat this irksome loss and gain. For those reasons, we've rated it only Worthwhile. Because this hike starts high at Cypress ski area, however, you can set out for Unnecessary and have the option of turning around, satisfied with your accomplishment, at any of several acceptable goals en route.

Hike as little as 30 minutes to Bowen Island Lookout, 1 hour to Strachan Meadows (Trip 8), or 2 hours to St. Marks. Reaching the top of Unnecessary takes about 3½ hours—a reasonable dayhike for many people. Ambitious hikers aim for the Lions (Trip 10), 30 minutes north

A Howe Sound view on the way to Unnecessary Mountain

along the Crest from Unnecessary. Over-achievers try to dispatch the whole Crest in one swoop (Trip 37).

On the way to Unnecessary, you'll repeatedly enjoy indelible vistas of ocean and islands. The first 1 ½ hours is in beautiful forest laced by frolicking creeks, brightened by lush understory. Virgin mountain hemlock, Douglas fir, and yellow cypress are as attractive as the distant views. But the steep, rooty ascents of St. Marks and Unnecessary are through dark, oppressive forest.

Return the same way. Or, if you can arrange a shuttle, make this a one-way trip by proceeding over Unnecessary, then descending the newer Lions trail (Trip 10) to Lions Bay. Before arranging a shuttle, make sure everyone in your party is capable of the rough scramble down Unnecessary's north side.

FACT

By Car
See Mt. Strachan (Trip 8) for directions.

On Foot
Follow the directions for Mt. Strachan (Trip 8) as far as Strachan Meadows. Reach the meadows in about 1 hour, at 3 km (2 mi), having gained only 155 m (508 ft). After crossing the small bridges over the creeks, stay left, following the Howe Sound Crest Trail (HSCT) north.

Gain 285 m (935 ft) to the top of a bump called St. Marks—2 hours from the trailhead and 1360 m (4461 ft) high. Enjoy views in all directions. Descend north 180 m (590 ft), then ascend 354 m (1161 ft) to the south summit of Unnecessary Mountain.

From the south summit, it's 0.6 km (0.4 mi) to the north summit. Between them, you'll lose and regain 50 m (164 ft). You'll also pass the old trail (Trip 22) coming up from Lions Bay.

To reach the Lions, descend the precipitous north side of Unnecessary, then proceed north. In about 10 minutes you'll pass the newer Lions trail coming up from Lions Bay.

Trip 16

Goat Mountain / Hanes Creek

Location	North Shore, Lynn Headwaters Regional Park
Shuttle trip	18 km (11.2 mi)
Elevation gain	273 m (895 ft) using Grouse Skyride
Time required	7 to 8 hours
Available	late June through October
Maps	Park map (at trailhead kiosk); ITM Vancouver's Northshore

OPINION

Wedged between water and wilderness, Vancouver is unique among big cities. And here's your chance to fully appreciate the setting: a route so rugged, that feels so isolated, it defies the reality of nearly 2 million people pressed up against the other side of the mountain. The trailhead is even on the city bus line. But that's no reason to leave your first-aid kit at home. This is a serious, back-country trip. Be prepared.

Most of the way is either atrociously rough or in deep forest, so don't expect an agreeable trail or sustained views. Your effort will have to be fueled by the joy of communing with nature, and the sense of accomplishment that comes from negotiating tumultuous terrain. The singular, panoramic vantage-point of Goat Mountain will tantalize you to explore the surrounding peaks on other trips. From Goat, the 1011-m (3315-ft) descent to Lynn Creek seems never ending. But after the unbridged crossing, the trail instantly improves, so you can look forward to cruising the rest of the way out on auto-pilot.

About that unbridged crossing. In spring, Lynn Creek is a raging torrent. To ford, you need a wetsuit, mask, snorkel, and a total disregard for your own safety. Don't even think about it until the treacherous water subsides in late summer or early fall.

Also, we suggest you ride the gondola to the Grouse Mountain Chalet, then begin hiking. From there, ascend Goat Mountain, then drop into Crown Pass, drop through Hanes Creek Valley, and exit Lynn Creek Valley. Most of the trip is downhill that way, and you'll be fresher when you plunge into the boulder chute beneath Crown Pass.

Descending the rockslide from Crown Pass to Hanes Creek

FACT

By Car

Drive or catch the bus up Capilano Road in North Vancouver. Follow the signs: GROUSE MOUNTAIN SKYRIDE. Capilano Road eventually becomes Nancy Green Way. From the parking lot at the end of the road, either hike to the Grouse Mountain Chalet via the Grouse Grind (Trip 66), or ride the gondola. If you have more energy than money, and don't want to forfeit the fare, you'll have to grind 854 m (2800 ft) up to where our *On Foot* description begins. To complete the shuttle trip described here, you'll need to leave a car (or have someone pick you up) at the Lynn Headwaters Regional Park entrance area. See the *By Car* directions for Lynn Valley (Trip 54).

On Foot

From the upper gondola station at 1128 m (3700 ft), walk past the Grouse Mountain Chalet. Go left at the large map/sign. Follow the wide, paved path to the Peak chairlift. Left of the lift is a dirt road; that's the way. The road leads you beneath a cliff face and affords views west down to Capilano Lake and out to Cypress Mountain and Howe Sound. In 1 km, reach the Grouse Alpine Area kiosk, soon after which you enter Lynn Headwaters Regional Park.

The kiosk states distances and times to destinations in the park. We've found these figures reasonably accurate, but keep in mind they don't include the 2 km round-trip between the kiosk and the Grouse Mountain Chalet. The Hanes Valley figures are misleading; they're for the one-way trip through Hanes *and* Lynn Valleys.

Confused? Don't be. If you're following our directions, here are the approximate figures you'll find helpful. From the Chalet, it's 3.9 km (2.4 mi) one way to the top of Goat Mountain. From there, the descent to Crown Pass is 1.7 km (1.1 mi). Reach the unbridged crossing of Lynn Creek at 10 km (6.2 mi), the bridge over Norvan Creek at 11.2 km (6.9 mi), the debris chute at 14.1 km (8.7 mi), and the park entrance area (at the end of Lynn Valley Road) at 18 km (11.2 mi). Start early and allow a full day.

From the kiosk, the steep, bouldery road soon dwindles to trail. Pass the left forks to Dam and Little Goat mountains. Continue straight for Goat Mountain. Reach a flat spot with views northwest to Crown Mountain and southeast to the Cheam Range. A trail descending right leads to Mt. Fromme. Continue straight, heeding the green-and-yellow signs and following the red-and-white blazes.

You're now walking the rim of a bowl, with Kennedy Lake below to the right. Approaching Goat Mountain, the ascent steepens to a scramble up a rooty route. Where it splits, stay right; it's a bit easier.

Allow at least 1½ hours to reach the summit of 1401-m (4595-ft) Goat Mountain, 3.9 km (2.4 mi) from the Chalet. If *you're* a goat, it's possible to continue farther northeast along Goat Ridge. But the route-finding is difficult, it's a descent requiring you to hoof it back up to the summit, and the views diminish. Leave it.

Drop off Goat Mountain the same way you came up, then turn right (northwest) descending very steeply to Crown Pass. It's a gnarly, slippery route. Follow the red flagging. After this mess, pick your way across a boulder slide to a more comfortable trail, soon reaching the narrow, tree-choked pass at 1080 m (3542 ft). At this junction, a dangerous route climbs left (northwest) up Crown Mountain (Trip 19). Go right (northeast), descending an enormous boulder field into Hanes Valley.

Watch closely for flagging and stakes marking the most efficient route through approximately 1.2 km (0.7 mi) of boulders. About 30 minutes down, where it appears you'll reach the bottom of the boulders within 15 minutes, flags mark a route heading left. Go left, following the flags toward a willow and bigger boulders. Be patient. It takes another 30 minutes to reach the actual trail on the valley floor.

Looking back up, you can see the sheer cliffs of Crown Mountain and the boulder-field you just clambered down. The valley trail is unmaintained and sometimes faint. Look for sporadic blazes. After hopping across upper Hanes Creek, the trail follows the creek downstream on its north side, eventually reaching upper Lynn Creek, at 390 m (1280 ft).

Approaching upper Lynn Creek can be disorienting, depending on how destructive the spring runoff was and how recently the park staff has cleared and re-blazed the route. There's no bridge, so expect a wet, frigid, potentially hazardous ford. If you're lucky, you can leap across on rocks.

Climb up the far (west) bank. The trail improves rapidly as it bends southeast. Cross the bridge over Norvan Creek at 11.2 km (6.9 mi). (Norvan Falls, 5 minutes upstream from the bridge, is worth a peek.) The now distinct, well-marked trail heads south, gently descending just east of Lynn Creek. A sign states this final leg to the park entrance will take you 2½ hours; strong hikers do it in 1½. At 14.1 km (8.7 mi), in a debris chute where Lynn Creek is visible, go right onto the Cedars Mill trail—it's more level and direct than the Headwaters trail higher on the slope. When you reach the park entrance area, cross the bridge to the west side of Lynn Creek and the parking lot just beyond.

Trip 17
Eagle Ridge/Dilly Dally Peak

Location	Fraser Valley North
Loop	24 km (15 mi)
Elevation gain	1370 m (4500 ft)
Time required	10 to 11 hours
Available	mid-June through early September; later there's not enough light for the loop
Maps	ITM Vancouver's Northshore; Coquitlam 92 G/7

OPINION

Adventure is a word of infinite interpretations. But most hikers attempting the entire Eagle Ridge traverse, especially in early summer, will agree this is an adventure. For some, it might be too adventurous. The trip requires a full day's stamina. The way is often rough, steep, or both. And if there's snow, route-finding is necessary. The reward? It's more than just a grand view. It's the emotional high of letting your wild self loose, and the physical joy of accomplishment.

Lindsay Lake and the other tannin-coloured ponds on the ridge are not a worthwhile destination. They're more appealing to bugs than to people. Set your sights higher, on Mt. Beautiful (Eagle Peak) and Dilly Dally Peak. The last one involves two more hours of hiking, but feels much farther into the mountains. From Dilly Dally, you can peer northwest, all the way up the glacier-carved fiord of Indian Arm, where the serpentine Indian River has created a gorgeous valley that looks like Xanadu.

So start early and don't dillydally at the ponds. That's the only way to complete the traverse in one swoop. Even with the increased daylight of early summer, you're likely to be racing to finish before sundown—especially if there's snow on the ridge, which you should expect through June. If you're not up for an epic, either plan on camping atop the ridge, or turn back after attaining the satisfying panorama from Mt. Beautiful's open, rocky summit.

None of the Eagle Ridge trail is dangerously exposed, though it does require light scrambling. If you have experience hiking in snow, it's possible to make this trek in June. Snow covered or not, however,

On Mt. Beautiful, high above Coquitlam Lake

an inept scrambler could take a serious tumble. The trail is fine up to the ridge. After that, it's not a marvel of engineering; it's just a decent, well-trod route. Use of all fours is sometimes required, especially on the descent west of Dilly Dally. You can view this either as a total annoyance or as a fun challenge that breaks the monotony of merely plodding.

FACT

By Car

Just east of Port Moody (26 km / 16 mi from downtown Vancouver), on Barnet Highway 7A, turn north at the traffic light onto signed Ioco Road. In 0.7 km (0.4 mi) turn left, staying on Ioco Road. (A sign here directs you straight, uphill on Heritage Mtn Blvd, to Buntzen Lake. But it's easier to go left into Ioco.) At a 3-way intersection, 4.8 km (3 mi) from Highway 7A, turn right (north) onto 1st Avenue. At 5.5 km (3.4 mi), turn right onto Sunnyside Road. At 8.5 km (5.3 mi), reach the entrance to Buntzen Lake Recreation Area. At 10.3 km (6.4 mi), pass gated Powerhouse Road and immediately turn to park at the southeast end of the first parking area. The elevation here is 180 m (590 ft).

On Foot

From the gate on Powerhouse Road, walk 20 meters north, then turn right (east) onto the trail signed HALVOR LUNDEN. In 10 minutes, reach a T-junction where you go left onto a gravel road/trail. About 70 meters beyond, where you pass under a powerline, turn right onto the small trail marked by an orange blaze. The ascent up Eagle Mountain is stiff. Strong hikers will reach Polytrichum Lookout in 1 hour. Here, at 780 m (2560 ft) elevation, you can gaze northwest over Buntzen Lake to Mt. Seymour, and Runner, Elsay and Bishop peaks. Then, after a short way in trees, the trail levels, entering an old logged area. You can now see Vancouver, including the peninsula of Stanley Park.

Proceed northeast. The tree-filled gorge of Buntzen Creek is on your left; a regrowing clearcut on your right. Where the gorge pinches out, re-enter beautiful forest. This is El Paso junction, about 1¾ hours from the trailhead, where you must choose one of two paths to Lindsay Lake. Left goes southwest, then north, past Buntzen Lake viewpoints and through some impressive old-growth trees. Right (signed LOWER LAKES) heads generally north, past several ponds. We describe the lower lakes route, because it's the fastest way to the optimal views.

Going right, soon reach small Foy Falls. Beyond, follow the main trail cutting between the lakes. Other paths veer off but soon lead back to the main trail. Pass Wren Lake. About 5 minutes beyond, stay left (straight) for the direct trail north to Lindsay Lake. (Right is signed EAST LOOP, SISKIN LAKE.) Pass Chicadee Lake, receding into meadow. About 2¼ hours from the trailhead, reach a junction at St. Mary's Lake. Ignore the West loop. Head north to Lindsay Lake. The East Loop trail rejoins at Nancycatch Junction beside a stream.

Reach Lindsay Lake after about 3 hours of determined hiking. It's a bit bigger and deeper than other lakes on the ridge. At the northeast end of the lake is Lindsay junction, where you go right for Mt. Beautiful, 2.8 km (1.7 mi) distant. Left leads back to El Paso junction, via the viewpoints trail.

Forging ahead, the trail undulates north along forested Eagle Ridge. Soon reach a good spot for a rest break—open rock slabs amid hemlocks. The area is signed TT TOP. From there, the trail descends north, dwindling to a route in places. Deadfall and eroding bluffs require gymnastic stretches, slowing your progress. Follow the orange blazes.

About 1½ hours from TT Top, reach 1280-m (4198-ft) Mt. Beautiful, the true summit of Eagle Ridge. Ascend a short distance over a rock outcropping. On top there's a rock slab big enough for a tent. Just north of and below the high point is another excellent vantage, and another tent site on rock. The view: Coquitlam Mountain is prominent east; Peneplain and Obelisk peaks are north of it; Coquitlam Lake is northeast; Indian Arm is west; Georgia Strait and Vancouver are southwest; Mt. Baker is south.

Continuing north toward Dilly Dally Peak, the route descends 150 m (492 ft) to a small, forested saddle. Here, the signed Swan Falls trail descends steeply left, eventually heading west to intersect Powerhouse Road just north of Buntzen Lake. If you're tired, or anxious about losing daylight, this is your escape route off the ridge. But if you bail out now, you'll miss the culminating views from Dilly Dally Peak.

Resuming progress north along the ridge, gain another 120 m (394 ft) to reach Dilly Dally Peak at 1250 m (4100 ft). Being the end of the ridge, it affords an unobstructed view north up Indian Arm and the Indian River valley, to the snowfields of Mt. Garibaldi. The nearest glacier in the north is the Meslilloet.

From Dilly Dally, the route plunges north off the ridge at roughly a 45° angle. Be careful. Slip here and you'll be cartwheeling until a tree stops you. The route is now more frequently marked with orange flagging than metal blazes. After dropping about 180 m (590 ft) in 1 km (0.6 mi) to a barely noticeable, forested saddle (Dilly Dally Pass), the angle eases to about 30°. Though still narrow, the path is now more obvious as it descends west.

Below the saddle, the trail crosses a couple creeks. Having hiked about 7 ½ hours (excluding rest stops) from the trailhead, reach an old road. Heading west toward Indian Arm, the descent is now moderate. Also visible are powerlines and the road you'll soon be walking back to Buntzen Lake. Continue descending through young forest with almost no undergrowth.

In a tight mess of deadfall and scrawny trees, a signed spur trail forks right (northwest) then bends southwest about 0.7 km (0.4 mi) to Croker Lookout. Forget it. You saw much more from above. Beyond this fork, the Dilly Dally trail turns south. Soon cross the third and biggest creek on the descent. It should pose no difficulties.

Finally, the trail crosses beneath a powerline tower and spills onto a rough road. Go left. It's initially steep, then fairly level. When you reach paved road near Trout Lake, go left (southeast)—away from the big green pipe. At the North Beach picnic area, you have a choice: (1) continue walking about 1 hour (4 km / 2.5 mi) on Powerhouse Road; or (2) hike the Buntzen Lake trail, which begins on the right, just south of the picnic area, past the Coquitlam Lake Tunnel Outfall. The lakeside trail takes about 15 minutes longer, but it's more pleasant. If there's sufficient light, opt for the trail.

Trip 18
Blowdown Pass/Gott Peak

Location	Lillooet
Round trip	14.4 km (9 mi) to Gott Peak
Elevation gain	874 m (2867 ft) up Gott Peak
Time required	6 hours
Available	mid-June through mid-October
Maps	ITM Stein Valley Trail;
	Duffey Lake 92 J/8

OPINION

Wander alpine slopes. Witness an eruption of glacier lilies. Stretch your eyes. Scope out the Stein Wilderness. You'll find Blowdown Pass worthwhile. But only if you drive an old beater. Bring your mountain bike. Carry a bear spray. And continue hiking up Gott Peak.

The narrow, brush-choked access road is a deterrent. Though 2WD is adequate, your car's likely to get scratched. Expect to stop repeatedly to break off the branches that lash out at your paint job. Weekend warriors, piloting ten-year-old Subaru wagons, won't care.

After the exasperating access road, you face a mining road— another 7.5 km (4.7 mi) round trip. It makes for C- hiking, B+ mountain biking. Or why not park beside Highway 99 and bike all the way to Blowdown Pass? That's the way to enjoy the road and the scenery. Just 2 km (1.2 mi) up, you can see glacier-laden Joffre Peak, southwest.

This side of the Coast Mountains, near the Fraser River, is decidedly un-coastlike. It's dry. Hot. And the peaks have lost their fizz, like a carbonated drink left open too long. Looking east into the Stein Wilderness, the bare, knobby summits bear no resemblance to the whipcream-dolloped Tantalus Range, or the nearby, canine-fanged Joffre / Matier massif. After the spring greenery withers, alpine slopes here have no crowning adornment. You might as well walk in a wheat field. Avoid this oven in July and August, unless you want to bake your enchilada. Talus, like pavement, radiates heat. You'll find little shade on the thinly forested ridges.

Because this is a high-elevation hike, it's not available in shoulder-season. Mid to late June is the time to come, when yellow avalanche lilies appear en masse. But—red alert—grizzlies love those lilies too. The area supports a healthy griz population. Read our *Bears* section.

The option of ascending Gott Peak for more expansive views is really a requirement if you want to make this a great trip. In June, you might have to walk in snow, but try to mush through. See all that you can see.

FACT

By Car

If you're heading northeast on Highway 99, drive 23.3 km (14.4 mi) past the Joffre Lakes Recreation Area parking lot. Or, if you're heading southwest on Highway 99, drive 41.3 km (25.6 mi) past the turnoff to Seton Lake, outside Lillooet. From either approach, turn east onto the Blowdown logging road. It's only signed NO THRU. Heading northeast, it's on the right, immediately after the yellow-and-black road closure gate. Heading southwest, it's on the left, immediately after a green highway sign PEMBERTON 52. Set your trip odometer to 0 again as you start on the Blowdown logging road.

The narrow road is initially steep, but the grade soon eases. Stay on the obvious, main road where spur roads branch off. If you decide to bail out, there are spots wide enough to turn around. At 8.4 km (5.2 mi) pass a road crossing to the west side of the creek. At 9.2 km (5.7 mi) reach a junction where most cars will have to park. Drive or walk up the left fork 1.5 km (0.9 mi) to the end of driveable road. The elevation here is 1616 m (5300 ft).

On Foot

Walk the private mining road. If the heat is oppressive, cool off at one of the snowmelt streams crossing the road. A little beyond 2 km (1.2 mi) reach a fork. Stay right (straight), on the older, narrower road. In another 15 minutes, at 3.0 km (1.9 mi), it's possible to descend right (south) to Blowdown Lake and scattered campsites. The lake is 45 m (150 ft) below.

Proceeding east on the road, reach 2180-m (7150-ft) Blowdown Pass at 3.7 km (2.3 mi), having gained 564 m (1850 ft). The South Cottonwood valley is east of the pass. The road continues, descending into the valley toward the Silver Queen Mine, eventually joining a trail that leads east into the Cottonwood Creek drainage, then southeast into the lower Stein River valley.

Gott Peak, 310 m (1017 ft) higher, is 2 km (1.3 mi) northwest of Blowdown Pass. Fit muscles will get you there in 45 minutes. Otherwise allow 1 ½ hours. Ascend steeply, directly north from the pass, then angle northwest on the open slope to the first summit at 2450 m (8036 ft). To reach the official Gott Peak, drop between the summits, then climb the southeast ridge, topping out at 2490 m (8167 ft).

Trip 19
Crown Mountain

Location	North Shore, Lynn Headwaters Regional Park
Round trip	9.6 km (6.0 mi) using Grouse Skyride
Elevation gain	695 m (2278 ft) using Grouse Skyride
Time required	5 hours
Available	July through October
Maps	Park map (at trailhead kiosk); ITM Vancouver's Northshore; North Vancouver 92 G/6

OPINION

A dangerous, exposed route slithers up wild and woolly Crown Mountain. Make a mistake here, and it could be your last. Only experienced scramblers should grapple with the final couple hundred meters of the ascent. The summit crown is small and uncomfortable. Descending the precipitous route is even riskier than the ascent. For most hikers, it's not worth it. Nearby Goat Mountain offers equally satisfying views.

FACT

By Car

Drive to the Grouse Mountain Skyride. See Trip 16 for directions.

On Foot

See Trip 16 for directions to Crown Pass, where the Hanes Valley Route intersects the Alpine trail from Grouse Mountain. Hiking the 3.6 km (2.2 mi) from Grouse Chalet to Crown Pass takes about 1 ½ hours.

From the trail junction in the narrow, forested pass, a rough route climbs northwest up 1501-m (4925-ft) Crown Mountain. The trail quickly diminishes to little more than a goat track, gaining 421 m (1381 ft) in 1.2 km (0.9 mi).

Trip 20
Mt. St. Benedict

Location	Fraser Valley North
Round trip	15 km (9.3 mi)
Elevation gain	1279 m (4195 ft)
Time required	6 hours
Available	June through mid-November
Maps	Stave Lake 92 G/8; ITM Lower Mainland

OPINION

If this were what hiking was about, you'd do better to take up caber tossing, jai alai, ostrich racing. Even lawn bowling would be more exciting.

We first explored the logging roads near Stave Lake while researching our book, *Camp Free in B.C.* We were disgusted by how heavily logged the area is, and alarmed by the rifle-brandishing clientele. We winced at the thought of returning but were obliged to check out this hike. At first, we were relieved to find a well-engineered trail switchbacking up through pleasant forest. But the trail ends within 15 minutes. You then have to climb over 366 m (1200 ft) on an ugly, recently-built logging road. Desecration surrounds you until the trail resumes in forest. Even then, the trees are scrubby and the scenery dominated by clearcuts until you reach 762 m (2500 ft).

Look at the ITM Lower Mainland Map. The tangle of red zigzagging lines is a warning to stay away. If you're in the area and want an outdoor diversion, visit nearby Cascade Falls Regional Park.

The summit panorama would have to be stupendous to justify such an appalling approach. It's not. Mounts Robie Reid and Judge Howay are visible northwest, but are too distant to overshadow the clearcuts below Benedict. McKay Lake, at the base of a buttress, is the ho-hum highlight on this dreary ascent. Murdo Creek is occasionally audible, but so is gunfire. Men without meaning like to target practice around here.

FACT

By Car

From Highway 11 in Mission, drive Highway 7 east 9.0 km (5.6 mi). Between Hatzic and Dewdney, at the Shell gas station, turn left (north) onto paved Sylvester Road. Reset your trip odometer to 0 here. In 3.7 km (2.3 mi) stay right at the fork. Continue toward Cascade Falls Regional Park. At 14.7 km (9.1 mi), a right turn on Ridgeview Road leads 1 km to the park. Stay straight (north) for Mt. St. Benedict. Pavement ends at 15.4 km (9.5 mi). Ascend on Lost Creek FS Road. At 16.1 km (10 mi), pass Murdo Creek Road. Enter Davis Lake Provincial Park at 16.4 km (10.2 mi) and cross a creek. After crossing another creek, park in the pullout on the left at 17.7 km (11 mi). The elevation here is 183 m (600 ft).

On Foot

Walk back over the bridge. The flagged trail is just south of the creek, on the left. Ascend the wood steps. The well-engineered trail switchbacks upward. Climb 122 m (400 ft) in 15 minutes to a logging road. Go left and continue ascending. At a bend, look northwest over Stave Lake. In 4-5 minutes, curve left on the main road where a smaller, older road forks right. The main road rises steeply. After about 20 minutes on the road, look for large numbers painted on boulders. Where you see massive clearcuts across the drainage, watch for a big "4". Just past it, look right. Where the bushes are festooned with flagging, there's a narrow, overgrown, awkward trail ascending the left bank of a creeklet. That's the way.

At McKay Lake (820 m / 2690 ft), cross the outlet on logs. Climb steeply southeast toward a 1060-m (3477-ft) low point on the ridge, then follow the ridge right (southeast). Pass a pond and start ascending steeply again to the final ridge. The trail turns north, then west to reach the summit of 1279-m (4195-ft) Mt. St. Benedict.

Trip 21

Mt. Steele

Location	Sechelt Peninsula
Round trip	18 km (11.2 mi)
Elevation gain	543 m (1781 ft)
Time required	4 to 5 ½ hours
Available	mid-June through mid-October
Map	Sechelt Inlet 92 G/12

OPINION

Enough Sunshine Coast hype. Average hikers, lacking cross-country navigation skills and all-day bushwhacking fortitude, will be dissatisfied with most scenery within easy reach. It has been, and continues to be, rampaged by loggers. You can see how badly from the open summit of Mt. Steele—if you get that far. The logging road to the trailhead is rough. The hike tedious. Don't let this mountain steal any of your time.

Still curious? Sections of the approach road are rocket-launch steep. The first 3 km (1.9 mi) makes for anxious driving in the rain. The final spur road is so ditch-riddled many drivers will give up and back down. Most of the way is high on a slope, next to a dizzying drop. All the valleys and mountainsides within view have been clearcut. Such a grim atmosphere won't buoy you up for a jolly outing. Neither will the choice of initial hiking routes: boggy trail, or more logging road.

To Edwards Lake, the trail winds through a narrow corridor of trees saved from the saw. It's a faint path across boggy meadows, beside a dainty stream, in a mossy, primeval-looking forest. Squishing and splashing through this mucky mess, we could only travel about 2.5 km (1.6 mi) an hour. Though it's drier in mid-summer, there's no excuse for hiking here then.

If you come despite our warning, bypass the initial stretch of boot-drenching trail. Drive to Tannis Lake, then walk the abandoned logging road 15 minutes to where a better trail leads to Edwards Lake in another 10 minutes. That way you'll feel like a hiker, instead of a salamander. You'll miss Gilbert Lake, but it's no loss. Edwards is more impressive, and even it won't be taking up space in your memory. What you might remember are the bugs. Swatting flies and mosquitoes is the big activity here. Beyond Edwards, the trail climbs steeply through unremarkable trees to the subalpine summit, where you'll find great views of nothing worth looking at.

FACT

Before your trip

Request the *Mount Steele Backcountry Ski Trails Map* from the Sunshine Coast Forest District office (604-485-0700).

By Car

From the Langdale ferry terminal, drive Highway 101 northwest to Sechelt. At 25.6 km (15.9 mi), slow down at the sign for Porpoise Bay Provincial Park. At 26.6 km (16.5 mi), turn right (north) on Wharf Road. At 27.2 km (16.9 mi), turn right onto Porpoise Bay Road. Soon pass the park entrance. At 36 km (22.3 mi), pass an unsigned Interfor logging road. At 36.2 km (22.4 mi), turn right on Upland Drive. Go 0.5 km (0.3 mi) and turn right on Carmel Place to get onto the Grey Creek Logging Road.

The road you want to stay on is periodically marked by ski signs. About 6.8 km (4.2 mi) up, stay right, where a narrower road ascends left to Mt. Richardson. Stay left on the main road at the next fork. At the MILE 7 marker (11.3 km / 7.0 mi), ascend right on a narrow, steep road. As you turn, look left for a sign in the trees: MT TETRAHEDRON. Drive up 1.1 km (0.7 mi) to a large information sign at a dirt lot on the left, shortly after the road levels. You can start hiking here or, as we suggest, avoid a miserable stretch of trail by driving 1.3 km (0.8 mi) farther up. As soon as you see Tannis Lake, park next to the big logs blocking an abandoned road on the left. A still driveable road continues contouring right, around the southeast side of the lake.

On Foot

If you park in the dirt lot with the large information sign and want to brave the bogs, start by walking the worn old road left of the sign. The actual trail begins in 75 meters. Follow the blazes and flagging. Those, plus a little directional sense, will get you to Gilbert Lake at 2.4 km (1.5 mi). Allow 1 hour. Edwards Lake is 0.9 km (0.6 mi) farther, at 3.3 km (2.0 mi).

If you park near Tannis Lake, go left on the grassy, old roadbed. Proceed for about 1 km (0.6 mi). In the valley to your left, below the clearcut, is a narrow band of trees. There's a mucky trail down there leading through bogs to Edwards Lake. You're bypassing that. In 10-15 minutes, where the road is again blocked by logs, follow the blazed trail descending left into forest. This broad, recently built path will lead you to the south end of Edwards Lake within 10 minutes. Continue 20 meters north to where the trail from Gilbert Lake joins from the left. There's a large, colourful, backcountry ski-trail map nearby. There's also a warning sign for people heading to the Mt. Steele cabin: THIS TRAIL RECOMMENDED FOR EXPERT HIKERS ONLY. RETURN TRIP TO THIS POINT APPROXIMATELY 5 HOURS. From this signed junction, proceed north/northeast.

Hike along the north side of the lake, through meadows and bogs. The trail gently rises, heading east. About 1.6 km (1 mi) from Edwards Lake, reach Edwards Cabin. The trail then switchbacks northeast before heading west into a pass between the lesser peak of Mt. Steele (west, to your left) and the greater peak (east, to your right). Views open up as you ascend. Follow cairns and poles northeast on the ridge to the Mt. Steele Cabin—4.7 km (2.9 mi) from Edwards Lake, and 6 km (3.7 mi) from where you parked your car near Tannis Lake. Hemlocks and heather grace the slopes. If you've come this far, be sure to climb 150 m (492 ft) higher, along the trailless rocky ridge east of the cabin, to the 1500-m (4920-ft) summit of Mt. Steele.

Trip 22

Unnecessary Mountain from Lions Bay

Location	Howe Sound
Round trip	9.5 km (6.0 mi)
Elevation gain	1310 m (4297 ft)
Time required	6 hours
Available	July through October
Maps	ITM Vancouver's Northshore; North Vancouver 92 G/6

OPINION

Heart-attack steep and steel-wool rough, the old trail up Unnecessary Mountain, from Lions Bay, entices few hikers. There are easier, more enjoyable routes. Only if you're preparing for the Eco-Challenge is this a worthwhile training hike. And only Wile E. Coyote would descend the mountain this way, careening between obstacles like a demon-possessed maniac.

You can reach Unnecessary Mountain in the same time by hiking the Lions trail (Trip 10), which also starts in Lions Bay, on Sunset Drive. That way you spread the elevation gain over 7.5 km (4.7 mi), rather than the compressed 4.8 km (3.0 mi). The popular approach to Unnecessary starts higher (Trip 15), at the Cypress ski area parking lot.

If you ignore our advice and assault this now unnecessary trail, you'll have to confront a dicey scramble down the mountain's north side to continue along Howe Sound Crest to the Lions. With only one vehicle in your party, you'd also have to ascend that 100 m (333 ft) on the return.

FACT

By Car

From the turnoff to Horseshoe Bay, just outside West Vancouver, drive 11.5 km (7.1 m) north on Highway 99 to Lions Bay. Turn right onto Oceanview Road. Proceed 1.3 km (0.8 mi) to the road's end. Parking space is limited.

On Foot

Walk up the gated road, past the water tower. The trail starts beside a sign NO TRESPASSING. It ascends steeply southeast. You'll encounter lots of deadfall. Expect to use your hands on several ragged stretches. Nearing the ridge, at 1200 m (3936 ft), the trail heads east. When you intersect the Howe Sound Crest Trail (HSCT), turn left (north) and soon attain the north summit of 1524-m (5000-ft) Unnecessary Mountain.

Continuing to the Lions? Carefully scramble 100 m (330 ft) down the north side of Unnecessary Mountain. Stay right at rock slabs in a dip in the crest, where the Lions trail joins from the left. It's 20 minutes farther, including an easy scramble over an outcropping, to the base of the West Lion.

Trip 23

Deeks and Brunswick Lakes

Location	Howe Sound, Cypress Provincial Park, North
Round trip	14.4 km (9 mi) to Deeks Lake, 20 km (12.4 mi) to Brunswick Lake
Elevation gain	90 m (3247 ft) to Deeks, 1120 m (3670 ft) to Brunswick
Time required	7 hours for Deeks, 11 hours for Brunswick
Available	mid-June through early September; later you won't have enough light for a round trip to Brunswick
Maps	ITM Vancouver's Northshore; Squamish 92 G/11

OPINION

Put your boots where the beauty is. Somewhere else. Deeks Lake is a popular destination only because it's close to Vancouver. People who recommend it haven't seen enough of the Coast Mountains to really know.

Slow hikers will endure four sweaty hours of arduous tedium to Deeks Lake. That makes it a full day's trip. And for what? The first two-thirds of the hike is on a viewless old logging road, through scrubby forest. Reaching the lake is merely a relief. It's nothing to marvel at. Just another forest-ringed basin filled with water. There's hardly even any place to sit on the stingy shoreline.

Where to go instead? This book is filled with superior alternatives. Wedgemount Lake (Trip 4), for example, requires only a little more effort but offers scenery that'll blow your hair back. Brandywine Meadows (Trip 1) is way easier, yet it's as captivating as Deeks is dull.

If you get dragged along on someone's lame choice for a dayhike, and you find yourself at Deeks Lake, be sure to continue around the west shore. Follow the inlet creek upstream into its narrow, intimate canyon. You'll find this the most pleasing sight of the trip.

Hiking to Deeks Lake is only justified if you're barreling by on your way to Brunswick Lake—a highlight of the Howe Sound Crest, but merely a footnote in the southern Coast Mountains. It's set in an impressive subalpine cirque, beneath the soaring walls of two-horned Brunswick Mountain.

From Brunswick Lake, the HSCT climbs 244 m (800 ft) to Hat Pass. Plugging all the way up there is unnecessary. The pass is a yawn. It is, however, worth ascending the first couple hundred feet above the lake for a better view.

FACT

By Car

From the turnoff to Horseshoe Bay, just outside West Vancouver, drive 22.5 km (14.0 mi) north on Highway 99 to a large pullout on the left. There's an information kiosk and a sign HOWE SOUND CREST, DEEKS LAKE on the right. Or, if you're heading south from Squamish on Highway 99, look for the paved parking lot beneath the Chief (the dominating cliff). From there, drive 19.2 km (11.9 mi) farther to the Deeks pullout, on the right. The elevation here is 60 m (200 ft).

On Foot

Starting on the east side of the highway, across from the pullout, the trail is initially steep. Quickly attain a view of Howe Sound. In about 15 minutes reach a T-intersection with an old road signed for Deeks Lake. Turn right. In another 5 minutes the road forks. Stay right.

In about 1 hour, stay straight at an unsigned fork. Five minutes later, the road forks again. Stay left.

About 5 minutes later, a trail branches right. Highway 99 is right. Go straight on the Howe Sound Crest Trail (HSCT), which at this point is still a road. It's 3.3 km (2.0 mi) farther to Deeks Lake. Reach yet another fork in about 5 more minutes. Stay left, on the main road.

A few minutes farther, after a total of about 1 ½ hours, come to another signed fork. Go left on the Bluff trail toward Deeks Lake. The road going right is the HSCT, which also leads to Deeks Lake. After about 2 hours of hiking, reach a fork. Go right, following another Deeks Lake sign. Ten minutes farther, enter big timber. Leave the salal and scrubby trees behind.

Roughly 2 ½ hours from the trailhead, reach a signed junction. Right is an older route, now blocked by a slide. Ascend left. You're again on an abandoned logging road, in scrubby forest. Climbing steeply, you'll soon be on a trail, re-entering big timber within 45 minutes.

After 3 ¾ hours of hiking, the trail is still climbing steeply, now beside a roaring cascade. Just after your first view of the water, the trail forks. Stay right.

Deeks Lake is at 7.2 km (4.5 mi). Total hiking time: 4 hours for slow hikers, 3 ½ hours for moderately fit hikers, 2 ½ to 2 ¾ hours for strong, determined hikers. According to a metal plaque on a tree, the elevation here is 1050 m (3444 ft), though it's higher on the topo map. Where you arrive at the northwest end of the lake, you'll find tent sites just above the shore.

The HSCT continues right, around the west shore of the lake. Cross the outlet creek on logs. At the south end of the lake, as you approach the inlet creek, the trail turns south, upstream. Enter a narrow canyon. Where logs span the creek, cross from the west bank to the east. There's an inviting pool here, big enough for plunging. Continue south.

An hour after leaving the north end of Deeks Lake, arrive at Middle Lake. Also called Hanover Lake, it's small, with steep, forested sides. The trail stays high above the east shore. Descending to the water isn't easy.

After climbing beside the waterfall that flows into Middle Lake, enter another canyon. Broader than the last, this one is garden-like, with a quiet, meandering stream. The trail then crosses heather meadows, passes a pond, and affords a view south to Brunswick Mountain and the shelter above Brunswick Lake.

About 30 minutes after leaving Middle Lake, arrive at Brunswick Lake. Total distance: 10 km (6.2 mi). The elevation here is 1180 m (3870 ft). Set in a subalpine cirque, the turquoise water rests at the base of towering Brunswick Mountain.

To proceed on the HSCT, when you reach the main body of Brunswick Lake, go right. Cross the outlet stream and ascend steeply right (southwest). Pass the shelter. It's tiny, Spartan, for emergencies only. Looking back north, you can see Hanover and Deeks lakes. After climbing about 45 minutes from Brunswick Lake, reach Hat Pass at 1424 m (4670 ft). The subalpine pass is short and narrow, but open, with a big tarn in the middle.

From Hat Pass, the HSCT contours around the west and south sides of Brunswick Mountain to Magnesia Meadows, then proceeds south. About 5 minutes beyond the pass, and again within 15 minutes, watch the trees for plaques stating times and directions to various destinations. About 20 minutes after leaving Hat Pass, Magnesia Meadows is visible southeast, across the Magnesia Creek drainage.

Trip 24

Deeks Peak

Location	Howe Sound
Round trip	16 km (10 mi)
Elevation gain	1613 m (5291 ft)
Time required	8 hours
Available	July through October
Maps	ITM Vancouver's Northshore; Squamish 92 G/11

OPINION

Mountains are as easily and frequently scarred as the human heart. What's impressive about the scars on Deeks Peak is their height. It's amazing loggers could build roads this far up the walls of Howe Sound. But hiking on them, through emasculated forest, is a waste of time. This trip is wearisome—mentally and physically.

It's stupidly steep. A lot of it's also a brushy, scratchy thrash, because the route is rarely if ever maintained. When an opening in the trees allows a glimpse west, all you see are the ho-hum humps of the Rainy River Peaks on the Sechelt Peninsula. The summit scenery is better, of course, but doesn't justify the trouble to get there.

Hike into Garibaldi Lake (Trip 27) or Mamquam Lake (Trip 30) instead. With imagination and effort, you can escape the crowds and worship unscarred nature in solitude.

FACT

By Car

See Deeks and Brunswick lakes (Trip 23) for directions.

On Foot

The trail starts on the east side of the highway. In about 15 minutes reach a T-intersection with an old road signed for Deeks Lake. Turn right. In another 5 minutes, follow the more eroded branch left. The road/trail switchbacks up the mountainside. Heading east and slightly north, the trail nears Kallahne Creek, then swings away from it. Cross the creek's west fork and soon get a view of Howe Sound. After crossing a rockslide, the old road ascends south to Kallahne Lake, at roughly 4.5 km (3 mi). The elevation here is 1160 m (3805 ft), so you've gained 1100 m (3608 ft).

Cross the log jam at the outlet and pass the west side of the lake. Just beyond the lake, stay on the right branch of the bedrock road. Enter big timber. You're now following a faint, rugged, taped route. Head slightly west of south before turning east and ascending—very steeply now—the ridge to the main (second) summit of 1673-m (5487-ft) Deeks Peak. Impressive Sky Pilot is nearby, northeast, followed by the king, Mt. Garibaldi. 1679-m (5507-ft) Mt. Windsor is southeast across a pass.

Trip 25

Place Glacier

Location	Birkenhead Road
Round trip	21 km (13 mi)
Elevation gain	1310 m (4300 ft)
Time required	9 hours
Available	July through October
Map	Pemberton 92 J/7

OPINION

This is not an Equal Opportunity trail. No handrails. No switch-backs. No moderate grades. Nobody responsible for your comfort and safety, but you.

It's a torturous trip, strictly for keen climbers gunning for Place Glacier. The primitive route will even work *them* hard, like a heartless Industrial Revolution factory boss.

Deadfall frequently blocks the route, forcing you to clamber up the extremely steep slope *and* over big trees. It's precarious. Achieving a better vantage of Mt. Ronayne and Sun God Mountain isn't worth the two hours of strain and risk required to reach the Vodka Rock view-point. And that's less than half way to the glacier.

Place Glacier is fantastic, especially if you're equipped to proceed onto the ice. And you're likely to have the Place all to yourself. But the aggressive 1310-m (4300-ft) ascent is almost entirely in trees. Most hikers will agree, it's just too much to ask.

FACT

By Car

See Trip 63.

On Foot

See Trip 63 for directions to lower Place Falls. Beyond, the steep, narrow route scurries heedlessly up the east edge of Place Creek gorge. After climbing 400 m (1300 ft), cross a rockslide. From a perch called Vodka Rock, views are northwest to Mt. Ronayne and 2315-m (7593-ft) Sun God Mountain. The rough route plows through more deadfall to reach a questionable log jam where you must cross to the west side of the creek at 1420 m (4660 ft). After that, the grade slacks off as the trail swings southwest. Later it approaches the creek again. Just beneath the glacier, scramble up the rocky headwall about 152 m (500 ft), then go left and cross the dam. The elevation here is 1830 m (6000 ft).

BACKPACK TRIPS

Mamquam Mountain, from Paul Ridge (Trip 30)

Trip 26
Lake Lovely Water

Location	Tantalus Range, Squamish
Round trip	10 km (6.2 mi)
Elevation gain	1128 m (3700 ft)
Time required	4 to 5 ½ hours up, 2 ¾ to 4 hours down
Available	mid-July through October
Maps	ITM Garibaldi Region;
	Cheakamus River 92 G/14;
	BC Parks handout

OPINION

The Tantalus Range has chutzpah. Starting nearly at sea level, wearing glaciers like armor, these bold peaks rear their heads as high as 2575 meters (8450 feet). Visible from Highway 99 and the Squamish Valley road, their defiant stance goads hikers to venture closer. This trail is one of the few allowing people of average strength and normal pain threshold to respond to that intimidating invitation.

At trail's end is a resplendent mountain cirque cupping a high sub-alpine lake that lives up to its name. It's the Coast Mountain equivalent of the Canadian Rockies' Lake Louise. The difference is that here you have to pay. The price of admission is a wickedly steep ascent. Though fit hikers can make this a rigorous day trip, it's worth hauling a full pack so you can make the most of your accomplishment.

The trail to Lake Lovely Water is even steeper than those to Wedgemount Lake (Trip 4) and Mt. Roderick (Trip 36). In places, you can look down and see the hiker behind you—between your legs. The trail is narrow, often no wider than two boots, but it's almost brush-free, and despite the radical grade it's in decent condition. Otherwise this trip would be a climb instead of a hike. Still, some hikers might be uncomfortable traversing the steepest slopes next to the creek gorge, where you have to grab hold of roots and haul yourself up.

Unless you have muscles like Popeye, the way to experience anything approximating pleasure on a hike this demanding is to clear your mind. Eliminate discomfort by relinquishing judgment and comparison. Hike with a zen attitude of calm alertness. If you're fully aware of

Lake Lovely Water

each moment, nothing more, the duration or difficulty of the hike is not an issue. The child in the back of your mind asking "When are we gonna get there?" disappears. You stop nagging yourself with progress reports and simply hike, one step at time. You just know you'll get there when you get there. Observe each beautiful, ancient tree in this lush rain forest, and your impatience to escape the trees will subside. (Good thing, since even the lakeshore is treed.) By not precluding enjoyment until you reach the destination, you might experience something even deeper en route.

About 1 ½ hours up, the trail is near Lovely Water Creek and crosses several tributaries. You'll occasionally see the creek cascading through the mossy gorge. Approaching the lake, you'll climb beside powerful falls generating a refreshing blast of mist. It's one of the few places on the entire trip where you can truly relax, without being annoyed by flies. Start preparing for them now. Practice flapping your arms around your head. Or bring a head net.

The hut is an inviting one—solid, spacious, clean, comfortable. And it has two rowboats. If you're an Alpine Club member, or if no members are around to use them, you could row into the middle of the lake for an IMAX perspective of this incredible setting. Also consider hiking to Lambda Lake. Round trip from the hut takes only half a day. Or you can camp there. From Lambda, continue exploring northwest into the basin beneath 2317-m (7600-ft) Serratus Mountain. Allow a full day for that if you're staying at the hut.

Omega, Pelops, Niobe, Pandareus, Ionia, Serratus, and Alpha peaks surround Lake Lovely Water. Like Sirens, they lure climbers onto the rock and ice. Hiking to the lake seems an impressive feat, until you look up and imagine scaling higher. Alpha and Omega mountains are favourites. Superheroes also travel the ridges from Iota Mountain to Mounts Sedgwick and Roderick.

In addition to all the little bugs, you might have some big bugs flying in. Currently two helicopter companies are licensed by BC Parks to land on the lake. But the frequent fly-overs by commercial and private planes are more bothersome.

FACT

Before your trip

To reach the trailhead, on the west bank of the Squamish River, you must canoe across. If you don't own a boat, you'll have to rent one or pay somebody to ferry you. Jay Bicknell of Kodiak Adventures in Squamish will take you across and meet you for the return at an appointed time. Cost: approximately $20 (1999) per person, round trip. Reservations: (604) 898-3356.

If you want to stay in the hut, make reservations with Ron Royston of the Alpine Club of Canada: 604-687-2711. Ask the BC Parks Garibaldi / Sunshine Coast District office (604-898-3678) for the park hand-out.

By Car

From Squamish, at the traffic light by Esso and McDonald's, drive Highway 99 north 10 km (6.2 mi). Or, if you're heading south on Highway 99, continue 31.6 km (19.6 mi) past Brandywine Falls Provincial Park. For either approach, turn west onto Squamish Valley Road, across from the Alice Lake Provincial Park turnoff. Just over 2 km (1.3 mi) from Highway 99, stay straight (right) toward Cheekeye. Left leads into Squamish. At 3.7 km (2.3 mi) cross the Cheakamus River. About 100 meters beyond is a junction. Stay left on Squamish Valley Road.

You'll then drive through Native reserve. Look for a dirt road on the left at 6 km (3.7 mi), as the road curves then straightens out. Turn left here. It might be posted NO TRESPASSING. Continue in 2 km (1.9 mi). Park by the BC Hydro right-of-way, where powerlines cross the road and a cable spans the river. The elevation here is 30 m (100 ft). There's no ladder up to the cable car, and the car is locked to prevent the public from using it.

On Foot

After canoeing to the west bank of the Squamish River, pick up the trail near the cable car tower. Follow it upstream (north), paralleling the river. Immediately stay left of an aluminum shed. In 30 minutes, cross a dry creekbed. Look for flagging on the other side. Clamber steeply over rocky terrain. The trail then improves and is frequently blazed. Soon reach the edge of a clearcut where you turn sharply left (southwest) and ascend.

Within 1 ½ hours, you'll see raging Lovely Water Creek. Within 2 ¼ hours, at about 565 m (1850 ft), a path forks right, dropping 10 meters to a good rest spot beside slick rock and a waterfall. This is roughly where you enter Lake Lovely Water Recreation Area.

Within 3 ¼ hours, cross a couple streams. The trail soon tilts skyward again. If you're ascending on a clear day, you'll be thankful you're not in the sun on the other side of the gorge. Thirty minutes after the last stream, reach a gentle waterfall. Several minutes farther, there's another good rest spot where you again cross a stream. The elevation here is about 975 m (3200 ft).

You'll cross one more stream before attaining the first view over the Squamish and Cheakamus river valleys. Diamond Head is just a bit north of east. The Black Tusk is northeast. Here, the Lovely Water Creek gorge is a deep gash. The falling water pounds explosively.

Reach Lake Lovely Water at 1160 m (3800 ft). The Alpine Club hut is 200 meters to the right, across the mouth of the creek. Visit the hut's lake frontage for an unobstructed view of the water and surrounding mountains. Starting right (northwest) and continuing counterclockwise, you're looking at Alpha, Serratus, Ionia, Pandareus, and Niobe. To your left (south and a bit east) is nearby Omega Mountain.

You have a choice of five campsites: behind the hut; on a sandspit on Lovely Water's southeast shore; above Lovely Water's north shore, near Lambda Lake; at the northwest end of Lovely Water, or in the basin above.

Where you arrived at the lake, the rough, blazed trail left (south) leads to the sandspit in about 20 minutes. Hike up and down through dense forest (gaining 60 m / 197 ft) to the top of a boulder field. Scramble down the boulders to the sandspit, visible below. There's room for several tents, but you'll have no privacy. A creek originating in Omega Bowl flows into the lake here. The impressive bowl—buggy meadows, steep walls, no camping allowed—is a 10-minute scramble up the east side of the creek.

The Lambda Lake basin, above where Lake Lovely Water narrows, is easy to recognize. To get there, pick up the path from the hut and travel above Lovely Water's north shore. On the way, about 10 minutes from the hut, you'll pass a small sandy beach ideal for swimming. Reach Lambda Lake in about 1 ¼ hours.

Trip 27
Garibaldi Lake/
Black Tusk/Panorama Ridge

Location	Squamish, Garibaldi Provincial Park
Round trip	35 km (22 mi), includes the ridge on Black Tusk, and Panorama Ridge
Elevation gain	2450 m (8035 ft) total
Time required	2 to 4 days (3 to 4 hours one way to the lake)
Available	mid-July through October
Maps	ITM Whistler and Region; BC Parks brochure; Cheakamus River 92 G/14

OPINION

Wilderness with the edges sanded off. That's Garibaldi Park. The beauty is raw, but it's easily accessible on gently graded, well maintained trails. Signposts are frequent but unnecessary; the park is so popular, there will always be someone you can ask for directions. The major campgrounds are huge, accommodating dozens of tents. There's even a contingent of rangers here all summer. That's the way it is with areas of outstanding natural beauty, like Yosemite, Chamonix, Banff. They draw crowds, which require management, which diminishes the qualities that made the place appealing to begin with. Diminish but not destroy. Garibaldi Park is still magnificent. Go. Whether you need those edges sanded off or want to rough them up, you'll be witnessing one of the world's strongholds of alpine grandeur.

The scenery here is what we're all after on a Pacific Northwest hike. Big trees. Big lake. Big glaciers. Big meadows. And big views of the whole sprawling expanse. Visible across Garibaldi Lake's vividly coloured glacial water are Guard Mountain and the Sphinx Glacier. Just above and a bit northwest of the lake are the Taylor Meadows, which you can swing through on your way to or from the lake.

After pitching your tent at the lake or meadows campground, your first dayhike should be to Panorama Ridge, high above the lake's north shore. As the name implies, this is the penultimate vantage point. So you'll need a clear sky to enjoy it fully. Here, the view magnifies to

Garibaldi Lake from Panorama Ridge

include the Warren Glacier on 2694-m (8837-ft) Mt. Garibaldi to the south, as well as countless other spires and patches of ice in all directions. We prefer Panorama Ridge to the Black Tusk. The Ridge is a gradual ramble that leads you closer to the big glaciers and gives you the option of forging deeper into wilderness. The Tusk overlooks Highway 99, and from the summit there's no place to go but down.

The Black Tusk is the oddest and most distinct volcanic peak in Garibaldi Park. Ascending the alpine meadows toward this striking monolith is worthwhile. But plodding over scree to its base is no joy. And reaching the summit requires serious scrambling up a chimney—it's not for everyone. Instead, we recommend heading northeast to the bizarre, fascinating, volcanic ash flats near Helm Lake. Continue at least as far as the unbridged crossing of Helm Creek to witness the bare surrealism of the black soil and voluptuous cinder cones. It's possible to hike there, explore Panorama Ridge, and approach the Black Tusk, all in a dayhike starting from Garibaldi Lake or Taylor Meadows.

Don't have a couple days to spend in the area? Fleet-footed hikers can see the highlights in a single day by hustling to Garibaldi Lake, charging up Panorama Ridge, then racing back down through Taylor Meadows. The challenge is leaving so much beauty after spending so little time in it. You really should backpack, even though you'll probably be camping with a gaggle of other admirers. Ideally, make this a more adventurous, 24-km (15-mi) shuttle trip by hiking the Helm

Creek trail (Trip 31) through a broad, subalpine valley, past the Helm Creek campground, then down into lush forest and out along the Cheakamus River. Allow at least an extra day for side trips. Experienced cross-country trekkers can escape the carnival atmosphere by picking their own route southeast from the Garibaldi Lake ranger cabin, to Mt. Price or Clinker Peak.

The campgrounds at Garibaldi Lake and Taylor Meadows are both in exquisite settings. Relaxing on the shore of the 300-meter-deep, 7-km-long lake is wonderful. So is ambling through the enormous, flower-dappled meadows. If you're lucky, you'll snag one of the choice campsites on the lakeshore, or beside Taylor Creek. The creek has the advantage of drowning out other campers' noise.

Noise. It's infuriating. You go backpacking to get away from civilization, and you find yourself lying awake, listening to other campers yuk it up. At campgrounds as big and crowded as Garibaldi Lake or Taylor Meadows, all you can do is bring earplugs and try not to be noisy yourself. After dusk, whisper, especially when passing other tents. If you speak loudly, stay in the cooking shelters. If you want peace, pitch your tent as far away from the shelters as possible. Slam the door on the pit toilet and you deserve to be locked inside the fetid contraption. At Helm Creek campground, where the sites are close together with no foliage in between, keeping quiet is even more important.

Before you commit to a one-way trip starting at the Rubble Creek trailhead and ending at the Cheakamus Lake trailhead, a warning: Muscling the cable car across the Cheakamus River might be impossible for a solo hiker. Two people can do it if they're strong, but it's still a struggle.

FACT

By Car

Driving Highway 99 north from Squamish, continue 28 km (17.4 mi) past the turnoff for Alice Lake Provincial Park. Or, if you're driving south from Whistler Village, continue 13 km (8 mi) past Brandywine Falls Provincial Park.

From either approach, look for the BC Parks sign indicating where you turn east toward the Black Tusk / Garibaldi Provincial Park trailhead. Proceed 2.6 km (1.6 mi) to the parking lot above Rubble Creek. The elevation here is 595 m (1950 ft).

If you're hiking one-way, exiting via the Helm Creek trail, read Trip 51 for directions to the Cheakamus Lake trailhead.

On Foot

Bring money. BC Parks rangers will charge you to camp at Garibaldi Lake and Taylor Meadows. There's no charge at Helm Creek campground.

The trail to Garibaldi Lake is posted with white and green signs indicating elevation, as well as the direction and distance to various destinations. The directions are correct on all the signs. But the elevation and distance figures are sometimes contradictory. Overall, the white signs seem to be more reliable.

Ascending east above Rubble Creek, the trail is moderately graded and wide enough to allow two people to hike abreast and talk. The trees in this ancient forest are stately Douglas fir and red cedar. Cross a bridged creek within 30 minutes. After gaining 770 m (2525 ft) in 6 km (3.7 mi), reach a signed junction with benches. The elevation here is 1350 m (4438 ft). Right leads to Garibaldi Lake campground in 3 km (1.9 mi). Left leads to Taylor Meadows campground in 2 km (1.2 mi).

Staying right toward the lake, the forest opens up as you approach evidence of the area's volcanic past. Garibaldi Lake was formed in the mid-1850s when a lava flow from Mt. Price hardened into a natural dam. Visible directly south, across the canyon, it's called The Barrier.

The trail levels, re-enters trees, passes Barrier Lake, then Lesser Garibaldi Lake, and reaches a junction. Left leads to Taylor Meadows. Stay straight for Garibaldi Lake. Cross Parnasus Creek on a major bridge with yellow rope railing. About 25 meters beyond is another junction and the bridge over the Garibaldi Lake outlet stream. Here, 9 km (5.6 mi) from the trailhead, the elevation is 1470 m (4822 ft).

Right (south, across the bridge) is Garibaldi Lake campground. After arriving at the lake's northwest shore, you'll see a cooking shelter and a campground map/sign.

Left (staying north of the outlet stream) ascends 105 m (344 ft) in 2.5 km (1.6 mi) to a signed junction and a pit toilet in Black Tusk Meadows. Turning left (southwest) there, you'll gently descend 2 km (1.2 mi) through heather meadows to the Taylor Meadows campground and cooking shelter. From Taylor Meadows, at 1479 m (4850 ft), you can turn left and loop southeast back to Garibaldi Lake in 2 km (1.2 mi). Or you can continue descending generally west to the Rubble Creek trailhead in 8 km (5 mi).

Turning right (northeast) at the Black Tusk Meadows junction, you can proceed to the Black Tusk, Panorama Ridge, Helm Lake, or the Cheakamus Lake trailhead. In 0.5 km (0.3 mi) you'll reach a fork. Left (north) leads to the Black Tusk. Straight (northeast) leads to the other points just mentioned.

On the way to the Tusk, you'll ascend through lush, marmot-mad meadows profuse with wildflowers and laced with creeklets. Within 40 minutes start crossing a boulder field. The trail switchbacks steeply toward a ridge. The south face of the Tusk glares down from above. Views of Garibaldi Lake expand. The trail then angles left (northwest). After 1 hour, at about 2.5 km (1.6 mi), you'll attain the 2012-m (6600-ft) ridge just southeast of the 2316-m (7596-ft) Tusk. Many people will be satisfied stopping here. The Fitzsimmons Range is visible northeast. South, across Garibaldi Lake, you can see Clinker Peak just right of Mt. Price. Left and farther south is the Warren Glacier on Mt. Garibaldi. Castle Towers Mountain is southeast, north of Guard Mountain and the Sphinx Glacier. To reach the summit of the Tusk, continue west under the south face, pass a few chimneys and ascend the one that's flagged.

From where the trail forked left toward the Black Tusk, if you proceed straight (northeast) you'll pass Mimulus Lake and reach another fork in 2 km (1.2 mi). Left (north) on the main trail is Helm Lake. Right (east, then south) is Panorama Ridge—365 m (1200 ft) higher and 3 km (1.9 mi) distant. It's a decent trail the whole way; even kids can handle it.

Turning right for Panorama Ridge, the trail initially descends and passes just east of Black Tusk Lake. It then climbs through trees and heather to the rib that leads south to the ridgecrest. Above treeline, follow the cairns. The 2105-m (6900-ft) summit affords a 360° view: Garibaldi Lake and Mt. Garibaldi are south, the Tantalus Range southwest, the Black Tusk northwest, the Cinder Flats north, Castle Towers Mountain southeast, ice everywhere. The mesa-like mountain in front of Mt. Garibaldi was named by a genius: it's called The Table.

Experienced cross-country travelers can follow the Panorama ridgecrest east, dropping 152 m (500 ft) then ascending to Gentian Peak on the south side of Helm Glacier. With overnight gear, you can descend to Gentian Pass and ascend the northwest slopes of Polemonium Ridge, just west of Castle Towers Mountain.

Continuing northeast on the main trail, from the junction with the spur trail up Panorama Ridge, you'll descend between Helm Lake and the Cinder Cone. Stay on the trail through here; bootprints in the cinder are like graffiti. When you reach unbridged Helm Creek, however, turn right (east) off trail for a level, 400-meter walk to a view of the Helm Glacier. As for negotiating the creek, if you don't want to de-boot and wade the calf-deep water, it's possible to hop across (try downstream) on boulders and sandbars. The trail north of the creek picks up downstream from where you arrived at the south bank. Ignore footprints heading upstream on the north bank.

Heading northeast from Helm Creek, you'll easily cross two more small creeks. The trail is adequate, though much narrower than it was near Garibaldi Lake. It's again well-marked: posts with reflectors keep you on track. The view ahead is of the U-shaped, subalpine Helm Creek valley.

Helm Creek campground (Trip 31) is 8 km (5 mi) from Garibaldi Lake. It's the same distance from the campground down to the Cheakamus Lake trailhead. Fill your waterbottles at the campground. The trail immediately drops into dense forest and pulls away from the creek.

Trip 28
Stein Divide

Location	Pemberton, Stein Wilderness
Round trip	28.6 km (17.7 mi) to Tundra Lake
Elevation gain	1265 m (4150 ft), includes the trek up the 4WD road; 305 m (1000 ft) going out
Time required	3 to 4 days
Available	late July through mid-October
Maps	ITM Stein Valley Trail, Garibaldi Region; Stein Lake 92 J / 1

OPINION

The Coast Range has higher mountains, bigger lakes, and more impressive glaciers elsewhere. Yet the totality of the alpine Stein moved us more deeply than anyplace else we trekked while writing this book. Check out the cover photo. It was taken from Tabletop Mountain, just above Iceberg Lake, looking east at the Stein Divide—where this journey leads.

Wandering the boulder-strewn benches and flower-peppered slopes between Arrowhead and Tundra lakes is a sublime alpine experience. Meltwater creeklets are omnipresent. Ponds, tarns and lakes are set just far enough apart so you continually feel the thrill of discovery. The peaks are not fierce, but they're sufficiently imposing to keep your eyes flitting across the rock and ice. Intent on no particular destination, it's easy to spend many happy hours rambling in a single exquisite basin or scrambling up just one of the smaller mountains.

Watching the sun perform its morning and evening ablutions on the cliffs and snowfields in this wide-open expanse is ethereal. In the course of a day, you can see the water surfaces shift hues like kaleidoscopes: iridescent pink and blue at dawn; brilliant turquoise in the morning, glassy mirrors reflecting the landscape in the afternoon; and finally bronze, silver and charcoal in the evening. There's one body of water that's unearthly: Tundra Lake. It's an impossibly vivid, Milk-of-Magnesia-bottle blue.

Some people, thinking they can adequately sample the area in an afternoon, turn around at Lizzie Cabin. Big mistake. The western Stein

Over boulder fields and meadows from Cherry Pip Pass to Caltha Lake

begins to climax just above, at Arrowhead Lake. That's where you enter the unique, magical alpine country. Though strong dayhikers can get there or perhaps farther before turning around, it's a waste to invest all that energy and miss camping in such blissful surroundings.

One of the rewards of backpacking in a wilderness area like this is camping where you please. Find a private, idyllic site, and you're home. It's a tension-relieving joy not to be forced to huddle next to others, as in the Garibaldi Provincial Park backcountry campgrounds. Here, your destiny is your own. Your sense of adventure deepens when you can opt to camp high on a ridge (like Tabletop Mountain) or near a lonely lake. Of course, with this freedom comes the responsibility of practicing Leave No Trace camping. Don't pitch your tent on grass or heather; limit yourself to bare dirt, gravel or rock slabs. Don't wash anything near a lake or stream; do it far enough away so you won't pollute the fresh water. Don't build a fire; carry a stove for cooking. Carefully bury human waste. Pack out all trash, including toilet paper.

Hiking the alpine Stein means facing rough-hewn trails and cairned routes. They work you hard, but they enhance the wild atmosphere. Children and neophytes will struggle here. You'll climb above Lizzie Lake on a narrow, slanted, muddy, deadfall-plagued, hacked-out gash of a trail. It often requires you to lift your boots as high as your waist. Past Lizzie Cabin, the going is easier though usually sloppy in the wet meadows. To reach the first alpine lake basin, you must then negotiate a steep, challenging boulder field. Following the intriguing, small trail from Arrowhead Lake toward Tabletop Mountain is easy. Later, the traverse from Cherry Pip Pass toward Tundra Lake is across more awkward, ankle-eating boulders.

Other negatives? Bugs, of course. The samurai warrior strain. Both flies and mosquitoes. Come prepared to do battle. Another potential enemy here is heat, despite the high elevation. Above treeline, there's no shade except your tent. Bring a lightweight, long-sleeve shirt to block out harmful rays, as well as insects. Sunglasses are essential unless cataract surgery appeals to you. Also, extended alpine terrain means exposure in severe weather. Pack storm-worthy clothing and shelter.

Though the Stein is much less crowded than Garibaldi Park, you'll still have to explore off the beaten paths if tranquility and solitude are your goals. Midweek you'll see maybe a dozen other hikers on the route described here. The vantage points you'll hit along the way will reveal possibilities for exploration. Long and Rainbow lakes, for example, are easy to reach, southwest and southeast of Arrowhead Lake. From Long Lake, you can continue cross-country to Sapphire Lake, Crystal Tarns, and other unnamed, inviting alpine ponds. Or, on your way to Caltha Lake, scope out the rough trek southeast, high above Rogers Creek canyon, to achingly beautiful Figure Eight Lake. The truly hardy venture past Tundra Lake to Elton Lake.

FACT

By Car

From the 3-way junction in Mt. Currie, drive 10.3 km (6.4 mi) northeast on Highway 99. Or, if you're heading southwest from Lillooet on Highway 99, drive 13 km (8 mi) past Joffre Lakes Recreation Area. From either approach, turn southeast at the bottom of a steep hill, onto the In Shuk-ch Forest Service Road. Drive this dirt road southeast along Lillooet Lake, past several free Forest Service campgrounds. At 16 km (10 mi) Lizzie Bay Recreation Site is on the right. At 16.6 km (10.3 mi) turn left onto Port Douglas—Lizzie Creek Branch FS Road. Set your trip odometer to 0 here.

Ascend the valley, now on a narrow, rough road, with Lizzie Creek on your right. At 1 km (0.6 mi), where a lesser road ascends left, bear right, staying with the creek. Fork right on the lower road at 7.4 km (4.6 mi). After 8 km (5 mi), the road gets much rougher and steeper. Most people in 2WD vehicles will want to park here, beside the road. Those with 4WD and the confidence to negotiate a narrow, steep road with a major dropoff on one side can continue 3 km (1.9 mi), gaining 320 m (1050 ft) to the road's end at Lizzie Lake.

On Foot

Without a 4WD vehicle, you'll be hoofing it at least 3 km (1.9 mi) up a steep, dusty road to Lizzie Lake, where the actual trail begins. There's no shade on these lower, clearcut slopes, so start early to avoid getting broiled by the sun.

Most people will start hiking the road at about 1005 m (3300 ft). (This is just before the orange road on the topo map intersects the broken black line designating a rougher road.) In a few minutes, come to a fork. Go left. There should still be a sign here pointing the way to Lizzie Lake. There's parking space here too, in case you kept driving and now want to bail out. Where the main road veers right (southeast) and a fork heads left up a ravaged slope into the East Fork of Lizzie Creek, stay right and start ascending steeply.

Strong roadbusters will cover the 3 km (1.9 mi) to the Lizzie Lake parking lot in about 1 hour. The elevation here is 1326 m (4350 ft). Follow the path toward the lake and turn left (southeast) where it intersects the trail paralleling the lakeshore. A third of the way along the lake (0.5 km / 0.3 mi), look for the tree stump cut like a throne. Take the blazed trail left (east) from there and start ascending away from the lake. Walk through dense timber with a lot of deadfall. If you need to camp now or on the way out, there's a private, lakeview campsite here. Then the trail steepens. As you ascend, the trail periodically divides for short stretches. Often the left path requires less elevation loss and gain.

The trail levels at 1585 m (5200 ft) as it enters the rocky defile of the Gates of Shangri-La. Before descending a huge boulder slide to the refreshing creek, you can look east and see Arrowhead Mountain, which is where you'll enter alpine country and reach the first lake. The trail drops sharply through the Gates. Watch your footing here. The creek has gorgeous pools with sandy bottoms—tempting on a hot day. You'll also find a couple bare tent sites in trees close to the creek. Then the trail resumes through forest, reaching Lizzie Cabin about 10 minutes past the Gates. The cabin is at 1615 m (5300 ft). It's 3.0 km (1.9 mi) from the Lizzie Lake trailhead. The rickety cabin has a woodstove, a loft, table, and old foamies. Treat it kindly.

Follow the trail east of the cabin and soon cross to the south side of the creek. Climb a grassy slope into a basin where the trail levels outs then forks. The minor path right (south) leads to Long Lake. Go left (southeast), aiming for the cascade visible on the rockface above. It's pouring out of Arrowhead Lake. As you get higher, nearing the lip of Arrowhead Lake basin, you can see glaciers north-west above Lillooet Lake.

After gaining 220 m (720 ft) from Lizzie Cabin, reach Arrowhead Lake, just above treeline, at 1835 m (6020 ft). Jump across the outlet stream and continue hiking north along the west side of the lake. There are good tent sites here, though you're likely to have company. From the short rise just west of the lake, you can see the Coast Mountains west and northwest. From the south tip of Arrowhead Lake, where you arrived, it's an easy 30-minute hike through rock-and-heather gardens to Heart Lake, in a bouldery, grassy bowl at 1935 m (6350 ft).

Ascend around the west and north sides of Heart Lake. Follow the cairned path toward the meadowy saddle visible to the east. Where the lake pinches out, there's a faint junction of paths. From here, a steep route heads directly up Tabletop. Look just east of north and you might recognize the namesake table. It's best, however, to stay straight and gently traverse east toward the saddle. Cross above and north (left) of the saddle's lowest point. If you want to go to Iceberg Lake (directly below the east side of the saddle), when the route starts rising steeply, stay lower, contouring southeast to the low point of the saddle. Keep in mind, Iceberg will lose the evening light earlier than Heart or Arrow-head lakes. Immediately southwest of Iceberg Lake, Arrowhead Mountain rises sharply.

From the saddle, as well as higher on the slopes of Tabletop Moun-tain, you can look east, across Rogers Creek canyon, at massive, ice-laden Mount Skook Jim. Caltha Lake is northeast in the large, level basin. With the aid of a topo map, you can pick out the cross-country route from Caltha Lake, southeast to the hidden Figure-Eight Lake basin.

Proceed north from the saddle, over the east shoulder of Tabletop, staying away from the steep drop into Rogers Creek canyon. Contour at about 2043 m (6700 ft), gradually curving northwest, then northeast. If you like to camp high, this is the place to do it—in favourable weather. Water should be available in meltwater pools and trickles.

To reach Caltha Lake, work your way northeast, gradually ascend-ing, until you're just below the northeast ridge of Tabletop Mountain. Follow cairns along the prominent, boulder-strewn benchland. You might pick up a path for a while. Reach about 2088 m (6850 ft) on the gentle slope before cairns lead you down, on the east side of the ridge, to the trail zigzagging through meadows and rocks to 1905-m (6250-ft) Cherry Pip Pass.

Arrive at the pass 1 ¼ hours after leaving the east shoulder of Tabletop. You're now at the head of Rogers Creek canyon and can look southeast down its course. From here, follow the cairned, boot-beaten path 75 m (250 ft) up the north side of the pass along the ridge. The path stays just left of a few trees as it heads east toward the base of Tundra Peak. Then gradually descend east toward the broad, gentle, Caltha Lake basin.

The angling descent to Caltha Lake is across an immense boulder field that requires a lot of leaping, dancing and balancing—hard work with a full pack. Occasionally you'll tag onto traces of dirt path through patches of heather, but mostly just follow the cairns. The lake is now in plain view anyway. You'll cross a few meltwater creeklets big enough to refill bottles. Looking back, you can survey the shoulder of Tabletop that you traversed. The wall of fluted cliffs southeast, off Arrowhead and Tynemouth mountains, is stunning from this vantage. About 1 hour from Cherry Pip Pass, reach good trail that descends steeply at first as you proceed toward Caltha Lake. You don't have to descend all the way to Caltha, at 1814 m (5950 ft), if you're heading to Tundra Lake. Stay north of Caltha and travel northeast, across heather.

Looking northeast, you'll see a stream flowing down from a pass, in front of stunted trees. Aim for the stream and you'll pick up a path climbing to the 1966-m (6450-ft) unnamed pass. Tundra Lake is 107 m (350 ft) directly below the northeast side of the pass. The pass is about 45 minutes from the west end of Caltha Lake and 11.3 km (7.0 mi) from Lizzie Lake.

Tundra Lake is an intense blue (some say purple) similar to Oregon's famous Crater Lake. Looking east beyond the lake, you can see the sharp, ragged, snowcapped peaks of the Coast Mountains dwindle into dull, dry, meadow- and glacier-less ridges.

Rounding Tundra Lake's north shore is difficult but possible. The only place near the lake that's flat enough to pitch a tent is at the far east end. To continue from there to Stein Lake, Elton Lake, or around the east side of Caltha Peak to Figure Eight Lake, requires a topo map, compass, and advanced cross-country skills. To ensure safety, you'd also want a couple days of bombproof blue sky.

On your return trip, descending from the shoulder of Tabletop Mountain it can take as little as 1 ½ hours to Lizzie Cabin, and another 1 ¼ hours to Lizzie Lake.

Trip 29

Southern Chilcotin/Taylor Basin

Location	Carpenter Lake / Gold Bridge
Round trip	37 km (23 mi) plus side trips
Elevation gain	1340 m (4400 ft)
Time required	3 to 4 days
Available	late July through late September
Maps	Spruce Lake Trails; Bralorne 92 J/15, Noaxe Creek 92 O/2

OPINION

The Southern Chilcotin is just a whisker outside the Coast Mountains. It's on the east edge, where icy peaks melt into the Interior Plateau. But we offer a sampling from this wondrous country, for several reasons: (1) any serious hiker in southern B.C. will want to know about the Chilcotin; (2) you'll find few long-distance, flexible-itinerary backpack trips farther south in the range; (3) there's still no guidebook devoted to the area; (4) the easy-to-ascend ridgecrests here are a unique vantage, where you can peer south into the snowcapped Bendor Range at the north edge of the southern Coast Mountains; (5) within a half-day drive of Vancouver, the Chilcotin is more accessible for most people than similar mountain terrain in Mt. Edziza or Spatsizi Plateau parks; (6) it's a satisfaction-guaranteed hiking destination.

This is an intriguingly inconsistent land. Dusty dry yet meadowy lush. A see-forever alpine vastness that's also forested for miles. Peaks coloured junkyard rust on one side, golf-course green on another. You'll see all these surprises and more within a day's hike. We came away fascinated, scheming to come back and trek the entire area.

The topography here is unique in southwest B.C. and unlike any in the southern Canadian Rockies. If most of your hiking has been in those ranges, you'll feel like a stranger in a strange land. The ridges are rounded; the peaks blunt; the slopes mauve, cinnamon, charcoal, cobalt. Many of the summits are gentle, cliffless, yet the immensity of these formations clearly defines them as mountains. We were initially confounded by the area, but it grew on us rapidly. It has a mysterious appeal, a beauty that haunts long after you've left.

The meadows are bigger than some airports. Brilliant flowers,

Overlooking Cinnabar Basin

wildly prolific and varied, keep your eyes dancing across the land-scape. Some of the flowers are common elsewhere: lupine, aster, arnica, fleabane, subalpine daisy. Thistle are so numerous here, their heads so big, they look like an alien invasion. Other species are more exotic. This is one place a wildflower identification book can be worth its weight. After a cool summer, flowers could still be fresh and vibrant into late August.

You might feel a lightness of being here, a sensation we associate with desert hiking in winter. It can permeate your body on a warm day. Occasional patches of sand in basins and on ridges enhance this desert atmosphere. You'll also find unusual scatterings of rock. In one respect, however, the area is typically Coast Mountain: the jumbo-jet horseflies are obnoxious.

Without a 4WD vehicle, you'll probably have to walk the initial 6 km (3.75 mi) on a mining / logging road. Don't get discouraged. Though it's not a pretty approach, views of distant red-soiled peaks will be the first few pieces of the mental puzzle you'll be building of the area.

Once you reach Taylor Basin, you'll need at least two days to explore nearby passes, ridges and basins. If you basecamp in Taylor, be sure to dayhike south over Cinnabar Pass into the flower-splattered meadows of Cinnabar Basin. If you camp higher, near the pass, pitch your tent on dirt, not on heather.

West of Cinnabar Basin, the trail is less scenic, ambling through subalpine fir, Englemann spruce and whitebark pine, before reaching the sprawling meadows of upper Eldorado Basin. It's possible to complete a 15-km (9.3-mi) loop in one day, linking all three basins—Taylor, Cinnabar and Eldorado—but you'll have to scoot, giving the scenery less attention than it deserves.

If you day trip from Taylor to Cinnabar one day, spend the next day hiking west of Taylor. From the nearby Lucky Strike mine, ascend the road to the 2110-m (6920-ft) pass between Taylor and Eldorado basins, then continue northwest to Windy Pass. From there, roam the spine rising southwest into the heavens. This is our favourite ridge in the area. It's gentle enough at both ends to allow you to make a circuit, and it gives you a great view of the jagged, snow-clad Coast Mountain peaks.

From Windy Pass, it's not far to the most popular destination in the Southern Chilcotin: Spruce Lake. Most hikers, mountain bikers and horse packers (expect to see them all) reach the lake via the Gun Creek trail, starting northwest of Gun Lake. Instead, we recommend hiking to Taylor Basin, then roller-coasting over Windy Pass to Spruce Lake. It's about 10 km (6 mi) longer than the Gun Creek approach, but you'll see the highlights of the area. The trail along Gun Creek is forested nearly all the way to the lake. From Taylor Basin, the trail to the lake is on open slopes and through showy meadows. En route, camp in lovely, wide open, upper Eldorado Basin. But if your time is limited, skip Spruce Lake and focus on Taylor, Cinnabar and Eldorado basins. Also, the side trip to Windy Pass is definitely worthwhile even if you don't continue to Spruce Lake.

FACT

Before your trip

There are so many hiking options here—on trail and cross-country—you should bring a map to supplement our description. Ask the Lillooet Forest District office (250-256-1200) to send you their *Recreation* and *Spruce Lake Trails* maps. The FS map provides enough detail for most hikers and eliminates the need to purchase topo maps.

Learn more about the Southern Chilcotin by contacting the Western Canada Wilderness Committee (WCWC): 20 Water Street, Vancouver, BC, V6B 1A4. Phone: (604) 683-8220. Fax: (604) 683-8229. They're working to gain provincial park status for the area. It's currently unprotected from mining and logging, which threatens to destroy more of this special wilderness. Ask WCWC for their newspaper explaining the issues and featuring colour photos.

By Car

There are two approach options: a 2½-hour drive from Pemberton, or a 1¾-hour drive from Lillooet. From Pemberton, travel north on the Hurley Road—60 km (37 mi) of dirt, rocks, washboards and potholes. It's passable but jittery in a 2WD car. From Lillooet, travel well-graded gravel road and long stretches of pavement northwest. If you arrive one way and leave the other, you'll complete a fascinating BC backroads tour. There are lots of free campgrounds along the Duffey Lake and Carpenter Lake roads. Read our *Camp Free in B.C.* for details.

To reach the Hurley Road, read the directions for Trip 33. Continue on the Hurley all the way to Gold Bridge. Cross the Bridge River to the Carpenter Lake Road and turn right (northeast). Drive 11.7 km (7.3 mi) to signed Tyax Junction, where you turn left (north) then proceed up the Tyaughton Lake Road, described below.

In Lillooet, set your trip odometer to zero on the west side of the Fraser River bridge (junction of Highways 12 & 99). Drive through Lillooet and turn left onto Moha Road at 2.9 km (1.8 mi). Follow signs for Gold Bridge. Stay left at the Yalakom junction at 33.8 km (21.0 mi). Reach the Terzaghi Dam junction at 50.9 km (31.6 mi). Stay straight. Proceed along the north shore of Carpenter Lake. At 69.6 km (43.2 mi) reach the BC Hydro campground at Bighorn Creek. The Jones Creek FS Recreation Site, is 2.4 km (1.5 mi) farther northwest, just before the Marshall Lake Road. Arrive at Tyax Junction 95.8 km (59.4 mi) from Lillooet. Turn right (north).

Both approaches merge here. Reset your trip odometer to 0. Ascend north on Tyaughton Lake Road. At the top of the climb, on your left, is Mowson Pond FS Recreation Site with 5 well-spaced campsites. At 3.5 km (2.2 mi) continue past rough Gun Creek Road on your left. Follow signs for Tyax Lodge. At 6.0 km (3.6 mi) pass a road going left. Immediately there's a fork. Curve left and descend the main road. Pass Hornal Road on your right. At 8.6 km (5.3 mi) stay straight. About 200 meters farther, ascend left. Tyax Lodge is below to the right.

Continue to a steep descent around a ridge at 13.5 km (8.4 mi). Reach a Y-junction at 14.2 km (8.8 mi). Mud Cr-Taylor Cr FS Road continues right (north). The extreme left fork might still be signed TAYLOR CREEK. That's the way.

But you'll need a truck, or at least a low-clearance 4WD vehicle, because the road can get very muddy and is deeply rutted in places. The alternative is to park in the pullout at the Y-junction, then walk the Taylor Creek road. With a capable vehicle, you can drive 6 km (3.75 mi) until the road reaches bridged Taylor Creek.

On Foot

The Taylor Creek road starts at 1128 m (3700 ft). Ascend the road, first a bit northwest, then north. Cross a regrowing clearcut that allows views. The Bendor Range is south, behind you. Shulaps Peak is the gentler, mauve-coloured peak nearby, southeast. To the west are rounded peaks. After 45 minutes, curve left (west) on the road, where an old road forks right. Rust-red 2448-m (8029-ft) Eldorado Mountain is northwest. More of the mauve and cinnamon mountains are visible northeast, across the valley.

After 1 hour, stay straight on the main road, still heading into the valley. Ignore the side roads. After 1¼ hours, strong hikers will reach what appears to be the end of the road. The elevation here is 1372 m (4500 ft). A sign points to a steep trail ascending north through a wide, ugly scar, to the edge of forest. Climb 60 m (200 ft), then go right, heading west onto another old road. This upper road is passable in 4WD and can be reached by turning left on a spur before the seeming road's end mentioned above.

At 6 km (3.7 mi), within 2 hours, cross to the north side of bridged Taylor Creek. The elevation here is 1494 m (4900 ft). If you've driven this far, park and start hiking. The bank is steep and rugged. Beyond, the road narrows and becomes more trail-like as it moderately ascends southwest. The scenery perks up as you enter the lower Taylor Basin.

About 2½ hours from the start of the Taylor Creek road, you can begin to see green, rust, and mauve slopes typical of the gentle Chilcotin peaks. After 3 hours, at 1787 m (5860 ft), you can look directly into Taylor Basin. The views rapidly expand.

At 11 km (6.8 mi) reach the old cabin in Taylor Basin at 1840 m (6040 ft). Strong backpackers can be here in 3¼ hours. Others might take up to 4½. The cabin is just below treeline, near the creek. Anyone can use the cabin, if it's vacant. Clean up after yourself and leave cut firewood. You can also pitch your tent nearby. There's a fire pit and a picnic table.

From the cabin, head straight south up the bench. In a few minutes, a road forks right (west). It's signed SPRUCE LAKE VEHICLE CLOSURE AREA JAN 1-NOV 30. That's the road you'll descend at the end of the loop we describe. It's possible to camp near here, in trees surrounded by meadows. Or head another 15 minutes south onto open slopes.

To reach Cinnabar Pass, proceed south. Pass the Lucky Strike mine on your right. The narrow trail through meadows is overgrown. Just past the mine, pick up a boot-beaten path climbing through lupine, lavender fleabane, and white mop tops. Continue ascending left (south and a bit southeast).

Arrive at 2122-m (6960-ft) Cinnabar Pass 2 km (1.2 mi) from the Taylor Basin cabin. Laced with streams, the meadows of Cinnabar Basin spread out below you. Looking southeast you can see the Carpenter Lake canyon and the snowcapped Bendor Range beyond.

From Cinnabar Pass the trail drops southeast through meadows into subalpine forest. At the junction with the Old Chilcotin trail, which descends the Pearson Creek drainage, turn right (west). Regain elevation via meadowed slopes to reach the 2050-m (6720-ft) unnamed pass above Cinnabar Basin. The pass is 4 km (2.5 mi) from the Taylor Basin cabin.

From the unnamed pass, the trail descends west into dry forest that can be dusty. After dropping 183 m (600 ft) reach a boggy spot. Horses stomping through here have made it worse. Where the indistinct trail splits, stay high (right). The trail resumes at a dip in the ridge, then drops toward Eldorado Creek.

Reach Eldorado Forks at 1750 m (5740 ft), nearly an 1 hour from the unnamed pass. The trail then curves north, heading upstream, soon entering the vast meadows of Eldorado Basin. Again you'll see cinnamon-coloured mountains. Where a faint trail veers left in the lower meadows, stay straight (north) on the main trail. Shortly after rockhopping across a shallow, upper fork of Eldorado Creek, ascend steeply to a junction at 1910 m (6260 ft). You've now hiked 9.5 km (6 mi) from Taylor Basin cabin. To complete the loop, go right, reaching Taylor in 5.2 km (3.25 mi).

Left ascends 2 km (1.2 mi) to 2200-m (7220-ft) Windy Pass. A red ridge juts northeast of the pass, separating Bonanza and Nea creek canyons. Castle Peak, Cardtable and Relay mountains are visible north. Spruce Lake is just north of west, but is blocked from view. A trail drops steeply west from the pass, through meadows then forest, to intersect the Spruce Lake trail in 5 km (3.1 mi). Turn right (north) to approach the south end of the lake in 0.5 km (0.3 mi). Bear right at the fork to proceed 2.5 km (1.5 mi) up the east side of the lake to the campground.

For more expansive views, ascend the grassy, rounded ridge southwest (left) from Windy Pass. Top out at roughly 2332 m (7650 ft), overlooking forested Gun Creek valley. Hummingbird and Trigger lakes are visible west, up the valley. The Coast Mountains are south and southwest. The nearby Leckie Range is southwest. The Shulaps Range is east. North of Relay and Cardtable mountains, the Chilcotin Range peters out into a plateau.

If you're intrigued and capable, it's possible to walk the ridgecrest southwest, then descend southeast, looping around the canyon you ascended from upper Eldorado Basin. Regain the trail at treeline and return to the junction where you previously went left to Windy Pass.

To return to Taylor Basin, head east on a narrow, old mining road. Soon pass the site of the Lucky Gem mine. Subalpine fir are on your right, red talus slopes on your left. Volcanic hoodoos line the ridges. About 3 km (1.9 mi) from the junction in upper Eldorado Basin, reach a 2110-m (6920-ft) unnamed pass. From there, the road drops northeast into Taylor Basin.

Trip 30
Elfin Lakes / Mamquam Lake

Location	Squamish, Garibaldi Provincial Park
Round trip	22 km (13.6 mi) to Elfin Lakes; 44 km (27.2 mi) to Mamquam Lake
Elevation gain	763 m (2500 ft) to Elfin, plus 152 m (500 ft) out; 1082 m (3550 ft) to Mamquam Lake, plus 473 m (1550 ft) out
Time required	6 ½ hours to 2 days for Elfin; 2 to 3 days for Mamquam
Available	mid-July through October
Maps	ITM Garibaldi and Region; BC Parks brochure; Cheakamus River 92 G/14, Mamquam Mtn. 92 G/15

OPINION

Awe. Annoyance. Joy. Disgust. Relief. Peace. At-one-ness. You might experience all these feelings here.

Starting as close to treeline as any Coast Mountain trailhead allows, you'll quickly cruise into the subalpine zone. Soon, the fearsome snowcapped Tantalus Range, west across the valley, shouts for attention. The scenic intensity escalates on Paul Ridge, as colossal Mt. Garibaldi and mammoth Mamquam Mountain roar into your life. (See the photo on page 103.) Beyond, the rocky, glacier-swept, creek-sliced barrens speak to the clarity that resides in us all.

The tiny Elfin Lakes, however, draw hikers from Vancouver like an Electrolux sucks dust. It often gets so crowded that a solitudinous soul can feel oppressed, alienated, claustrophobic. Sound like you? Trek past the lakes, where most people turn around. On a typical, teeming weekend, it wasn't until reaching glacier-fed Ring Creek that we felt liberated from the clutches of civilization. There, with nobody else in sight, we relished a moment of catharsis. Beyond: wilderness.

You can't expect tranquility at an alpine destination as beautiful and accessible as Elfin, unless you come mid-week. Easy backpack trips like this are scarce near Vancouver. The other obvious choice, Garibaldi Lake (Trip 27), is also inundated on weekends. Three-day weekends are worse, so stay away unless you're a Westender who only

Ring Creek

hopes to diminish the noise level a decibel and reduce the human factor by a few thousand faces. Use the extra time to drive farther into the mountains. Arrange to visit these places when most people are at work in the city. It's a hassle, but a private audience with the mountain gods will more than compensate.

Another disappointment here is the road-walk most of the way to Elfin. The rough trail cutting off 15 minutes along is no better; it's more difficult and locked in trees. The scar of the road is ugly, but lift your eyes: roads provide views. This one also enables hikers and bikers to accommodate one another. Yes, bikers. BC Parks allows them to pedal as far as Elfin. It's phenomenal cycling country—another reason you'll have to forego any sense of hinterland until after the popular lakes.

Next problem. There are only two desirably-located campgrounds. One is just below Elfin Lakes, the other at Mamquam Lake. On weekends, the Elfin campground can be a hikers' ghetto. If it's full, you'll be exiled to an overflow lot where you and other refugees must pitch your tents next to each other. You're likely to find a vacant site at distant Mamquam Lake, but if your time is limited, camping there might preclude the side trip to Little Diamond Head, which starts near Elfin. Backpacking all the way to Mamquam in a day is a challenge, but possible if you're exceptionally fit.

The Mamquam campground is in a wonderfully wild setting. Getting there you'll traverse a fascinating moonscape. So at least dayhike from Elfin to the ridge above Mamquam Lake for Holy Cow! views of the lake, Mt. Garibaldi and skyscraping Pyramid Mountain. If you have time and energy on your way back, dash up the Opal Cone, remnant of an extinct volcano.

Okay, lecture time. Since this is a busy area, go out of your way to give others a little space. On the trail, turn your conversation volume down. At campgrounds, lower the cone of silence. And after dark, shut up!

FACT

Before your trip

Call the BC Parks Garibaldi District office (604-898-3678) and ask about the snow level along Paul Ridge. It could be snowbound through July if there's been heavy spring snowfall.

By Car

From Squamish, at the traffic light by Esso and McDonald's, drive Highway 99 north 3.1 km (2 mi). Cross the Mamquam River and watch for the BC Parks sign (GARIBALDI) DIAMOND HEAD. At the traffic light, turn east (right) onto Mamquam Road. About 10 km (6.2 mi) from the highway, bear left at the sign. Arrive at the trailhead parking lot at 15 km (9.3 mi). The elevation here is 914 m (3000 ft).

On Foot

First, a geographic clarification. Diamond Head is the southernmost major peak on the Mt. Garibaldi massif. The main summit of 2679-m (8787-ft) Mt. Garibaldi is farther north. Atwell Peak is between them. From Paul Ridge, you can see Diamond Head nearby to the north. The trail curves around its southeast side to the moraine near Ring Creek. Mt. Garibaldi is visible from there. You're hiking in the Diamond Head area, which comprises Elfin and Mamquam lakes.

From the trailhead parking lot, start walking northwest on the logging road. Soon turn northeast, ascending moderately. The short, regrowing forest offers no protection from sun or rain. Within 20 minutes, the Tantalus Range is visible west. Eventually bigger trees line the road. Cross a creek 45 minutes up. After 1 hour, views of the Tantalus are better. At 5 km (3.1 mi), after about 1¼ hours, arrive at the tidy Red Heather shelter. It has tables and a woodstove. You're now in subalpine meadows punctuated by western hemlock. The Red Heather campground is 100 meters past the shelter. It has 6 tent platforms, a line for hanging food, and a brook nearby. Diamond Head is visible north.

Reach a junction at 1455 m (4775 ft). Hikers go left on trail, bikers go right on road. Elfin Lakes are 6 km farther. The trail ascends more gradually than the road did below the shelter. Soon, you can see the Lake Lovely Water cirque, west beneath Omega and Alpha mountains. After 1 km (0.6 mi) on trail, rejoin the road and continue northeast along the northwest slope of Paul Ridge. Sky Pilot Mountain, Mt. Habrich, and Goat Ridge are visible, all slightly west of south. After rising to 1677 m (5500 ft) on Paul Ridge, the road drops 150 m (500 ft) to Elfin Lakes. Descending, you'll see clearcuts up Cheekeye Ridge (northwest) and throughout Mamquam valley (south). The Elfin campground is in the green basin below. About 1 km down Paul Ridge, you can look north and pick out a trail—a possible side trip from Elfin—climbing a meadowy slope to the saddle between Columnar Peak and the Gargoyles.

Reach Elfin Lakes at 11 km (6.8 mi). Total hiking time: about 3 hours. The lakes are on the edge of a little plateau. Swimming is allowed in the first, larger lake. Only use the second, smaller lake for drinking water; definitely purify it. The moraines and glaciers of Garibaldi are north. Mamquam mountain and icefield dominate east across Skookum Creek valley. The Diamond Head Ranger Station and an old lodge are beside the lakes. The Elfin Lakes shelter (34 bunks, propane and wood stoves) is 200 meters beyond. There's a fee for sleeping there. From the ranger station, the campground is 1.2 km (0.7 mi), Mamquam Lake 11.2 km (6.9 mi), the Saddle trail 1.5 km (0.9 mi), and the Opal Cone 6 km (3.7 mi).

The road descends northwest from Elfin Lakes to the campground turnoff (left). Five minutes past that turnoff, the signed Saddle trail forks left (northwest), gaining 457 m (1500 ft) in 2.5 km (1.6 mi) to the saddle between the Gargoyles and Columnar Peak—about a 2-hour round trip. To make it more challenging, ascend 170 m (558 ft) above and beyond the Gargoyles to 2100-m (6888-ft) Little Diamond Head.

Continuing north to Mamquam Lake, stay straight, still on an old road. Gradually descend along subalpine slopes into Ring Creek canyon, bounded by steep lateral moraines. The view of Mt. Garibaldi improves here. Orange posts in cairns atop boulders show where to rockhop across a fork of Ring Creek, at 1402 m (4600 ft). You're on trail now. Head north, descending 107 m (350 ft) to a bridged crossing of Ring Creek—roughly the halfway point between Elfin and Mamquam lakes. Fuschia monkeyflower and yellow asters flourish in the moraine soil.

Above the east side of Ring Creek, 17 km (10.5 mi) from the trailhead, reach a cairned junction. The smaller trail left leads north 20 minutes on the barren, rocky slopes to a viewpoint of the Garibaldi Névé and the 1738-m (5700-ft) volcanic Opal Cone. For Mamquam Lake, stay right on the main trail. Proceed generally east.

Soon, cross flat, open barrens scratched clean by glaciers. Snow might linger here until mid-August, but there should be no difficulty hiking over it. From atop the next major moraine, at 1463 m (4800 ft), the trail drops to Zig Zag Creek at 1372 m (4500 ft). Continue 30 meters upstream for a narrower place to rockhop across. Then gain 152 m (500 ft) in about 30 minutes to crest the last moraine near 1524 m (5000 ft). The best views yet of Mt. Garibaldi (northwest) are from this moraine. The Rampart Ponds are a short distance north on the plateau. East are nearby Pyramid and Mamquam mountains. A steep talus slope on Pyramid drops to the forested shore of Mamquam Lake, visible below. To the south, clearcuts encroach on Garibaldi and Pinecone-Burke parks. From a cairned saddle on the moraine, the trail switchbacks 250 m (820 ft) down to the lake. The campground is at the south end, 22 km (13.7 mi) from the trailhead.

Trip 31
Helm Creek

Location	Whistler, Garibaldi Provincial Park
Round trip	16 km (10 mi) to Helm Creek campground
Elevation gain	717 m (2352 ft)
Time required	7 hours to 3 days
Available	mid-July through October
Maps	ITM Whistler and Region; BC Parks brochure; Cheakamus River 92 G/14, Whistler 92 J/2, Brandywine 92 J/3

OPINION

Here's the backdoor to three celebrated sights: Garibaldi Lake, Panorama Ridge, and the Black Tusk. Though longer and steeper than the popular approach (Trip 27), it's far less crowded. And it allows you to basecamp at a sweet little campground in a meadow beside Helm Creek. Accommodating about seven tents, it's a veritable hermitage compared to the monster campgrounds at Garibaldi Lake and Taylor Meadows. You shouldn't expect the Helm Creek trail to be yours alone, but you can look forward to a quieter, wilder trip than most hikers experience in this famous chunk of Garibaldi Park.

The Helm Creek trail climbs steeply through lush, dense forest before breaking into subalpine meadows between two ridges. It continues at a more modest grade through a gloriously open alpine expanse, then across fascinating volcanic cinder flats near Helm Lake. The trip requires more stamina and back-country experience, however, than is needed for the popular approach to Garibaldi Lake. This is a trail, not a groomed path. Anyone who's reasonably fit should have no trouble. But the lake attracts lots of once-a-year backpackers and families with kids who are better off on the hikers' highway that languorously switchbacks up from the Rubble Creek trailhead.

For a round trip, camp beside Helm Creek, dayhike from there, then return to your car at the Cheakamus Lake trailhead. Even if you're making this a through trip and exiting west of Garibaldi Lake, spend your first night at Helm Creek campground.

Helm Creek meadows

FACT

By Car

See Trip 51 for directions to the Cheakamus Lake trailhead, at 838 m (2750 ft).

On Foot

Begin hiking southeast on the Cheakamus Lake trail. In about 20 minutes, reach a junction at 1.5 km (0.9 mi). Descend right and cross to the south side of the Cheakamus River. You have to muscle your way across in a cable car. It can be a struggle for only two people to pull it up at the other end, but it's possible if you're both strong. Getting in or out of the car is easier if you first hook the car to the tower. Be sure to unhook it when you leave, so the car is retrievable from either side.

Tight switchbacks ascend the south side of the river valley. The trail then approaches the Helm Creek canyon and parallels it, climbing southwest. As you ascend, the trees change from red cedar, Douglas fir and western hemlock, to mountain hemlock and subalpine fir. About 2 hours from the trailhead, you can hear the roar of Helm Creek, though the water is rarely visible.

At 8 km (5 mi) the trail leaves dense forest, enters a wide valley and reaches Helm Creek campground in a subalpine meadow. The elevation here is 1555 m (5100 ft). Five tent platforms are just above the creek. There's another large site across the creek. You'll find a pole for hanging food and a fire pit, but no cooking shelter. The Black Tusk is visible southwest. Comparatively small Helm Peak is the ridgecrest summit to the south. Empetrum Ridge, just west of Helm Creek, allows easy scrambling. Empetrum Peak (1950 m / 6400 ft) affords a unique view of the Tusk's north wall.

Following the trail southwest from Helm Creek campground, you'll gain 180 m (590 ft) in 2 km (1.2 mi) to a point where Helm Lake is visible. For directions to Panorama Ridge, the Black Tusk or Garibaldi Lake, read Trip 27. It describes the more popular approach east, then northeast to Helm Creek.

Trip 32
Rainbow Lake

Location	Whistler
Round trip	16 km (10 mi)
Elevation gain	850 m (2788 ft)
Time required	6 hours
Available	July through October
Maps	ITM Whistler and Region; Rainbow Madely Trail; Whistler 92 J/2, Brandywine 92 J/3

OPINION

Lakes lure hikers. Especially lakes with tantalizing names. But this one is a clever disguise for a hateful trail. Before marching up here to see the end of the rainbow, be prepared for an ugly, monotonous road, clearcut lower valley slopes, nearly a kilometer of tiresome boardwalk across boggy meadows, and a tedious trail through uninspiring forest. Some will enjoy the view of sprawling Whistler. Others will think it's a blight on the landscape.

So, why is this trip outstanding? Because the Rainbow Lake basin, beneath its soaring namesake peak, is magical. The small lake, fed by lilting creeklets, is clear near the edges, teal where it's deep. Plunge in for mental cleansing and physical revitalization; it will dilute the sourness of getting here. Surrounding the lake are idyllic grass-and-heather meadows full of luscious flowers in rainbow colours. Looking east, over the lake and across the valley, you can see 2905-m (9527-ft) Wedge Mountain, highest in Garibaldi Park. As you rise to the pass west of the lake, the scene grows more wondrous. It's an image you'd find in a Sierra Club calendar. Or on the back of this book.

Even dayhikers should continue to the pass above the lake. It's a brief, sweet, alpine interlude on an intimate path. From the pass you can look across the Callaghan Creek valley to snowcapped Brandywine Mountain (southwest) and Mt. Callaghan (northwest). If you're well-organized and arranged a vehicle shuttle, you can make this a one-way trip by proceeding northwest from Hanging Lake, 7 km (4.3 mi) through forest, to Madely Lake. But the road to Madely requires 4WD.

Though you can easily enjoy Rainbow Lake and its immediate setting on a dayhike, you'd spend most of your day plodding the dismal

Mt. Sproatt

trail. Instead, make this an overnight trip; allow at least another day to explore the alpine surroundings. Scramble up the agreeable slopes of Rainbow or Sproatt mountains. For a more tranquil tentsite than at nearby Hanging Lake (no camping allowed at Rainbow), head to Beverley Lake. It's an elysian alpine ramble, 5 km (3 mi) north of Rainbow.

A drudgery reduction device—a mountain bike—shortens the Rainbow approach and descent by 30 minutes each. But the 240-m (787-ft) climb, to where a fence bars bikes, is for robust cyclists only. Bring a sturdy lock to secure your steed to the rack.

On a clear summer day, you can feel like a bug under a magnifying glass during the initial, steep, open-road ascent. Start in the cool of the morning. Also, steel yourself for battle: an army of fiendish flies will attack from the trailhead all the way to the lake.

FACT

By Car

From Highway 99, at the southwest end of Whistler, turn left (northwest) onto Alta Lake Road. Cross under powerlines, over railroad tracks and proceed north. Trailhead parking is on the left, at 6.2 km (3.8 mi). There's also a lower parking lot just ahead on the right. The elevation here is 660 m (2165 ft).

If you're entering Whistler from the north, turn right (west) at the traffic lights where a sign directs you to Alpine Meadows. At the stop sign in 0.2 km, turn left onto Rainbow Drive, which later becomes Alta Lake Road. Follow it 3.3 km (2 mi) southwest to the trailhead.

On Foot

Pick up a map and brochure at the trailhead bulletin board. When you return, replace the map for someone else to use. Keep in mind, camping at Rainbow Lake is prohibited because it supplies Whistler's drinking water. Hanging Lake, just west of Rainbow, has a campground.

If hiking, ascend west on the trail starting at the bulletin board. If mountain biking, ascend west on the dirt road just south of the trailhead.

A few minutes up the trail, go right at a sign RAINBOW FALLS. Ascend steeply another 10 minutes to a junction. A spur trail drops right to the pretty but not stupendous falls. From the spur, ascend left and immediately reach another trail. Go up right, into a tunnel of scrawny regrowth and soon reach a dirt road at a curve.

Ascend left on the road, away from the creek. Here in the open, you can see the Fitzsimmons Range above Whistler. Continue straight past the cement pumphouse. At a curve in the road, just above the pumphouse, a 2-km (1.2-mi) trail leads downhill to Rainbow Park. For Rainbow Lake, keep right on the road.

After 20 minutes of steep road-walking, enjoy a short, level reprieve before reaching a watershed boundary fence at 915 m (3000 ft). Mountain bikes and campfires are prohibited beyond. Total hiking time to this point is 45-60 minutes. Southeast across the valley, you can see the Horstman Glacier on Blackcomb Peak. Your next view is an hour up the trail. Continue ascending northwest, on the south side of Twenty-one Mile Creek.

Soon enter a brushy area, usually trimmed by mid-summer. Stay right where a spur trail forks left to a creek. Finally, an hour or more from the trailhead, at 1037 m (3400 ft), enter a forest of old-growth mountain hemlock and Douglas fir. On hot days, the shade is a welcome relief.

Just past the sign 4 KM is a bridged creek crossing at 1128 m (3700 ft). Look left (south) for a cascade flowing down from Mt. Sproatt. Flies seem to be less bothersome near moving water, which makes this an appealing rest stop. Next, long sections of boardwalk lead you across boggy meadows for about 1 km (0.6 mi). Soon get a clear view north to Rainbow Mountain. Its cliffs and ridgecrests are more impressive from here than at Rainbow Lake.

At 6 km (3.7 mi), elevation 1280 m (4200 ft), the trail crosses Tonic Creek on a suspension bridge. Near 6.5 km (4.0 mi), a rough trail leads left (south) to Gin & Tonic lakes in less than an hour. Continuing northwest, the trail crosses to the north side of Twenty-one Mile Creek at 1433 m (4700 ft). It then ascends steeply to a small waterfall flowing from the east end of naturally dammed Rainbow Lake. Reach the east end of the lake at 8 km (5 mi), 1465 m (4805 ft).

To fully appreciate the lake basin, follow the path right, around the north shore. It leads 1.3 km (0.8 mi) through meadows and across streams, to a 1520-m (4986-ft) pass west of Rainbow Lake. From the pass, Hanging Lake is visible farther west, 105 m (344 ft) below. Having to camp at Hanging Lake seems unattractive, but it's only a 10-minute walk back up to the pass for panoramic views. If you planned a one-way trip and arranged a shuttle, proceed from Hanging Lake 7 km (4.3 mi) northwest to Madely Lake at 969 m (3178 ft).

From the west end of Rainbow Lake, just before the pass, a route leads north 5 km (3.1 mi) to Beverley Lake, at 1610 m (5280 ft). Gain 152 m (500 ft) crossing the saddle beneath Rainbow Mountain's southwest ridge, then stay low in the little valley.

Before ascending 1845-m (6051-ft) Mt. Sproatt or 2328-m (7636-ft) Rainbow Mountain, assess your ascent options from the vantage point of the pass west of Rainbow Lake. Sproatt is an easier scramble than Rainbow. A faint path leads south from the pass toward the northwest ridge of Mt. Sproatt, which juts far north to Rainbow Lake from its main peak farther southeast. Ascend just 244 m (800 ft) for improved views. Head south, then maneuver east to overlook Gin & Tonic lakes. The moderately steep slope of heather and berry bushes allows you to choose a safe descent route into the Gin & Tonic basin. From there it's a short hike north to the trail you originally ascended to Rainbow Lake.

Trip 33

Tenquille Lake

Location	Pemberton
Round trip	12 km (7.5 mi) if you have 4WD;
	19 km (11.8 mi) if you don't
Elevation gain	457 m (1500 ft) with 4WD,
	additional 340 m (1115 ft) without
Time required	5 hours with 4WD; 7 hours without
Available	mid-July through October
Map	Birkenhead Lake 92 J/10

OPINION

Sex... but no orgasm. That's the trip to Tenquille Lake. There's the long, slow, sweaty build-up. Then the gorgeous meadows at Tenquille Pass—a definite turn-on. But the mountain scenery never climaxes. And the trail drops to the small, disappointing, forest-shrouded lake. The anticipated ecstasy remains unrealized.

Dayhiking here is merely worthwhile. It's easy if you turn around at the meadowy pass, where glimpsing the lake should convince you it's not worth continuing. Most people plod lemminglike down the trail to the lake, some pitching their tent in the trees or sleeping in the hut. But hiking, like love making, can be more satisfying when you're creative. This is an outstanding adventure if you backpack to the meadows, then veer off the beaten path into higher, more stimulating terrain.

The trip begins with stirring scenery as you drive through the Pemberton Valley. On both sides, peaks rise 2010 m (6600 ft) from the valley floor. While coaxing your vehicle up the Hurley Road, you can stare at the Pemberton Icefield and the peaks marching northwest along the Upper Lillooet River toward Meager Mountain.

Without 4WD, you'll face at least an hour's trudge on rough road, compensated by a hang glider's view over the steep-walled Pemberton Valley 915 m (3000 ft) below. Actually, the panorama here is more impressive than what you'll see from Tenquille Pass. Having overcome the road, you'll proceed from the 4WD-accessible trailhead. It's a forgettable hike through viewless forest until you reach subalpine greenery. Bionic mountain bikers, some starting at the bottom of the Hurley Road, cycle through here to the pass, then scream 1463 m (4800 ft)

Tenquille Pass

down the old trail to the Lillooet River. If you ride, dismount through the delicate meadows. The eroded, braided trail is being churned into slop.

Tenquille Pass is justifiably esteemed. In July, the broad, lush meadows are a crazywild pastiche of colours. You'll see red-orange columbine, yellow asters, lime-green corn lilies, pink thistles, white Sitka valerian, and lavender lupine, all floating in an emerald sea of grass. But looking up, the mountains resemble globs of talus hardened into lumps—no looming cliffs, no spearhead spires—which is why you can and should ascend them.

Venture northeast from the pass to Finch Ridge. Or head south to Fossil Pass, between Copper Mound and Mt. McLeod. With a topo map, scrambling ability and route-finding experience, you could spend a week happily wandering the alpine heights southeast of Mt. McLeod. Work your way to Gingerbread Lake beneath Mt. Barbour, on to Ogre Lake, maybe even over to Cerulean Lake. Consider making this a through trip by descending to Owl Lake and the 4WD road that leads to the D'Arcy Road. All you need are a few capable friends, two vehicles, and time. From the ridges you can look east across the Pemberton Valley toward the humongous Pemberton Icefield

FACT

By Car

Set your trip odometer to 0 at the edge of Pemberton, at the 3-way intersection on Highway 99, by the Petro Canada station. Drive north into town and cross the railroad tracks. At 1 km (0.6 mile) reach a T-junction. Turn right, heading toward the Hurley River FS Rd. At 2.8 km (1.7 mi), turn left (northwest) on Pemberton Valley Road.

At 25.0 km (15.5 mi) there's a sign for Meager Creek, Gold Bridge and Lillooet. Turn right here onto the Hurley River / Upper Lillooet River FS Road. At 26.5 km (16.4 mi), cross the small bridge over the Lillooet River. Immediately right, above the north bank, is the trailhead for an old, very steep trail ascending the entire Wolverine Creek drainage 1460 m (4800 ft) to Tenquille Pass.

Reset your trip odometer to 0 and proceed left on the Lillooet River FS Road. At 7.6 km (4.7 mi) turn right and begin ascending the Hurley Road on a long switchback. The Hurley continues 60 km (37 mi) over washboards and potholes to Gold Bridge and Carpenter Lake. It's jittery but doable in a 2WD car. For this trip, however, drive only to the 20-km (12.4-mi) marker, at about 975 m (3200 ft). Here, just beyond a rounded switchback, a spur road cuts back sharply right (southeast). You can also access this spur road a bit earlier, at the end of the switchback, but this unhelpful shortcut is too steep and rough for 2WD.

Drive the nearly-level spur road 2.1 km (1.3 mi) to a parking area. 2WD cars should stop here. 4WD vehicles can continue left, up the rough, steep road for another 3.5 km (2.2 mi) to a small parking lot at the actual trailhead. In this last stretch, ignore a rougher road going left.

On Foot

Starting at the first parking area, gain 340 m (1115 ft) in about 1 ¼ hours hiking up the 4WD road to the trailhead. Then, on trail, ascend steeply through a clearcut. The scarred, stumped hillside on your left will likely be covered with fireweed. After gaining about 100 m (330 ft) enter forest, where the grade eases.

Your general direction of travel will be east, curving northeast, as the trail swings around the south side of Goat Peak and ascends the upper Wolverine Creek drainage.

About 30 minutes from the trailhead, ignore the minor trail cutting back left. Continue straight, rockhopping across the stream. The grade is gentle, often contouring at about 1524 m (5000 ft), through whitebark pine and Englemann spruce.

About 1 hour from the trailhead, reach an open view south over Pemberton Valley. Ascend to cross a feeder stream, ignoring a rougher, flagged trail forking left. Step across a creeklet in a defile. Much larger Wolverine Creek is audible across the canyon. Views from here are southeast to nearby Copper Mound and south to distant peaks. Undergrowth is now thick and lush.

About 1¾ hours from the trailhead, at 1537 m (5040 ft), reach a fork. Right is the old trail that started way down by the Lillooet River. Just below this fork, it crosses boisterous, unbridged Wolverine Creek. Bear left, gently ascending northeast through subalpine meadows.

After hiking 6 km (3.7 mi) in about 2¼ hours from the trailhead, arrive at the meadows of Tenquille Pass at 1692 m (5550 ft). If you started hiking at the first parking area, you've now covered 9.5 km (6 mi). Proceed 0.5 km (0.3 mi) east through through the verdant pass. You can glimpse Tenquille Lake, 60 m (197 ft) below. The trail drops to the lake.

Northwest of the pass is 2480-m (8134-ft) Goat Peak. It's connected to Tenquille Mountain, directly north of the pass. Northeast is long, meadowy Finch Ridge—a possible destination for experienced off-trail ramblers. The easiest and most obvious ascent from Tenquille Pass is directly south to Fossil Pass. It lies east of Copper Mound and northwest of Mt. McLeod.

Trip 34

Coliseum Mountain

Location	North Shore, Lynn Headwaters Regional Park
Round trip	24.5 km (15.2 mi)
Elevation gain	1239 m (4064 ft)
Time required	10 hours to 3 days
Available	July through October
Maps	Park brochure (at trailhead kiosk); ITM Vancouver's Northshore; North Vancouver 92 G/6

OPINION

Smashed by a god's fist? It looks like it. Coliseum is the one North Shore summit that's nearly flat, and big enough to keep a hiker happily roaming the rocks for hours. Two small lakes on top—goblets of blue nectar—are held skyward in a toast to the sun. And the mountain-ocean-city panorama could lure Zeus from Olympus. Nevertheless, we've given Coliseum a lowly Worthwhile rating because it's demandingly far, excruciatingly steep, irksomely rough.

Elastic-lunged, steel-legged mountain mongers can dayhike Coliseum: 6 hours up, 4 hours down. Attempting this trip without a tent and sleeping bag is unsafe for most people. It's too long and nasty. Besides, the summit is a vast, alpine playground that cries out for campers. Yet few respond; you're likely to have the mountain to yourself. Under the burden of a full pack, the ascent is a grueling, day-long slog, but if the weather's fine, wow! Overnighting on Coliseum could be the most delicious memory you create all summer. After sunset, the city lights below are dazzling.

A three-day trip is ideal, allowing you a full day to rejoice on top. Just start early the first day: there's precious little space for a tent until you're on the shoulder of Coliseum, above Norvan Pass.

FACT

By Car

See Lynn Valley (Trip 54) for directions to the trailhead.

Coliseum Mountain rock is made for rambling.

On Foot

From the parking lot, cross the bridge over Lynn Creek. Go left (north) on the Lynn Loop trail. After 30 minutes reach a signed junction at 1.8 km (1.2 mi). Stay left on the Cedar Mill trail. Proceed north, following Lynn Creek upstream. After 1 hour reach a debris chute at 3.9 km (2.4 mi). To this point, the tread is broad, smooth, nearly level. Ascend right, across the rocks, to where the obvious path is signed. Go left here on the Headwaters trail. After 1 ¾ hours of easy striding reach a junction at 6.8 km (4.2 mi), where the Headwaters trail descends left and Norvan Falls is 5 minutes straight ahead. The falls is worth a peek, but your route—and it is only a route from here on—ascends right (northeast), upstream through the Norvan Creek drainage.

Climb steeply, following occasional red flagging. Forest debris is soft underfoot. Where rooty, the surface is slick when wet. A round, yellow sign depicting a hiker is reassuring. Watch for more of these signs. One hour above the junction near Norvan Falls (2 ¾ hours from the trailhead), the ascent eases. When the yellow signs are scarce, follow the flagging. The route is obvious, but still rough. Three hours from the trailhead, Norvan Creek is visible on the left. Reach it by descending a rocky gully. A pool here is big enough for swimming.

After 3 ¼ hours come to a mucky stretch that quickly opens into Norvan Meadow—an avalanche swath, luxuriantly green in summer. Re-enter trees and negotiate more muck. After 4 hours the route is again near the creek. Ten minutes later reach big timber and a comfortable spot for a rest break. The forest is prettier and the route improves. This far, you've stayed just south of Norvan Creek. Now rockhop to the north side.

Cross back to the south side of the creek after almost 4½ hours. Another 15 minutes of uphill effort will bring you to Norvan Pass, at 1050 m (3444 ft), roughly 9.8 km (6.1 mi) from the trailhead. There might still be small, hand-written signs on the trees: (1) LOOKOUT RIGHT 5 MINUTES; (2) PARK ENTRANCE VIA NORVAN FALLS — 4 HOURS, ELEV. CHANGE 700 METERS; (3) COLISIUM MTN. 1 HR. The elevation gain from the trailhead is closer to 840 meters (2755 ft).

Technically, Norvan isn't a pass. It's more like a hang glider launch. The east side is a sheer drop to the Seymour River. Mt. Seymour, Runner Peak and Mt. Elsay are visible southeast across the valley. Go right (south) 5 minutes for a view north to Coliseum's rounded, rocky summit. To continue to Coliseum, turn left (north) at the pass and follow the flagged route.

About 20 minutes beyond the pass, enter subalpine. Finally, views. Vancouver is southwest and big mountains are farther north. There are suitable tent sites here, but no water source except a few unreliable tarns. The scenery rapidly expands as you climb. A few steep pitches require light scrambling. Flagging indicates the easiest route, but the terrain is now open, so you can navigate your own way. Just proceed upward. Eventually there's an abrupt but short drop, after which the ascent resumes. Rocks daubed with paint help guide you the final distance.

Reach the enormous, alpine summit, at 1446 m (4743 ft), about 1 hour and 20 minutes from Norvan Pass. You've now hiked 12.25 km (7.6 mi) from the trailhead. If the big tarn on top is dry (unlikely), the two Cornett Lakes just north of the summit are a reliable water source, as well as an ideal place to camp. Solid rock in all directions allows easy wandering and scrambling.

The panorama is 360°: Hanes Creek valley is below. Crown and Goat mountains are southwest, with Georgia Strait and Vancouver Island beyond. Vancouver and Boundary Bay are south. Mount Baker draws your eyes farther south. Just east of it is Mt. Shuksan. Mt. Seymour is southeast, Seymour Lake northeast. Mt. Burwell is immediately north, and Cathedral Mountain is beyond it.

Allow at least 45 minutes to descend to the pass. From there it's possible to reach the parking lot in 3 hours, but most people should allow 4 or more.

Trip 35
Golden Ears Mountain

Location	Golden Ears Provincial Park
Round trip	24 km (15 mi)
Elevation gain	1500 m (4920 ft)
Time required	11 hours or overnight
Available	mid-July through October
Maps	BC Parks brochure; Coquitlam 92 G/7; Stave Lake 92 G/8; ITM Lower Mainland Road Map (to identify distant peaks)

OPINION

It's not a trail. It's a trial. Attempting to bag Golden Ears in a single day will severely test your resolve and endurance. Even if you backpack, which most people should, it's a demanding journey on a viciously steep route—a real bastard. The elation summiteers feel is due to the accomplishment almost as much as the scenery. Yet it's a popular trip, crowded on summer weekends.

This was our first high-elevation hike early one July after months of walking in forest with only prison views of distant ridgetops. What a relief. We blissed out on the vertical rockscape. Finally, we were home again, above treeline. If alpine country is your touchstone, you know the feeling. And Golden Ears offers it earlier than many mountains in the range.

The trek is initially through mature but unimpressive second-growth forest—western hemlock, red cedar, Douglas fir. As far as Alder Flats (just over a third of the way), the agreeable trail gains only 245 m (804 ft). Diversions include a waterfall, creeks, and glimpses of peaks. Beyond Alder Flats, everything changes. The views get better and the going gets worse. Golden Ears Mountain, Edge Peak, and Blanshard Needle soon confront you. Their cliffs, visible from way out in the Fraser Valley, are stupendous up close. For a short dayhike (10.5 km / 6.5 mi round trip), turn around here, on the slope above Alder Flats. The trail then dwindles and steepens to little more than a boulder chute. Once you reach Panorama Ridge, the sweeping view over titanic Pitt Lake liberates your mind from the struggle to get there. Though the summit remains distant, the rest of the route is in the open, where

Ascending the permanent snowfield on Golden Ears

you're instantly rewarded for upward progress. The Coast Mountains seem to grow as you go.

You'll climb 1255 m (4116 ft) in 7 km (4.3 mi) to the summit—a test worthy of Sisyphus. Strong, determined, experienced hikers, however, can surmount Golden Ears carrying only a daypack. Do it in early summer, when you'll have enough daylight. Start by 9 A.M. and allow 11 hours for the round trip. Those lacking an iron will and legs to match should camp overnight at Alder Flats or Panorama Ridge. Under the burden of a full pack, allow an entire day to attain the ridge. The logical 2-day trip involves camping on the ridge, then summiting the next morning and hiking all the way out the second day.

Mountaineering experience is necessary to safely ascend the final ridge of Golden Ears Mountain. A half-kilometer-long permanent snowfield bars the way. Looking up at it from below, the angle of ascent appears terrifyingly steep. In reality, it's not so radical. That becomes apparent once you're on it. But the consequences of a slide could be serious without an ice axe and the know-how to use it. Above the snowfield, you must scramble along the narrow ridge of the east Ear, with precipitous drops on both sides. If you're comfortable on airy terrain, it's a thrilling climax.

Here, as in most of the range, it was hard maintaining our vegetarian diet: black flies were constantly zooming into our mouths. On a clear day, which is mandatory for this trip, also be prepared for searing heat. The sun can cook you on the unshaded ascent. Rivulets of sweat coursed down our bodies, almost washing the pesky flies off. If you're that hot, take a rest break every half-hour and drink lots of water, to avoid heatstroke. Reaching the year-round snow on Panorama Ridge should bring sweet relief from the flies and provide a welcome source of ice-cold refreshment.

FACT

By Car

Golden Ears Provincial Park is 41.0 km (25.4 mi) east of Vancouver. If you're driving east on Lougheed Highway 7, as you enter Maple Ridge, turn left onto Dewdney Trunk Road. Follow it to 232nd Street and turn left (north), where BC Parks signs indicate. Farther east in Maple Ridge, BC Parks signs identify other places where you can turn north off Highway 7 toward the park. From the north end of 232nd Street, cross the South Alouette River. After passing Maple Ridge Park, go right on Fern Crescent. About 4 km (2.5 mi) farther, enter Golden Ears Park at a giant carving of a mountain goat. The park gate is open 7 A.M. to 11 P.M. Grab a park map/brochure at the information kiosk, 250 meters beyond the gate. Proceed 11.0 km (6.8 mi) to a junction, where you fork left toward the West Canyon Trail. It's another 0.5 km (0.3 mi) on gravel to the large trailhead parking lot on the left. The elevation here is 205 m (672 ft).

On Foot

The trail is initially an old logging road, lined with ferns, through mixed forest. It starts at the south end of the parking lot, by the signboard and pit toilets. Immediately pass a minor trail on the right, leading to the Gold Creek parking area. Within 10 minutes, pass the Viewpoint trail, ascending left to a glimpse of Alouette Lake. Continue north into the Gold Creek valley. The creek is out of sight. In 0.5 km (0.3 mi) ascend to a bridge over a gorge that's dry in summer, then descend. After 30-40 minutes of mostly level walking, reach a signed junction at 3.1 km (1.9 mi). Detour right to see the Lower Falls.

From the Lower Falls fork, ascend the rocky trail left toward Alder Flats. Stepping over roots and rocks is awkward for the next 10 minutes. At 3.8 km (2.4 mi), elevation 320 m (1050 ft), there's a view north up Gold Creek and northeast to 2113-m (6930-ft) Mt. Robie Reid. The trail then heads northwest. You'll see yellow blazes, but you won't need them; the path is obvious as it winds through scrawny secondgrowth. Negotiate a gorge with the help of a sturdy ladder. If it's missing, try crossing above, where the embankment is less steep.

After 1¼ hours, at 4.5 km (2.8 mi), a boardwalk spans the creek. Blanshard Needle is visible southwest. Ten minutes later, cross more racing water. Notice the aluminum-blue pool, deep enough for plunging, 20 meters downstream from the bridge. After another bridge, a sign warns that drinking water is scarce beyond Alder Flats. Fill your bottles. In summer, the next available water will be snowmelt, high on Panorama Ridge.

After 1¾ hours, reach Alder Flats at 5 km (3.1 mi), 440 m (1443 ft). There are many tent sites beneath alders, beside a dry creekbed, within earshot of a distant waterfall. When you reach a fork in the campground, go right (north) following yellow blazes. Just beyond the flats, the trail is more rugged as it ascends earnestly northwest, often in the open. Views are west to Golden Ears Mountain, and southwest to Edge Peak and Blanshard Needle.

For long stretches you must clamber upward on all fours. The eroded, bouldery route is often unshaded, hot on a clear summer day, but even more difficult in rain. Be careful not to tumble rocks onto hikers below you. After 2½ hours (including 20 minutes of resting) strong hikers will arrive at a viewpoint on the ridge, just before the route drops 25 meters. Mounts Robie Reid and Judge Howay are northeast; you're as close as any hike in this book will bring you to those formidable peaks. Waterfalls across the valley drain the now visible snowfields on Golden Ears and Edge Peak. You'll have to cross that snow en route to the summit.

About 20 minutes beyond the viewpoint, reach a sign MOUNTAIN SHELTER directing you to the cabin on the north end of Panorama Ridge, at 1200 m (3936 ft). It's a small, miserable, metal hut, best left for emergencies only. To continue, turn left (southwest) and ascend above treeline. Pitt Lake is visible below to the west. Starting just past the shelter, you'll find flat dirt or rock tentsites along the ridge. Don't crush the heather by pitching your tent on it. Purify water from snowmelt pools. There's no place for a tent above the snow or on the summit.

You're now travelling generally south onto the eastern shoulder of Golden Ears. Stay on the ridgecrest, following the obvious, worn path and a few cairns. Near the snowfield, flagging directs you left onto rock. Avoid the snow as long as possible. Eventually you must cross the permanent snowfield. It's not difficult if the snow is soft, but it's no place for novices. Walk slowly, kicking footholds. It takes about 30 minutes to ascend southwest and attain the ridge above the snowfield.

Work your way to the south side of the mountain, onto rock. Follow orange flagging on trees as you turn right (northwest) and climb the ridge of the east Ear. A short but vigorous scramble through krummholz (stunted trees) and over rocks will grant you the 1706-m (5596-ft) summit and a well-earned panorama.

Pitt Lake is west; that's Cozen Point at the far north end. West, above the lake, is Widgeon Peak. Northwest is Peneplain Peak, above the out-of-sight Widgeon Lake (Trip 40). A bit farther north is Obelisk Peak. Raven Lake sits in a pristine bowl, below you and a bit north. A parade of mountains marches north and northeast to the horizon. Mt. Baker and Mt. Shuksan reign across the border, southeast.

On the summit of Golden Ears

Trip 36

Mt. Roderick

Location	Squamish
Round trip	20 km (12.5 mi)
Elevation gain	1476 m (4840 ft)
Time required	10 hours to 3 days
Available	early July through October
Map	Squamish 92 G/11

OPINION

The summit vantage is terrific. Even the preceding ridge offers frequent views. But Mt. Roderick itself is disappointing. It's not a mount, it's merely a mound. And the name Roderick sounds noble, which this runt definitely is not, so we'll just call it Rod. Mound Rod. But go anyway. If you're up for a stiff hike, you'll be rewarded with grand scenery.

Don't be put off by the industrial trailhead: Woodfibre mill. Though it's unsightly and loud, you'll leave it behind quickly. And the 1 ½ - hour road walk is less onerous than you might think, because the forest is surprisingly beautiful. If you go with friends, you can stride abreast and enjoy deep conversation until the trail demands single-file attention.

Think of Rod as your humble servant, who simply hopes to please as an open viewpoint, or perhaps a campsite from which you can launch deeper into the mountains, particularly toward the compelling and attainable ruggedness of Mt. Sedgwick.

An even better campsite, however, which you'll pass on the way to Rod, is lovely Sylvia Lake. From there you can explore a different and far more open, exciting ridge than the one leading to Rod. Ascend open slabs above Sylvia's southwest shore, then wander at will. This ridge has no official name. We call it Sechelt Lake Ridge, after the lake beneath its northwest and west walls. It's wild, unforested, fascinating terrain, ideal for ambling. No trail required. No trail desired.

An excellent adventure would be to basecamp at Sylvia Lake, then devote one day to Sechelt Lake Ridge and another to Rod and Sedgwick. But even if you're only dayhiking to Rod, be sure to say hello to Sylvia.

On Mt. Roderick

FACT

By Car

Drive Highway 99 to the Darrell Bay turnoff. It's 40.3 km (25 mi) north of the Horseshoe Bay turnoff. Look for it 4.2 km (2.6 mi) north of the lake at Murrin Provincial Park, or immediately southwest of Shannon Falls Provincial Park.

Park at the Woodfibre ferry-terminal public parking lot, which is free of charge. So is the ferry ride across Squamish Harbour to the Woodfibre mill, where the hike begins. The ferry runs frequently. Usual morning departures from Darrell Bay are 7:15, 8:30 and 9:30. Afternoon and evening returns from the mill are 4:15, 5:15, 6:15 and 8:10.

On Foot

Disembark the ferry, angle left, walk over the railroad tracks, and cross the road. Stop at the first-aid station, where hikers are required to register. When you come out, turn right (southwest), ascend the stairs, then walk between the building and the trailer to the higher road, where you go right.

One hour up, the roar of Woodfibre Creek replaces the stressful noise of the mill. Another 15 minutes and you're among big trees, at about 503 m (1650 ft). After 1 ½ hours, the creek is visible and you soon reach the road's end, at 610 m (2000 ft). Cross the metal bridge and ascend a steep trail with minimal switchbacks.

About 45 minutes from the bridge, reach Henrietta Lake at 863 m (2830 ft). There's a table and tent sites above the shore. To continue, don't cross the dam. Follow the path to the right of the old building. Continue along the right side of the wooden helipad. Head northwest, passing rock slabs and another campsite. Watch for blue and red flagging where the trail drops into the bush. For the next 30 minutes, the trail is steeper, narrower, rougher, rootier, and brushier.

Nearly 305 m (1000 ft) above Henrietta, the trail plows through knock-you-off-your-feet berry bushes before entering subalpine. You soon get views north to Mt. Sedgwick and east to a pristine, forested slope. About 1¾ hours from road's end, attain the ridgecrest at 1280 m (4200 ft). The trail levels now but also diminishes to a boot-beaten path requiring you to sidehill on the east side of the crest.

Head northwest, passing several tarns. Within 15 minutes of reaching the ridge, watch for the side route left to Sylvia Lake. The lake is not visible from the path to Rod, so it's easily missed. Yellow flagging on the bushes might alert you to it. A 7-minute, 30-meter descent through heather and across a small boulder field will bring you to the lakeshore. The way to Sechelt Lake Ridge begins on the far (west) side of Sylvia.

From the Sylvia fork, continuing north toward Rod, in about 1 hour you'll reach the ridgeline's 1360-m (4460-ft) high point. Tiny Woodfibre Lake is visible below, to the right. Sedgwick rises in the north; Conybeare northeast; Garibaldi far northeast. Rod is the insignificant bump just ahead, above the lake. So don't stop here; the so-called summit is nearly yours.

Drop very steeply to 1280 m (4200 ft) (not all the way to Woodfibre Lake), then begin the final 183-m (600-ft) ascent. Follow the treed path, around Rod's west shoulder to its north side. The way becomes faint as you leave the trees, so look for cairns. From where you first attained the ridgecrest, to 1476-m (4840-ft) Mound Rod, allow 2 hours hiking time.

The serviceable mound provides a glimpse of the Taquat Lakes basin far below, to the northwest. Mt. Sedgwick beckons immediately north. Looking east, you can see the western countenance of the Tantalus Range.

Rod has lots of flat areas for tents, but with little natural shelter, camping here could be disastrous in a severe storm. And if you're staying, haul lots of water from Sylvia or Woodfibre lakes; Rod is dry, except for snowmelt. From a basecamp on Rod, a daytrip up Mt. Sedgwick is easy for capable scramblers who can forge their own route.

Trip 37

Howe Sound Crest

Location	Cypress Provincial Park
One way	30 km (18.6 mi)
Elevation gain	1185 m (3887 ft)
Time required	1 to 3 days
Available	mid-July through October
Maps	BC Parks brochure; ITM Vancouver's Northshore; North Vancouver 92 G/6, Squamish 92 G/11

OPINION

The Howe Sound Crest is a feral, shaggy, hump-backed beast, beautiful from a distance, but a demon to ride. Especially if you're carrying a full pack. The trail bucks violently from start to finish, always working you hard. Hang on 'til the end and you'll be smiling, but only because you're glad the ordeal is over. Views of Howe Sound are superb, though not frequent. The savage spine is bristling with trees; you're rarely above them. Yet there's a zoo atmosphere at Unnecessary Mountain, the Lions, and Deeks Lake, because these vantages en route are accessible by Vancouver dayhikers. If you've got the juice to thrash this ripsnorting trail in a single day, go for it. The accomplishment of bolting from Cypress ski area, past Deeks Lake, to Highway 99, will make you feel like a dragonslayer.

Bravehearts intent on vanquishing the Howe Sound Crest end to end will gain an advantage by starting high at Cypress ski area, heading north, and ending at nearly sea level, on Highway 99.

Heavy fog and low-flying clouds are frequent here and can quickly reduce visibility to zero. In places, the rugged, faint route is easy to lose at the best of times. Don't risk traveling if you can't see.

Carry more water than you think you'll need. Fill up at every opportunity. Water is scarce for long stretches.

The best camping is at Magnesia Meadows and Brunswick Lake, but they're so close you'll probably have to pick one or the other. And Magnesia is too far for most hikers, fully packed, to reach in one day from Cypress ski area. The ridge between Unnecessary Mountain and the Lions, at 9.5 km (5.5 mi) is a reasonable goal for your first night. It has scenic yet reasonably sheltered tent sites. Just no water. Shoot for Brunswick Lake the second night, at 17 km (10.5 mi).

Because we've rated this viperous trail Don't Do, and because most of the trip is described elsewhere in the book, directions here are minimal. Read Mt. Strachan (Trip 8), Unnecessary Mountain from Cypress Ski Area (Trip 15), The Lions (Trip 10), and Deeks and Brunswick Lakes (Trip 23) for details. Keep in mind, the Deeks route is described south to north, so on this trip you'd be hiking it in reverse.

FACT

By Car

See Trip 8 for directions to the trailhead at the south end; Trip 23 for the north end.

On Foot

Start and stay on the Howe Sound Crest Trail (HSCT), heading generally north. It's well-signed through the initial confusion of Cypress ski area. It's periodically signed or blazed the rest of the way, past Deeks Lake.

Reach Strachan Meadows in about one hour. Cypress Park continues north, but narrows to a strip, barely wider than the trail. At Magnesia Meadows, the park boundary widens again, encompassing Brunswick, Middle, and Deeks lakes.

From Strachan Meadows, climb to St. Marks, descend, then climb the south summit of Unnecessary Mountain. Drop into the cleft, then ascend the 1524-m (5000-ft) north summit—highpoint of the trip. Scramble 100 m (330 ft) down the ragged north side of the mountain, then angle northeast toward the Lions.

Drop beneath the south side of the West Lion, proceed through the gap between the West and East Lions, then head north. Lose about 240 m (787 ft) between the Lions gap and Enchantment Pass, along the way hitting Thomas Peak. Enchantment Lake is east of and well below the pass. Bump over James Peak. From a meadowy pass between it and David Peak, the HSCT drops some 160 m (525 ft) around the east side of David toward Hanging Lake before ascending again.

Continue north through Magnesia Meadows, then contour around the south and west sides of Brunswick Mountain to Hat Pass. From here on, you're descending.

Drop northeast to Brunswick Lake, north to Middle Lake (also called Hanover Lake), northwest to Deeks Lake at 1050 m (3444 ft), and from there curve west then north to Highway 99. The trail reaches pavement just south of Porteau Cove Provincial Park.

Trip 38
Elsay Lake

Location	Mt. Seymour Provincial Park
Round trip	20 km (12.4 mi)
Elevation gain	885 m (2903 ft)
Time required	11 hours or overnight
Available	mid-July through October
Maps	BC Parks brochure; ITM Vancouver's Northshore; Coquitlam 92 G/7

OPINION

This is Bigfoot territory. His long, loping steps would easily propel him on this ornery route through tangled forest. Those of us less adapted to wilderness might feel more like slithering slugs on the exhausting, punishing venture.

If the route led to a sight like Wedgemount Lake (Trip 4) or the Cougar Mountain Cedar Grove (Trip 13), then the travails could be justified. But Elsay is only a forest-ringed lake of medium size and moderate interest. If solitude is your goal, you'll have a good shot at it here. Our recommendation, however, is nearby Coliseum Mountain (Trip 34), a trip of equal difficulty offering premier scenery as well as solitude.

Before you commit to clambering through the trees down to Elsay Lake, hike up to Second Pump Peak on the way to Mt. Seymour. From there, you can survey the terrain you'd be spending two days in. You'd have to descend 610 m (2000 ft) beneath Mt. Seymour, crossing over a ridge off Runner Peak, and the long, eastern buttress of Mt. Elsay.

The trail is in decent shape for roughly the first 2 km after departing the Mt. Seymour trail. Then it narrows to a challenging, rooty, muddy route. Searching for the bright blazes and flagging, it helps to adopt the spirit of a kid on an Easter egg hunt. If you relish getting messy, you might maintain the good-natured persistence necessary to complete this trudge. In fog or heavy rain, the route could easily evade you. In such conditions, proceed warily and slowly.

FACT

By Car

From Mount Seymour Parkway in North Vancouver, drive up Mount Seymour Road to the end. Park in the upper lot near the chairlift, at 1003 m (3290 ft).

On Foot

Follow the directions for Mt. Seymour (Trip 9) as far as the signed junction at 3.0 km (1.9 mi), on the east side of First Pump Peak. Then turn right on the Elsay Lake trail. The remaining 7.0 km (4.3 mi) to the lake require at least 4 hours one way. It becomes faint and rugged 3.5 km (4.6 mi) beyond the signed junction, but you should be able to follow the blazes.

Soon after the signed junction, the trail descends in tight switchbacks. It eventually levels, contouring a rocky basin beneath Mt. Seymour. From there, it bobs over a ridge off Runner Peak and drops to Canadian Pass at 960 m (3150 ft). There's a pond here, at the bottom of a bouldery basin.

After crossing the pond outlet, the route heads northwest, then curves around the forested buttress of Mt. Elsay. Reach the geographic low point of the trip at 650 m (2132 ft), as you near unbridged Elsay Creek. Fording can be a difficult if the water's high. Try upstream.

On the north bank, the route curves left (northwest), paralleling the creek. Follow blazes through open forest and bog. It's about 1 km (0.6 mi) from the creek crossing to Little Elsay Lake. Big Elsay Lake is just beyond, at 770 m (2526 ft). Your total distance: 10 km (6.2 mi). Proceed along the northeast shore to reach a small backcountry shelter.

SHOULDER-SEASON TRIPS

On the Chief's second summit (Trip 43) in mid-April

Trip 39

Hollyburn Mountain

Location	Cypress Provincial Park
Round trip	8.0 km (5 mi)
Elevation gain	405 m (1328 ft)
Time required	3 hours
Available	mid-June through mid-November
Maps	BC Parks brochure; North Vancouver 92 G/6

OPINION

Hollyburn Mountain offers the most accessible stand of ancient fir, cedar, and western and mountain hemlock within 120 kilometers of Vancouver. This unlogged forest is a refreshing relief from the dismal second growth that now disgraces most of the North Shore mountains. The trees here are noble and lovely. The well-maintained trail is a joy to walk. By starting at the ski area at the end of Cypress Parkway, the elevation gain is minimal to the top of Hollyburn, where you'll enjoy a 360° mountain-city-ocean panorama.

If you want to treat visitors to a special hike, but feel they'd be intimidated by the demanding routes typical of this rugged range, tote them up here. It's one of the few Coast Mountain trails that don't require a grueling ascent on a cantankerous trail, yet still reward you with views.

FACT

By Car

Driving Highway 1 through West Vancouver, turn off at Cypress Bowl, Exit 8. Continue 16 km (10 mi) up the Cypress Parkway to the ski area. Near the end of the road, just before it curves south into a huge parking lot, on your right is a big map of the ski area. That's the trailhead, at 920 m (3018 ft).

On Foot

Walk between the gate and the ski-area map, onto the gravel road. In 20 meters, go right (east) on the road. Pass the big, white diesel tanks. Now on the blazed Baden Powell Trail (BPT), cross a boardwalk, then descend a bit.

At about 0.6 km (0.4 mi), cross a stream, ascend the far bank and reach an unsigned junction. Stay right (level) on the trail that's blazed on both sides. (The left fork ascends steeply to join the old Strachan trail.) You're now heading east, traversing the slopes of Hollyburn. About 20 minutes along, cross another stream, this one with pool-and-drop cascades.

Steadily ascend to a gorge where a stream is spanned by a heavy-duty bridge. Just before the bridge, pass the old Strachan trail ascending left. Stay on the BPT, crossing the bridge and continuing another 7-10 minutes to a junction with the Hollyburn Mountain trail. Snow might persist above this point until mid-June.

About 35-45 minutes from the trailhead, reach a junction, park map, and a sign stating it's 50 minutes more to Hollyburn Mountain and 40 minutes back to Cypress Bowl. Go left toward Hollyburn Mountain. Right descends Hollyburn Ridge south to a parking lot by Powerline Road, which joins the Cypress Parkway at about 880 m (2885 ft).

Ascending through berry bushes and forest, you'll see trails branching right toward the ski run. Stay left on the wider, main trail. Coming into view southeast are Port Moody, Burnaby, and Second Narrows bridge; south is Boundary Bay; southwest is Georgia Strait.

A blaze marks the 4-km point. There are no blazes beyond, but the trail, now steeper, is obvious. Just before reaching the summit knob, the trail hugs the west side of the mountain. Scramble over a 2-meter band of rock before topping out at 1325 m (4350 ft).

Nearby to the southeast, you can see the sails of the Vancouver Convention Centre downtown. In the distance is Mt. Baker, and the flatlands of Washington. South and slightly west is Point Grey, and beyond it, across the strait, is Vancouver Island. Langdale and the Sechelt Peninsula are west. The rock pillars of the Lions are directly north. Farther north are snowcapped Mt. Garibaldi and Mamquam Mountain. To the east and a bit north, across the Capilano River valley, is 1501-m (4923-ft) Crown Mountain—its dramatic rock wall unusual for the North Shore.

Trip 40

Widgeon Lake

Location	Pinecone-Burke Provincial Park
Round trip	18.5 km (11.5 mi)
Elevation gain	815 m (2673 ft)
Time required	1½ to 2 days
Available	mid-May through early September
Map	Coquitlam 92 G/7

OPINION

Want to cleanse your mind of city craziness? You need only go as far as Pitt Lake to start a purifying adventure. You'll travel via canoe, then on foot, and sometimes on all fours. It gets rough, but that's what scrapes all the gunk out of your head. Like steel wool.

If you make it to Widgeon, you'll be generously compensated for your persistence. It's a magnificent lake cupped in a cirque of bright rock. The question is, should you haul a full pack all the way up so you can camp? On the ascent, you'll say no way. After arriving, you'll say absolutely.

We recommend dayhiking up from a basecamp at Widgeon Slough, for several reasons: (1) There aren't enough easy exploration options around the lake to warrant camping there; (2) Backpacking to the lake requires strength of mind and body that few people can muster; (3) Extending the trip necessitates a more expensive canoe rental, unless you own one.

On a sunny day, you'll have company as you paddle across Grant Narrows and up Widgeon Slough. It's more like a teenage pool-party than a trip into the wilds. Lots of people enjoy this first leg of the journey, but few continue on the rumpled road and sketchy route to Widgeon Lake. Everyone should at least walk the first 6 km (3.7 mi) to see a cascading creek pound through a stunning gorge. The rest of the trip is not for softees. It's for hardened hikers, and those whose youthful nonchalance makes them immune to misery.

If all you're seeking is an opportunity to mix a little paddling with a bit of hiking, the Widgeon Wildlife Reserve is ideal. An entertaining

Widgeon Lake cirque

trail leads through pleasant forest to the cascading creek. You'll pass a deep, green channel begging for swimmers. You'll see gargantuan bigleaf maples cloaked with luxurious moss. From the Widgeon Slough campground, walk the trail to the falls, then loop back via the old logging road. It takes about two hours and is nearly level the whole way (7 km / 4 mi). Paddling up the slough, walking the loop, then paddling back to your car is a full but comfortable daytrip.

For hard-core adventurers, the trail along Widgeon Creek is the south approach to the demanding 50-km (31-mi) hike northwest through Pinecone-Burke Provincial Park, to the Mamquam FS Road about 20 km (12.4 mi) outside Squamish. Buy the Boise Valley map produced by the Western Canada Wilderness Committee.

FACT

By Car

If you're heading east on Lougheed Highway 7 to Pitt Meadows, immediately after crossing the Pitt River bridge, turn left onto Dewdney Trunk Road. In 6.2 km (3.8 mi), turn left on Neaves Street (also 208th St.), which becomes Rannie Road. Arrive at the public boat ramp and parking lot at Grant Narrows (the beginning of Pitt Lake), 18 km (11.2 mi) from the Pitt River bridge.

If you're heading west on Highway 7, in Maple Ridge turn north on

Laity. In 2 km (1.2 mi), go left on 128th. At 3.7 km (2.3 mi), go right on Neaves. There's a sign AYLA'S CANOES 14 KM. You'll arrive at the public boat ramp and parking lot at 16.6 km (10.3 mi). Pitt Lake is at sea level.

By Boat

Bring your own canoe, or borrow one, so you'll have the freedom to return whenever you like. The less attractive option is renting one from Ayla's Canoes (941-2822), beside the Pitt Lake public boat ramp. If you rent, your trip will not be relaxing; you'll constantly be checking your watch. A one-day rental grants you a canoe, paddles and life jackets, from 8 A.M. to 6 P.M. For the same one-day fee, you can take a canoe at 4 P.M. the evening before, then return it by 6 P.M. the next day. That's the minimum time you'll need to paddle up Widgeon Slough (about 1 hour), camp there the first night, then dayhike (starting by 7 A.M.) to Widgeon Lake and paddle back to Pitt Lake by 6 P.M. Ayla's charges $10 for each hour you're late after 6 pm. If you want a comfortably-paced trip, or you plan to camp at Widgeon Lake, rent a canoe for the whole weekend.

The public boat ramp is at Grant Narrows, where the Pitt River flows out of Pitt Lake, and where Widgeon Slough empties into the river. (Widgeon Creek feeds Widgeon Slough farther north. The slough is a marsh that's part of an inlet.) From the boat ramp, paddle northwest (across the narrows, bearing left) to the slough entrance, which is visible from the boat launch. Once you're in the slough, it's easy to follow the main channel through the Widgeon Wildlife Reserve. Don't worry about finding the route on weekends—just follow the crowd. You'll paddle along the north tip of Siwash Island. After 0.8 m (0.5 mi), curve right around a point and head north. The channel will get narrower and the water will at times be so shallow you can see the sandy bottom. Stay in the obvious, main channel as it curves left then right to continue north. After about 1 hour of determined, steady paddling (1½ hours for moderate strokers), drag your canoe ashore at the BC Forest Service campground, on your left. It's obvious: a big, worn-out dirt area with fire rings. On weekends, you'll see lots of tents set up here. There are a couple secluded tentsites a few minutes farther up the left bank. The slough narrows beyond the campground. You'll know you've paddled too far when the tree branches arch overhead, and it begins to feel like a Louisiana bayou.

Along the way, it can be tempting to jump out and swim, or sun yourself on one of the sandy beaches. You might have time for that while heading up the slough, but not on the way back if you're hoping to return a rental canoe without penalty.

On Foot

Behind the BC Forest Service campground on Widgeon Slough, there's an old logging road. Follow it north (right). In about 200 meters, turn right at the WIDGEON FALLS sign. This trail, marked with orange, metal blazes, winds through forest to Widgeon Creek and rejoins the road within 40 minutes. Ten minutes along, go right at the junction and continue to the cascades (left returns to the road). Figure at least an extra 20 minutes hiking time on the trail compared to staying on the road. On the return from Widgeon Lake, keep to the road and enjoy easy striding beneath giant bigleaf maples.

The lower cascades churn through rock clefts. From here, you can see forested mountainsides to the east. The trail ascends from the lower cascades, reaching a rooty junction in 3 minutes. There's a green pit toilet on the left. Stay right, following the orange blazes to the upper cascades. After viewing them, return to the rooty junction and stay right. Ascend 40 meters on stairs. You'll reach an old road. Go left to rejoin the main road, where you turn right at the green BC FS litter barrel.

The road soon crosses an exciting, 50-meter cascade on a creek running off Coquitlam Mountain. Just beyond, where a minor road forks left, a sign points the way to Widgeon Lake. Heed the sign and say right on the obviously larger road as it descends slightly.

About 4 km (2.5 mi) from the campground (not including the trail detour to the cascades), reach a junction. Go left on the flagged, old road. There's an open, sand-pit area 250 meters up. Stay right where a minor road forks left. There's a white sign straight ahead on a tree. The road dwindles to trail near 5.5 km (3.4 mi). When you hit a streambed, go left toward the hiker sign, into the forest. A hefty wood bridge spans a riotous fork of Widgeon Creek, where another cascade shatters onto rock slabs. This is a good place to refill water bottles and cool off in the spray. (See the photo on page 264.)

Beyond the bridge, turn left and ascend the trail (an overgrown road) paralleling the creek. Soon you can peek out of the forest over the cascade you just crossed. The trail climbs steeply for 0.4 km (0.25 mi) then eases to a moderate grade on an old road through re-growth. About 30 minutes from the bridge, you'll get a glimpse of unspoiled wilderness. Looking across Widgeon Creek valley, four waterfalls are visible streaming off high cliffs. The trail will probably still be overgrown through here, so expect to get thwacked by bushes and branches. There are a couple tricky spots to pull yourself over, but no dangerous drop-offs.

So far, it's merely been steep. But at 16.7 km (10.5 mi) you must storm the bastille of Widgeon Lake. A sign marks the beginning of this final assault and indicates the distance remaining: 1.8 KM. It's not a road. It's not a trail. It's a wickedly steep, muddy route, up a wall of roots and deadfall. Follow the orange flagging. Don't expect to see the lake for another hour.

Nearing the lip of the cirque, you'll face a 2-meter high bluff. Go left, descending slightly, rather than clinging to the base of the bluff. An old ladder that washed away used to facilitate the ascent to the right, directly over the rock. Another 7-10 minutes will bring you to a flat patch of dirt at 815 m (2673 ft), and there it is: Widgeon Lake, 45 m (150 ft) below you, in a semi-circle of granite cliffs.

Descend left or right to the lakeshore. A sign points left to a toilet. There's a campsite down that way, near the water. Astonishingly, campers had trashed the site when we were there. Pack out all your garbage.

Trip 41
Stein River Canyon

Location	Stein Wilderness, Fraser River Canyon
Round trip	27 km (16.7 mi) to lower cable crossing; 42.6 km (26.5 mi) to Ponderosa Shelter
Elevation gain	355 m (1165 ft) to cable crossing; 415 m (1360 ft) to Ponderosa
Time required	3 hours to several days
Available	April through November
Maps	ITM Stein Valley Trail; Stein River 92 I/5

OPINION

Roaring hydraulics, shouting rapids, slurping holes. The lower Stein River is an outrageous entertainer, and you'll see it, often up close, throughout the first 13 km (8 mi) of this trip. Following the speeding river upstream, the trail penetrates the deep valley and eventually leads to the headwaters, high on the Stein Divide. The river is hyperactive from mid-May through June.

Except where traversing a couple talus fields, the path is excellent all the way to the lower cable crossing. You can stride confidently and vigorously—a delicious sensation after a long winter spent mostly indoors. We used to drive here from Calgary to thaw out and backpack over the long May weekend. It's liberating to wear shorts again, feel your skin swoon at the sun's touch, and hear the crunch of gravel underfoot.

Sun is dependable here on the eastern edge of the Coast Mountains. The few clouds that sneak overhead are mostly running on empty. The infrequent showers are usually light or brief. But only desert rats should hike here when the furnace is cranked up, mid-June through early September.

Families and beginning hikers will enjoy this trail because the boisterous river dispels boredom. Walking even just a few kilometers is memorable and will give you the flavour of the Stein Valley. Keep going, and you can see remarkable pictographs. For an excellent two-day, shoulder-season backpack trip, hike 13.5 km (8.4 mi) to the lower cable car crossing, camp there and return the next day.

Stein River

Beyond the cable car, the river loses its vigor, meandering slowly through the mid-valley. Hiking is not as pleasant or interesting here. The trail is often brushy, pushing through dense, mixed forest: black cottonwood, birch, Douglas fir. The river is visible only occasionally. Possible campsites are scarce. Though not always beside the river, the trail is often at water level, so sections get flooded in spring. Also be prepared to ford swollen tributary creeks with multiple channels.

FACT

By Car

From Hope, drive 108 km (67 mi) north on Trans-Canada Highway 1 to Lytton. Follow signs for Highway 12. Drive through Lytton and proceed north. Cross the Thompson River bridge, drive another 0.7 km (0.4 mi), then descend left to the Fraser River ferry. The ferry runs daily, on demand, 6:30 A.M. to 10:15 P.M., except for half-hour breaks mid-morning and early evening. It also stops during periods of extremely high water caused by spring runoff. Check with B.C. Highways (604-660-9770) before you go.

Ride the ferry across the river, to the West Side Road. From the ferry, go right and head north. Ignore a road intersecting from the left at 0.6 km (0.4 mi). At 1.4 km (0.9 mi) pass Earlscourt Farm on the left. Just after a sharp bend in the road, at 4.0 km (2.5 mi), watch for your turn. At 4.8 km (3.0 mi) turn left, cutting back on a rutted road that's little more than a track. You'll see a house on your right, across from the turn. This is Native land. Be respectful. Drive 1 km / 0.6 mi to the trailhead, on the south side of the river. The elevation here is 230 m (750 ft). If you missed the turn, you'll come to a bridge over the Stein River, 0.6 km / 0.4 mi too far north.

On Foot

At the trailhead, on a bench above the river, there's a large map/sign. The trail begins and continues in open forest: stalwart ponderosa pine and Douglas fir. Descend toward the river. At 0.3 km (0.2 mi) cross bridged Stryen Creek. At 1.5 km (0.9 mi) rock slabs provide comfortable seating where you can let your eyes run the rapids. Proceed across flat benchland. At 4 km (2.5 mi), switchback 180 m (590 ft) up to a valley viewpoint. Then cross a talus slope, descend into a gully, and enter the riparian area of Christina Creek. In 10 minutes, cross another talus slope. Near the bottom of the descent, you can take a quick side trip to enjoy a remarkable sight. Look for a fallen log on the right. Cross it and go downstream about 75 meters to the base of the cliff, where you'll find numerous pictographs.

Back on the main trail, 10 minutes beyond the pictograph turnoff, you can see a tight bend in the river. Pass through a cool cedar grove. After crossing a small creek and ascending a boulder field, reach the Wigwam campsite, on a large river flat at 8.3 km (5.1 mi). Walk through another cedar grove. At 10.7 km (6.7 mi), reach a possible campsite in a clearing near a reconstructed prospector's cabin. Just beyond, cross Earl Creek on a solid bridge.

After hiking river flats for 1.25 km (0.8 mi), look closely for pictographs on the rock walls where the trail nears the river. Fifteen minutes beyond, reach the lower cable crossing of the Stein River, at 13.5 km (8.4 mi). The elevation here is 585 m (1920 ft). When you leave, be sure the cable car is not secured at either end.

Up for a longer trip? It's 7.8 km (4.9 mi) and a gain of only 60 m (197 ft) to the next obvious destination: Ponderosa Shelter. Near 18 km (11 mi), the trail starts crossing the river flood plain. Cresting bluffs, you'll gain views of the river and valley. Ponderosa Shelter is at 21.3 km (13.2 mi), just east of Ponderosa Creek. If you plan to hike through to the Stein Divide, you're almost a third of the way at this point. In total, it's a 75-km (46.5-mi) trek from the east end of the Stein Valley near the Fraser River, to Lizzie Lake (Trip 28) at the west end. Take the Stein Valley topo map or refer to a Stein Valley Wilderness guidebook.

Trip 42

Mt Gardener / Bowen Island

Location	Howe Sound
Round trip	16 km (10 mi)
Elevation gain	750 m (2460 ft)
Time required	7 to 8 hours, excluding ferry travel
Available	all year, except after a serious snowstorm
Maps	Crippen Regional Park brochure; North Vancouver 92 G / 6

OPINION

Play hookey from winter. Catch the ferry to Bowen Island—a short, easy crossing that adds a sense of escape to the trip—then enjoy a full day's ramble to a summit with spectacular views. It's an exuberant workout, and vastly fulfilling, especially on a dauntless blue day.

Island forests have been ravaged like those on the mainland, so there are no lovely trees here to inspire your ascent. But an unrestricted panorama awaits you on Mt. Gardner's North Peak helipad. Looking northwest, over Keats Island, you can see the town of Gibsons; beyond is the Sechelt Peninsula. Gambier Island and Howe Sound are north. The mainland Coast Mountains arc across the horizon, north to northeast. English Bay and Vancouver are southeast; beyond is the Fraser Valley. On a clear day, you might see the Lucky Four peaks in the distance, east-southeast, above Chilliwack, and Mt. Baker crowning the nearer southeast horizon. Southwest, across the Strait of Georgia, is Vancouver Island. Snow on the distant mountains adds to their beauty—another reason to come here between December and May. In winter, just be sure to catch the early ferry, so you can start hiking by 9:30 A.M. and finish before dark.

A messy maze of old logging roads and intersecting trails presents many routes to the summit. The one we describe is fairly direct, has fewer junctions, and should eliminate confusion. You'll be on trail most of the time, rather than road, and you'll pass through prettier forest. You'll also ascend the east and southeast sides of the mountain, where in shoulder season you'll enjoy more sunlight than on the longer route up the northeast and west sides.

We recommend ascending and descending the same route. The

Mt. Baker and the Vancouver metropolis

other options are less pleasant, offering only one extra viewpoint on the northwest side—which adds nothing new to the summit vista.

FACT

By Car

West of Vancouver, Highway 1 turns north and becomes Highway 99. Near here take the Horseshoe Bay exit and drive down to the ferry. You can pay to park at the terminal, or hunt for a free spot on the roads above. Walk onto the Bowen Island ferry. Round trip: $4.25 per person in 1997. While on the ferry, orient yourself to the island by looking at the map of Crippen Park. There's also a map near the park entrance at Snug Cove.

On Foot

Be patient with all these directions to the actual beginning of the trail up Mt. Gardner. During the 3 km (1.9 mi) to that point, there are lots of junctions. Basically, follow signs to Killarney Lake. Fast walkers can get there in 30 minutes from Snug Cove. Leaving the ferry terminal, walk Government Road straight west. Where you see a sign announcing Crippen Regional Park, turn right on signed Cardina Drive. In a couple minutes, go left through the park on a trail signed for Killarney Lake, but before you do, continue north to the lagoon for a look across Deep Bay and Howe Sound to the looming wall of mainland mountains.

Back on the trail, follow signs to Killarney Lake. Within 100 meters reach a junction at the Bowen Memorial Garden. Continue straight on the unsigned Alder Grove trail toward Killarney Lake and Terminal Falls. In 5 minutes, pass the fish ladder and falls on your right.

A couple minutes farther, the trail comes to Miller Road and a sign. You can go either way, but it's more enjoyable going straight across the road to follow the Hatchery trail through the meadows. Though this takes 5 or 10 minutes longer than using the more direct Killarney Creek trail, it eliminates a 5-minute road-walk. About 10 minutes along the Hatchery trail, reach a junction. Mt. Gardner Road is on your left. Go right to pass the Equestrian Ring and head northeast through meadows to meet the Killarney Creek trail. At that junction, go left (northwest) onto a gravel path. A couple minutes farther is a fork; stay left toward the picnic area.

In another five minutes reach Magee Road (dirt) at the south end of Killarney Lake. Go left, pass the dam, then turn right onto the lakeshore trail heading around the southwest end. Follow signs toward the picnic area. In about 5 minutes look for numbers on the poles beside the road. Leave the trail at pole 490, cross the paved road, and go left onto Bow Pit Road—by pole 491. About 1 minute up, stay left on a minor road.

About 5-7 minutes later, turn left toward the creek, onto the signed Skid trail. Ascend 20 minutes. Go left onto the Mt. Gardner Shortcut trail. This is before the Skid trail rejoins the gravel road. Shortly, stay left again and ascend the Mt. Gardner South trail. Don't go right onto the rocky logging road. Ascend steadily, traversing the east and southeast slopes. At the next junction, go left.

Farther along you might notice an old trail cutting right, ascending steeply. It leads directly to the South Peak. We recommend continuing about 10 minutes farther to a 3-way junction on the south side of the peak. A trail drops left (west) to Bowen Bay. Don't descend unless you have a sailboat waiting. Continue straight (right), to the west side of a rock outcropping on the ridge just before the South Peak. You might not even notice passing the forested, viewless South Peak. Beyond it, hike up and down 15-20 minutes through hollows on the west side of South Peak ridge. Be looking on your right for metal sheds and helipads both marring and marking Mt. Gardner's 719-m (2358-ft) North Peak. Descend the way you came.

Trip 43
Stawamus Chief ✓

Location	Squamish
Round trip	6 km (3.7 mi) to the Chief, 9 km (5.6 mi) to second summit, 11 km (6.8 mi) to the third summit
Elevation gain	612 m (2007 ft) to the second summit
Time required	3 hours for the Chief, 4 ½ hours for third summit
Available	March through November
Map	Squamish 92 G/11

OPINION

The Chief is aptly named. It dominates. Everyone looks up to it. At its base, passers-by stop and stare, mentally grappling with the mighty monolith.

The Chief's strikingly sheer granite wall is in your face as you drive Highway 99 north or south into Squamish. It's the most dramatic sight on the entire trip between Vancouver and Pemberton. Though you'll see higher mountains along the way, none has such a sustained cliff.

Climbers claw their way to the top. But if you're a mere mortal and cannot ignore the call of this Homeric stone, you don't have to scale any cliffs. You can walk up the back side, only occasionally using your hands on the rooty, steep route. You'll encounter no threatening drop-offs until you're standing on the summit.

Now here's an unusual suggestion: skip the Chief's first (south) summit. Like us, you might prefer the second (middle) and third (north) summits. They're always less crowded, yet afford equally marvelous panoramas that will draw your vision north and east, away from the Woodfibre mill and the pollution wafting across Howe Sound. But, if you have time, participate in the full drama and ascend all three summits.

If you reach the third summit, you'll enjoy the descent more if you retrace your route over the second summit. The other option is to loop back via the steep, rough, challenging East trail in the gorge between the second and third summits. The only advantage of the loop is that you'll encounter fewer people. By returning over the second summit,

Stawamus Chief and Howe Sound, from the second summit

you'll be in the open longer before plunging into dark forest. You'll also descend more gradually, on a more comfortable trail.

It's not just the epic views that attract hikers here again and again. The Chief's proximity to Vancouver makes it a viable destination for weekend days when you don't get around to deciding what to do until noon. Plus, the trail launches you out of the forest and into the open more quickly than the typical Coast Mountain trail. And the Chief's relatively low elevation ensures that it's snow-free most of the year. As a result, this trail is probably the most frequently hiked, and certainly the most talked about in the range.

FACT

By Car

From the Horseshoe Bay turnoff, just outside West Vancouver, drive Highway 99 north 40.5 km (25.4 mi) to Shannon Falls Provincial Park. You can start hiking here, or drive 1.2 km (0.75 mi) farther north to the large, paved viewpoint beside the highway, beneath the cliff face of Stawamus Chief.

If you continue to the Chief viewpoint, you can park there, or if the gate is open, drive up to the BC Parks campground and park across from the entrance. It's only a 5-minute walk from the viewpoint up to the campground, where the elevation is 40 m (130 ft).

On Foot

From the parking lot at Shannon Falls, follow the path straight past the right side of the washroom. Go left at the sign directing you to the Stawamus Chief trail. Soon, another sign tells you it's 2.5 km and a 550-m elevation gain to the Chief. Follow this trail 10-15 minutes to the substantial bridge over Olesun Creek. After crossing it, turn right and ascend steeply. You're now on the trail reached via the Chief viewpoint.

At the BC Parks campground just above the Chief viewpoint, bear left. Walk through the campground to the end of the road, where Olesun Creek charges down a steep gorge. Look for the route (probably still unsigned) on your left, before the creek. Start with an awkward but brief climb over a large boulder. Then ascend well-constructed steps of wood and stone. In 5 minutes reach the bridge over Olesun Creek. The trail joining from the right started at Shannon Falls. Don't cross the bridge. Continue ascending on the left side of the creek gorge. You'll soon leave the creek and climb northeast beneath the back (east) side of the Chief.

About 15-20 minutes from the bridge, continue straight (left) where a trail forks right (south) to Upper Shannon Falls—another worthwhile trip. A couple minutes past that junction, reach a well-signed choice of trails.

Right leads to the Stawamus Squaw (Trip 72) and provides, en route, more difficult, less exciting access to the second and third summits. Go left, following the popular, direct route to all three Chief summits. It's about 45 minutes to the first (south) summit, and 70 minutes to the third (north) summit. You'll pass directly beneath the granite walls of the first summit.

In 10-15 minutes, the trail divides once more and is again signed. Ascend left to attain the first summit (signed South Peak here) in about 15 minutes. The view is superb. The Cheakamus and Squamish valleys are north, beyond the townsite. The Tantalus Range is northwest. Squamish Harbour is west. Shannon Falls is south. Goat Ridge is southeast. Mt. Garibaldi is northeast. The one smudge on this grand scene is the smoke-belching Woodfibre mill, across the harbour.

Back at the last fork, where left ascended the first summit, right leads to the second and third summits. You'll come to a rock cleft between granite walls. Follow the chained route ascending the rock on your right. At the top of the chain, cut back right, along the narrow ledge. Stay on the lower ledge where another would lead you higher. Drop slightly and curve left, following blazes into a rock defile. Scramble up through it and climb the metal ladder.

Beyond the ladder, it's easy walking over rock to the 652-m (2138-ft) second summit. Total distance: 4.5 km (2.8 mi) from the BC Parks campground. Hiking time: about 2¼ hours. The views are similar to those from the first summit, which is now slightly below you, southwest.

To reach the third summit, continue northeast over the open, airy second summit. Follow the blazes back into forest, soon reaching the signed North Gully, where you can look left into a hair-raising abyss that drops all the way to Squamish. A minute beyond North Gully, pass a mossy rock face on your left, and a signed, rough route descending steeply right. It loops back to the trail you ascended beneath the first summit. To reach the third summit, continue ascending the faint, blazed route through trees. You'll soon be on rock again, walking along the edge of the cliff until scrawny trees and salal undergrowth close in on you. There, look right for blazes and orange paint on trees where the route drops 10 meters into another forested gully. (Left ascends over more rock to another viewpoint.)

In the forested gully, ascend left (north), following blazes. The route then turns right (south) through messy forest cluttered with deadfall. Still following blazes, work your around to the south edge of the third summit. There, go sharply left onto the narrow rock ridge and head north. The route is now marked with orange paint. Once in the open, angle left, then right. The third summit is about 50 m (165 ft) higher than the second summit. Mt. Habrich looms across the canyon.

If you insist on a loop and choose not to return the way you came, you can descend the East trail in the gorge between the second and third summits. It departs your ascent route from near North Gully and leads, in about 45 minutes, back to the trail you ascended, just above Olesun Creek. From there, it's 15-20 minutes to the BC Parks campground.

Though blazed, the ornery East trail is rooty, bouldery, and black-diamond steep. The gorge shelters huge cedars and Douglas firs, some of them growing out of sheer rock. As you descend, bear right, so you don't end up heading left to the Stawamus Squaw (Trip 72). You'll soon be on familiar ground, heading southwest back to the trailhead.

Trip 44

High Falls Creek

Location	Squamish River Valley
Round trip	12 km (7.5 mi)
Elevation gain	640 m (2100 ft)
Time required	4 to 5 hours
Available	late April through early November
Map	Cheakamus River 92 G/14

OPINION

High Falls Creek is gorges. A natural turbine is gnawing a ragged slice through the forest here, and you'll witness it, after a steep, 40-minute hike. The 30-meter falls will churn exhilarating negative ions your way, recharging you for the remaining ascent. Above, you'll see massive glaciers cloaking the astounding Tantalus Range—a sight that convinced us these wild B.C. Coast Mountains, rather than the Swiss Alps, should be the international benchmark for alpine grandeur. No cows wearing big bells here. Just big-balled grizzlies. So be wary.

The rambunctious, rocky route is not for acrophobes. It will engage your mind, and occasionally your hands, as you flank the gorge. And while the falls are a satisfying destination, don't stop there. Follow the trail through lovely forest, to where it ends at a logging road. Continuing up to the road is easier than reversing the steep ascent route. Looping back down on the road takes a bit longer, of course, but the gradual descent provides eye-popping, heart-stopping views of the Squamish River Valley, Mt. Jimmy Jimmy, and the Tantalus.

Come gorge yourself in spring, when the Tantalus peaks are glistening white and High Falls is plummeting at maximal volume. After your mini-adventure here, you'll know why the Tantalus Range is now a provincial park. Its boundaries are roughly from Brackendale in the south to Sigurd Creek in the north. The east side of the park includes most of the lower slopes.

High Falls

FACT

Before your trip

Request the *Squamish Forest District Recreation Map* from the Squamish office (604-898-2100).

By Car

From Squamish, at the traffic light by Esso and McDonald's, drive Highway 99 north 10.6 km (6.6 mi). Across from Alice Lake Provincial Park, turn left onto Squamish Valley Road. From the turnoff, continue 3.6 km (2.2 mi) to a bridge over the Cheakamus River. Cross it and go 100 meters beyond to a junction, where you stay left on Squamish Valley Road. The pavement ends 23.0 km (14.3 mi) from Highway 99. At 24.2 km (15.0 mi), stay right on Squamish River Road. At 26.5 km (16.4 mi) pass a powerhouse and cross a creek. Reach High Falls Creek at 27.3 km (16.9 mi). Park off the road. Look 100 meters beyond the creek, farther along the road, for the small trailhead sign on the right. The elevation here is 75 m (250 ft).

On Foot

The trail starts and stays on the left (northwest) side of the creek. It immediately heads to a rocky bluff. Go right up the bluff through a narrow, boot-worn chute. You'll then confront the creek gorge. This might appear to be the end of your hike, but look closely for a fixed rope on the left, and a cairn above the tricky part. You'll soon reach a spot where there's an alarming view into the gorge, directly beneath your toes.

Within 40 minutes, you'll see the falls. Beyond, the route heads toward a rocky bluff. Go up its spine for a view of the Squamish Valley. Soon a sign marks another viewpoint. Near here, don't follow the clear trail that goes off right. The main trail bears left at a junction marked by a big cairn. Another fixed rope helps you ascend a steep spot.

Come to a small, rock gully with a bluff on your right. Here are the best views of the valley and peaks, including 2205-m (7231-foot) Mt. Jimmy Jimmy. After that bluff, the trail drops into deep forest—big firs and cedars, with moss and salal undergrowth. Hop over a creek here, then ascend across slopes above High Falls Creek to a minor saddle.

Roughly 1 hour after your last view of the falls, the trail slinks out of forest to meet a small creek and a clearcut. You can see a logging road up to your left; that's your immediate goal. The trail now heads east, across the clearcut and over a rockslide. Stay high, to your left, until a brushy gully filled with tree trunks rises to meet the slide. Then, on the lower part of the slide, head toward what looks like a saddle. Follow the cairns. When you reach the road, go left. Cloudburst Mountain is southeast, behind you. You're now heading west, back into the Squamish Valley.

About 2 km (1.25 mi) of road-walking will bring you to a junction. BR 220 goes steeply right. Bear left, continuing downhill on BR 200. When you reach the main road on the valley floor, bear left again. From there it's about 1.5 km (0.9 mi) back to High Falls Creek and your car.

Trip 45
Diez Vistas

Location	Fraser Valley North
Loop	13 km (8 mi)
Elevation gain	455 m (1490 ft)
Time required	4 ½ to 5 ½ hours
Available	March through November
Maps	ITM Vancouver's Northshore; Coquitlam 92 G/7

OPINION

The name *Ten Viewpoints* is a stretch. Yes, there are fine views from Buntzen Ridge, high above Indian Arm. But ten of them? Each one distinctly different? Naw. And the trail is entirely in forest—scrawny, second-growth the whole way. What makes this an outstanding shoulder-season option is its length. In March, hiking the whole 13-km (8-mi) loop, traversing the shaggy ridge, can feel like a real adventure. Wimps will enjoy just walking the first 4 km (2.5 mi) of the loop, along the east shore of Buntzen Lake, to the pretty, grassy, North Beach Picnic Area.

We describe the loop counter-clockwise. By initially hiking up the east shore, your trip will build to a ridgetop climax. If you get a late start, however, follow our directions in reverse and ascend the ridge first. That way, come twilight, you'll be on the well-marked, nearly-level lakeshore trail, or if it's dark, you could resort to walking back on Powerhouse Road.

It's important for inexperienced hikers to start early—especially if it's shoulder season, when daylight is severely limited. The area is laced with trails and old logging and hydroelectric-project roads. Allow plenty of time to sort your way through by calmly following our directions.

FACT

Before your trip

Pick up the BC Hydro brochure *Buntzen Lake Reservoir Recreation Area* from the warden office at the far west parking lot.

By Car

See Eagle Ridge (Trip 17) for directions to Buntzen Lake Recreation Area. After passing the gated Powerhouse Road, proceed to the northeast end of the first parking area. The elevation here is 140 m (460 ft).

On Foot

There's a reason this description is so long: to help you negotiate the tangle of routes you'll encounter. Experienced hikers won't need so much detail. But if you're a beginner, bear with us.

The trail starts at the small bridge over Buntzen Creek (possibly dry), at the east side of the South Beach Picnic Area. Look for blue signs directing you to North Beach. The Buntzen Lake trail (BLT) is a wide, well-maintained path through mixed second-growth forest—alders, cedars, ferns, and lots of stumps. You'll pass a couple side trails down to the lake and fishing docks. Take the major trail signed VIEWPOINT. After looking, continue right, gently uphill on the BLT. You'll cross several creeks.

Two-thirds up the lake, the trail gets rockier and rootier, though it's not seriously rough. When the trail dumps you onto the road, next to the Coquitlam Lake Tunnel Outfall, go left. About 40 meters farther, at the end of a wood fence, go left down the steps to arrive at the North Beach Picnic Area, 4 km (2.5 mi) from the trailhead. Beyond the picnic area, go left and cross the suspension bridge over the north end of the lake. From the bridge, curve left (southwest) for a few minutes. When the trail again approaches the lake, just before the sign POWER-HOUSE ROAD (pointing back the way you came), cut right. Left is the BLT. Above you is a powerline. Ascend the narrow, rocky, possibly brushy path.

Your trail rises north toward a powerpole, where you reach a junction. Left is the Lakeview trail, which stays above and roughly parallel to the BLT and the power lines. Go right. You might soon notice on your right a rough trail emerging from deadfall. That's another way to get up to this point from the suspension bridge. The trail, now broad, rejoins the road at a powerhouse intake. Go left (west), at least 100 meters. Where the road starts descending, there's a white sign on your left DIEZ VISTAS TRAIL (DVT). Turn left (south), through mixed, scrawny forest.

Shortly after starting up, there's an orange blaze where the trail cuts back left, up a narrow rib. Reach a flat stretch on the ridge about 1 km up the DVT. After crossing logs in a bog, the main trail curves right toward a blaze. A small side trail leads to a campsite in alders. (An obscure trail descends past the campsite.) At about 2 km (1.2 mi), reach a good viewpoint on a rock knob. From here, you can look southeast over Buntzen Lake to Eagle Ridge (Trip 17). To the west, Indian Arm is still blocked by trees. During the next 45 minutes, you'll hit all the viewpoints that gave this trail its name. Your highest elevation on the ridge will be 540 m (1771 ft).

Beyond the sign NO. 10 VISTA, the trail drops a little. Pass a bog in a hollow as you descend. Cross and go down an outcropping in the open, then return to forest. Reach a totally open viewpoint. A sign on a log safety-guard states DESVIACION (detour). At the signed VISTA PRIMA, you can look southwest over Deep Cove, to Second Narrows, downtown Vancouver, and Georgia Strait. Continuing, pass a sign facing south on a tree: CON LOS MEJORES DESEOS (with best wishes).

As the trail heads southeast, it becomes obvious you're on Buntzen Ridge. Descend steadily five minutes to Punta del Este (the east point) and a view over Buntzen Lake's South Beach. Then a steep, rough descent begins. The trail turns northwest—the opposite of where logic would suggest it should go. You'll pass Punta Largueza (the long or generous point). After descending about 60 meters, cross a steep rock band that might require you to use your hands. Then you're back in forest.

When you arrive at an intersection of blazed paths, go left to descend to Buntzen Lake. Soon reach a flat area where there's a power-line and pipeline. Cross the old roadbed. A sign marks the trail, which now re-enters forest. In about 15 meters, go left onto a roadbed/trail marked by a square metal blaze. Proceed downhill. (It's also possible to go straight here, following the flags and eventually joining the Horse-shoe trail, but it's a rougher route, through darker, scrawnier forest.)

Having gone left onto the roadbed/trail, come to a large sign depicting a horseshoe. You're now on the switchbacking Saddle Ridge trail. About 10 minutes down, where the Bear Claw trail forks left, continue curving right on the Saddle Ridge trail. At a T-junction, pass the Lakeshore trail (signed on the left) and go right. Hit a gravel road where the Horseshoe trail joins the Lakeshore trail. Go right. Along here, the Lakeshore trail merges with Pumphouse Road. Continue walking south until you see on your left the floating bridge across the south end of Buntzen Lake. The rougher route off Diez Vistas (Buntzen Ridge) comes out of the forest here, on your right, directly across from where you turn left to go over the floating bridge. On the east side of the narrow south end of Buntzen Lake, the trail angles left (northeast). Reach the southwest end of the parking lot in another 10 minutes.

Trip 46
Alouette Mountain

Location	Golden Ears Provincial Park
Round trip	22.6 km (14 mi)
Elevation gain	1116 m (3660 ft)
Time required	8 to 9 hours
Available	late May through November
Maps	BC Parks map; Port Coquitlam 92 G/7, Stave Lake 92 G/8

OPINION

Most of the way up, we wondered if Alouette was worth the bother. Negotiating a tangle of logging and fire-access roads, and hiking a long, persistent ascent mostly through unremarkable, second-growth forest, is a drag. But because we managed to do it in mid-May of a late-snowfall year, the summit views excited us more than if we'd waited until summer. So give Alouette a shot in late spring, when you'll covet the achievement.

The route climaxes on a broad, gentle ridge that, even when snow-covered, allows safe walking, or at least post-holing. No worries about plummeting off into space. The forest is open here, and the route blazed, so if the trail is buried in snow, the sensible direction is still apparent. For these reasons, Alouette might be feasible when snow makes steeper trails hazardous.

If you dislike walking in snow, however, which might entail plunging up to your crotch, wait until late June to hike here. Summitting then is unlikely to elicit joyous "We made it!" outbursts, but the alpine meadows up top will be green.

Until you're near the summit, roots are the obstacle. They *are* the trail for long stretches. Thick, intertwined, annoying to hikers, they look like pythons slithering through the brooding forest. And only near Lake Beautiful, which should be called Pond Homely, are the trees inspiring: virgin mountain hemlocks and yellow cedars.

The culminating scenery? Big city and bigger ocean, in the distance. Up close are Blanshard Needle and Edge Peak, stark reminders that these mountains walling the Fraser Valley do have cliffs. Mounts Judge Howay and Robie Reid are also visible northeast—close enough to tantalize, too far away to impress.

Blanshard Needle

FACT

By Car

See Golden Ears (Trip 35) for directions to the park. From the information kiosk, 250 meters beyond the gate, proceed 4.3 km (2.7 mi). Turn left toward Mike Lake, ignoring the fork to the park head-quarters. About 0.4 km (0.25 mi) after turning off the main road, come to the Eric Dunning trailhead. Park in the pullout across the road. The elevation here is 250 m (820 ft). It's also possible to drive 1.2 km (0.7 mi) farther and begin this hike on the Incline trail.

On Foot

Start on the Eric Dunning horse trail. Travel northwest, steadily ascending through a forest of bigleaf maples, hemlocks and cedars. During spring, you'll cross several creeklets. After gaining 140 m (460 ft) in about 1.3 km (0.8 mi), reach a T-junction with the Incline trail. Go right. (If you came up the Incline trail from Mike Lake, stay left and continue ascending.)

Soon pass a fire access road on the left. Go right at a T-junction. Proceed on a fairly level fire-road heading northeast. After a sharp turn left (west), look immediately right for a sign ALOUETTE MT. Ascend this rooty Short Cut trail north. At a seeming junction, go left or right: both paths soon rejoin. Your route goes back onto the fire road at a T.

Go right, and in 10 minutes get a view east over Alouette Lake. When you reach the next sign ALOUETTE MT, and a trail going right, stay straight on the road. The Short Cut trail is no benefit here.

Reach the next junction at about 6.8 km (4.2 mi). Go left. (The road continues right.) You're now on trail for the remaining 4.5 km (2.8 mi) to the summit. Less than 1 km (0.6 mi) from the last junction (and just past the signs NO HORSES, NO MOTORCYCLES), there's a signed spur trail left to Lake Beautiful. This tree-ringed, tannin-coloured, shallow pond is little more than a swamp. The shoreline is inhospitable. For a more comfortable rest, continue 15 minutes up the trail and stop at the creek crossing (possibly dry in summer). In the vicinity of Lake Beautiful, virgin mountain hemlocks and yellow cedars make the hike enjoyable, despite the rough, rooty trail.

Soon, stay left on the trail where the fire road for horseriders joins from the right. The trail climbs steadily on the west side of the ridge crest for nearly 3 km (1.8 mi) to the summit, passing other acceptable rest areas en route. Cross a flatter stretch of alpine meadows during the final 1 km (0.6 mi), then resume the steep ascent through open forest punctuated by hemlocks.

Reach the 1366-m (4482-ft) summit of Alouette at 11.3 km (7.0 mi). North, across a deep, narrow canyon, is Blanshard Needle. Behind it is Edge Peak (1646 m / 5400 ft). Southwest is downtown Vancouver. Southeast, across the Fraser Valley, are Mounts Baker, Shuksan and Cheam.

Trip 47

Bear Mountain

Location	Fraser Valley North
Round trip	17.7 km (11 mi)
Elevation gain	1008 m (3306 ft)
Time required	6 ½ to 7 ½ hours
Available	early May through late October
Map	Harrison Lake 92 H/5

OPINION

A sweat-wrenching ascent is a fair trade for this trek's sweeping views. On the way up, you'll survey the inland fiord of Harrison Lake and the distant snowcapped peaks of the Lillooet Range. Later, you'll look down on Fraser River Valley farmland between Hope and Chilliwack, and across at eye-throttling Mt. Cheam and the Lucky Four peaks. Though all but the final half-hour of the trip is on an old logging road, it's shady, thanks to overarching deciduous trees, and colourful, thanks to lush roadside grass and flowers. That makes it a surprisingly agreeable road-walk.

Bear Mountain, seen from below, is an unremarkable lump rising above the southeast end of Harrison Lake. So the helicopter views you'll enjoy once you're perched on the mountain's southernmost knob are startling. Definitely wait for a day of guaranteed clear weather before you commit to this demanding hike.

Fast hikers can jam to the top in 3 ½ hours and descend in just over 2 hours. If you're unwilling to keep the pedal to the metal, expect a 4- to 4 ½- hour ascent. View-mongers will want at least an hour up top. In spring, sun worshippers might want an additional hour to sprawl on the accommodating rocks and warm their winter-weary souls.

Just reaching the initial viewpoint over Harrison Lake requires you to be reasonably fit or extremely determined. The ascent is unrelenting. Attempt it only if you have strength of body or mind, preferably both.

The Fraser Valley

FACT

By Car

Drive Lougheed Highway 7 east from Vancouver, or take Exit 135 off Highway 1, to Harrison Hot Springs. From the Highway 1 exit, drive 6.4 km (4.0 mi) north on Highway 9, then jog left toward Agassiz on 7W & 9. From either approach, turn north on 9N and drive to the T-intersection in the village of Harrison Hot Springs. Go right on Lillooet, following signs toward Sasquatch Provincial Park. About 5.0 km (3.1 mi) from the T-intersection in Harrison, turn right onto what appears to be a private road. Ahead is a gate barring vehicles from the Bear Mountain FS Road, which you'll be hiking up. Park near the gate. The elevation here is 40 m (130 ft).

On Foot

Four minutes beyond the gate, stay on the main logging road. Pass a rough road ascending right. Then, just before another gate (a rusty one that might be open), take the steep, rugged road right (south) that's blocked by boulders. There's a fence on your left. Another road in five minutes comes in from the left. Ignore it. Continue ascending straight ahead.

In 15 minutes, attain views east over Harrison Lake. About 35 minutes up, the road curves left (north) before jogging south again. You'll pass a small cascade coming off the mountainside. In this lush area shaded by overhanging trees, look for wildflowers: orange columbine, pink-and-white spring beauty, bleeding hearts, elephant's head. Also, beware of stinging nettles—hidden in the grass on the road, and among the roadside foliage.

About 1 hour up, the road curves northeast, and in another 10 minutes it curves south again. You've gained about 480 m (1575 ft) to this point. After 2 hours, the road slices across a rock band. The view is wide open: back to Harrison Village beach, southwest to Mt. Agassiz, northwest over Echo Island and Harrison Lake, to logged, regrowing mountainsides, and north to the peaks and glaciers of the Lillooet Range. Your goal, the summit of Bear Mountain, is nearby to the south. Harrison Lake, though it dominates the scene here, is not visible the rest of the hike.

About 10 minutes beyond this viewpoint, stay on the main road as it curves right (south). An overgrown road goes left. Five minutes farther, stay left. A fork right quickly descends to insignificant Bear Lake. In another 3 minutes, stay right, on the level, where a road forks left. Your way rises just a bit. Pass a marshy pond and views south across the Fraser Valley to the North Cascades. The road becomes so overgrown through here it feels like a trail as it heads west of south. About 30 minutes from the pond, the road peters out. Turn left, onto a faint, boot-built route marked with orange flagging. You're now within 30-40 minutes of the summit.

The route drops left (southwest) through timber. Devil's club is profuse here. Though flagged, the way is easy to lose; stay alert. Cross a mucky brook and ascend a forested hillside. Cross a small ridge and drop slightly to curve back right into a hollow. Riding a narrow ridge at 1048 m (3437 ft), you'll glimpse sky and distant mountains. The route gently descends to the end of the ridge. A good campsite is just inside the trees. Immediately beyond is the open, rocky viewpoint, where Mt. Cheam, across the Fraser River Valley, will monopolize your attention. The farmlands of Agassiz are directly below. Harrison Lake, however, is blocked from view by Bear Mountain.

Trip 48
Mt. Hallowell

Location	Sechelt Peninsula
Round trip	15 km (9.3 mi)
Elevation gain	1020 m (3346 ft)
Time required	5 to 7 hours
Available	May through October
Map	Sechelt Inlet 92 G/12

OPINION

Hold this image in mind: ocean inlets far below, fanning out to penetrate the sheer slopes of furry-green coastal peaks. It will fortify your resolve to trudge up this mangled mountainside. If you make it, you might find the reality more awesome than you imagined. But the ascent is also worse than you'd expect. Most of the way is on old industrial roads. Only the last half hour is through pretty forest. Steel yourself. Cling to your talisman—visions of the wondrous panorama above.

Mt. Hallowell is the Sunshine Coast's premier vantage point for non-climbers, where you can sense the limitless expanse of B.C.'s fiord-riddled coast. From here, it continues 800 km (500 mi) to Alaska. Of all the inlets and channels you'll see, the most memorable sight is north into the shriekingly steep-sided Hotham Sound.

Tramping up this mean, blasphemous route, we almost turned around a couple times. The roads are dismal. The chewed-up trails are appalling. The logging debris and scraggly regrowth are hideous. Our determination to write an accurately opinionated guidebook kept us going. We warn you: set out only if you're determined to see it through. Turning around part way is pointless. And don't bother hiking here unless a clear sky ensures you'll enjoy the view up top.

Flagging and arrows help you follow the challenging route. If you're fit and fast, you can conquer Hallowell in 2½ hours. "Conquer," a word we've long thought inappropriate for mountain vocabulary, seems fitting here. It summarizes the attitude necessary to deal with all the ugliness. We felt no gentle affinity for this peak; only sorrow. The logging companies have left little to admire. But the incredible view remains.

Hotham Sound

After seeing how thoroughly the Hallowell area has been logged, you might be surprised to learn you can still walk in a vestigial ancient forest nearby, in the recently protected section of the Caren Range. The oldest-known tree in Canada was found in the Caren. It was a yellow cedar, cut down in its 1,835th year. It's criminal, even sacrilegious, that this God-like tree and countless others like it were laid waste. Visit the Western Canada Wilderness Committee in Vancouver's Gastown (20 Water Street, 604-683-8220) to see a cross-section of the Caren yellow-cedar.

FACT

By Car

From the Langdale ferry terminal, drive about 65 km (40 mi) northwest on Highway 101 toward Earls Cove. From the Pender Harbour turnoff, where Garden Bay Road joins the highway, continue north 6.5 km (4.0 mi) and turn right at the green sign MALASPINA SUBSTATION. About 1 km (0.6 mi) up the gravel road, veer right onto a narrower road that bypasses the power station. You might have to prune alders as you go, if you don't want your vehicle scratched. Continue southeast, joining the Hallowell FS Road just above the powerline. Turn left, ascending steeply. Many cars will only make it another 0.4 km (0.25 mi). Beaters and low-clearance 4WDs can make it another 1 km. Full-on, high clearance 4WDs will make it the remaining 2 km to a washout. The statistics above include the additional 300 m (975 ft) you'll have to gain if you plod that last 1.5 km (0.9 mi) up the road. The starting elevation for most people will be 230 m (750 ft).

On Foot

Most people will have to walk about 1.5 km (0.9 mi) to a large washout that bars all vehicles from continuing. This stretch is seriously steep, causing us to wonder how logging trucks could be geared lower than a person. Strong hikers can cover it in 30 minutes. Another 30 minutes beyond the washout, reach a view southwest over Mt. Daniel and Pender Harbour. About 1 ¼ hours up, you can refill waterbottles at a second washout. Then there's another view, this one of long Texada Island. Several minutes after the last washout, go left. (Right leads along Caren Ridge to Halfmoon Bay.) A couple minutes farther, ignore the ridiculously steep road veering right. The road you're ascending soon curves steeply right.

Mt. Hallowell's insipid profile comes into view after 1 ½ hours of uninterrupted hiking. About 10 minutes beyond the Halfmoon road, fork right. Approach a small lake—spiked by silver, skeleton trees—on the right. The open road peters out here. Look left for a blue arrow on a stump. It points out the obvious: continue on a spur road overgrown with grass and bushes. In a couple minutes, come to a little log bridge over the left side of a boggy stretch. Stay on the remnants of the road, just right of the forest edge, through shrubs and wood-chip debris. Reach another bog before getting back on rockier ground. Though you might be discouraged by this mess, don't give up now. The summit is less than an hour away.

At a fork of old roads, a second blue arrow on a stump points left. You're now rounding Hallowell's southeast side. A few minutes after the second arrow, cross a large, section of crude corduroy over a bog. Then look for the third blue arrow. This one points left to an overgrown path through pretty forest. Red flagging now marks the route. Head toward what looks like a pass. After crossing through slash, go left at the flagged, skinny tree.

A pink-flagged route then descends gently, heading to a flat, open area with rock slabs. This is a comfortable place to rest. There's a partial view east over logging slash to Sechelt Inlet. Facing the inlet, look left for a cairn sporting a big, blue arrow. It indicates where a rough trail ascends left into a cutblock. From there, it's 2.5 km (1.5 mi) to the lookout atop Hallowell. After a couple minutes on trail, you again find yourself on the remnants of a road, which then dwindles to a rough trail ascending steeply through the regrowing cutblock. Follow pink flagging, and the occasional blue dot or arrow, as you ascend the obvious though narrow trail. Approaching the summit, enter a tiny area of beautiful, virgin forest.

After 2½ hours, strong hikers will be enjoying the view from Mt. Hallowell's 1250-m (4100-ft) summit. The trees thin out on top, so you have a choice of viewpoints. A path leads north from the lookout building to a rocky bluff. Directly below (northwest) is Ruby Lake. Sakinaw Lake is south. Malaspina Strait is your side of Texada Island. Georgia Strait and all its islands are farther west. Jervis Inlet and Prince of Wales Reach are north. Steep-sided Hotham Sound is just west of north. Mt. Drew (1885 m / 6183 ft) rises in the northeast above Sechelt Inlet, which stretches 25 km (15.5 mi) southeast.

On the descent, about 15 minutes below the summit, watch for where the trail turns sharply left. A blue arrow on a blazed tree marks the turn. Fast hikers will reach the slabs along the road in about 30 minutes. Maintain a fleet-footed pace and you'll be all the way back to your car at the bottom of the road within another hour.

Trip 49

Tin Hat Mountain

Location	Powell River
Round trip	12.5 km (7.75 mi)
Elevation gain	732 m (2400 ft)
Time required	4 hours
Available	May through October
Map	Haslam Lake 92 F/16

OPINION

You'll need a tin soul not to be depressed by the utterly dull tramp to the top of this mountain. And upon arriving, you could be attacked. The flies and gnats here were the worst we've experienced in the Coast Mountains. Nevertheless, endure. The dramatic summit panorama is enough to make a tin man break into song.

What you'll see is the famous British Columbia land-and-water-scape that only a few countries, like Norway, can rival. Specifically, you'll peer down at fiord-like Powell Lake, and northeast to the alpine Powell Divide, where 1811-m (5940-ft) Beartooth Mountain plunges into Goat Lake. Thirty-two lakes dot the scene. Count 'em. Lewis Lake is back near the trailhead. Dodd and Horseshoe lakes are southeast. Beyond Dodd are the Knucklehead Mountains. If you want to sit long enough to fully enjoy the spectacle, delay your trip until late September, or come prepared for a bug infestation. We wore head nets.

FACT

By Car

After disembarking the Saltery Bay ferry, drive 11.5 km (7.1 mi) west on Highway 101. Just before (east of) the steel bridge over the Lois River, turn right onto the MacMillan Bloedel BR 41 logging road. A sign POWELL FOREST CANOE ROUTE marks the turn. The ensuing maze of logging roads necessitates lengthy directions.

Reach a junction 1.1 km (0.7 mi) from the highway. Go left. At 1.7 km (1.1 mi) stay right. Proceed straight on Stillwater Main at 3.9 km (2.4 mi) and again at 5.2 km (3.2 mi). At 12.3 km (7.6 mi), go left toward

Powell Lake and the Powell Divide

Nanton Lake. At 13.1 km (8.1 mi) stay right on Goat Lake Main. At 17.6 km (11 mi), Tin Hat Mountain is visible ahead.

Reach a junction at 18.9 km (11.7 mi). Turn left here and head uphill northwest. (If you plan to camp first, go right 1.2 km / 0.75 mi, then turn right again onto the access road for the free campground on beautiful Nanton Lake.) After turning left, uphill, on signed TIN HAT MTN RD, watch for tiny Spring Lake on your right. (It's not labeled on the 1976 topo map.) Stay left on the main road. About 450 meters beyond the lake is a spur road forking right. If you miss the spur road, you'll come to a gate announced by warning signs. The spur road, which serves as the trail, is marked by orange blazes high on a tree on the left. There's no parking area, so just park along the spur road without blocking it; overzealous four-wheelers might try driving farther in. The elevation here is 488 m (1600 ft.)

On Foot

Start walking the spur road. It's an old logging road (aren't they all?) lined with overhanging deciduous trees—some of them flagged. About 20 meters in, on the left, a small, handwritten sign TIN HAT MTN confirms you're not lost yet. Eroded to bedrock much of the way, the road heading north is the trail for the 1 ¾ hours it takes strong hikers to reach the base of the summit. The grade soon steepens. About 30 minutes along, a fork ascends very steeply straight. Go right, climbing more gradually. Pink flagging might still mark the right fork.

Strong hikers will reach a flat spot in about 1¼ hours. The rocky bluffs of Tin Hat Mountain are directly ahead. Stay on the road as it heads toward the southwest side of the bluffs, then turns northeast. About 10 minutes beyond the flat spot, the road ends. Blue flagging in a brushy area marks the faint trail left. A rock slab across from here offers partial views south. About 15 more minutes of hiking will earn you the 1220-m (4000-ft) summit. The trail ascends via the easterly mound. Possible tent sites on top could allow you a memorable night out. But there's no water here, or anywhere en route, so pack what you'll need.

Trip 50
Skyline Loop / Levette Lake

Location	Squamish
Loop	8 km (5 mi) for the Skyline; 11 km (6.8 mi) including Levette Lake
Elevation gain	300 m (984 ft) on Skyline; 540 m (1770 ft) including Levette Lake
Time required	3 hours for Skyline; 4 ½ with Levette
Available	early April through mid-November
Maps	ITM Garibaldi Region; Cheakamus River 92 G/14

OPINION

Zen-like, the trail is in no rush to go anyplace. And if you aren't either, you'll find right here, right now, is just fine. You'll meander into hollows, over outcroppings, through pleasant forest. And you'll attain ridgetop views of the glacier-dripping Tantalus peaks—close enough to create the illusion that you're higher and deeper in the range than you really are.

Only a stretch of the Skyline loop rides a ridgeline, however, and the ridge itself is not high. So the name Skyline is a bit misleading. It's the ridge's location, between the Squamish and Cheakamus river valleys, that makes it a noteworthy perch for viewing the Tantalus (west), Sky Pilot (south), and Mt. Garibaldi (east).

The detour to Levette Lake is worthwhile. The glaciers above and beyond the lake are a memorable sight. The fact that you must walk a road to get there is mitigated by a frolicking creek nearby for two-thirds of the way. The road also allows sun to reach you and brighten your walk—a rare, fleeting delight on most shoulder-season trips. Though 4WD vehicles can negotiate the road, you're unlikely to encounter many.

Alpha Mountain looms above Levette Lake

FACT

By Car

From Squamish, at the traffic light by Esso and McDonald's, drive Highway 99 north 10.6 km (6.6 mi). Across from Alice Lake Provincial Park, turn left. Continue 3.6 km to a bridge over the Cheakamus River. Cross it, go 100 meters beyond to a junction, and go right on the Paradise Valley Road for 2.1 km (1.3 mi). Turn left, opposite the North Vancouver Outdoor School. Ascend the rough, steep road 1.3 km (0.8 mi) and park in the middle of a fork. Here, at about 152 m (500 ft), a map-sign states the distances to several possible destinations. See the private road descending left? That's your return route, through the forestry camp at Evans Lake, if you hike the loop we describe.

On Foot

Walk across the main road to the trailhead. Ascend steeply for 10 minutes through young forest. The trail is again level as it passes a marshy area (skunk cabbage and a creek) and reaches a signed junction. Before going left on the main trail, follow the overgrown Silver Summit trail straight, cross the creek, and quickly reach a viewpoint on a bluff. You'll also see what appears to be a grave up there, covered with rocks.

Back on the main trail, in 3 more minutes, go right to see Copper-bush Pond. From the pond junction, the trail wanders through a hollow, ascends around the base of an outcropping, then climbs onto a rocky slope. This is a terrific sunning spot affording views of the glacier-drapped Tantalus peaks across the Squamish Valley, the Stawa-mus Chief (south, Trip 43), and Sky Pilot (southeast). Continuing north, the route is flagged. Descend slightly to cross a creek just before reaching the road. You've hiked 2.5 km (1.5 mi) so far.

To continue the Skyline loop and make the side trip to Levette Lake, go right on the road, soon recross the creek, and walk uphill 0.6 km (0.4 mi). Immediately north of a low, wood bridge over the creek, the Skyline trail cuts sharply back left. This is the point you'll return to after visiting Levette Lake. Heading for the lake? Continue north 1.5 km (0.9 mi) on the gravel road.

After about 20 minutes, ignore two private roads forking left. The third road left is the one you want, just beyond where the main road crosses a creeklet. Don't go right, up the rough, bouldery road—that's the way to Hud Lakes. A couple minutes after curving left, you'll reach the public side of Levette Lake, where there's a primitive campground on the shore. The elevation here is 420 m (1375 ft).

Now walk the road back to where the Skyline trail angles right, off the road, just before the bridge. The trail is initially level, following an old logging road. Ten minutes along, approach a ridge and turn sharply left (south). Ascend a bluff and gain views. Descend the bluff with the aid of stairsteps hacked out of a fallen tree. Heading generally south, the trail undulates along the ridge, providing several Tantalus Range vantage points.

Having walked 1.8 km (1.1 mi) and gained 245 m (800 ft) from where the Skyline trail left the road, you'll reach a trail junction. The left fork rejoins the road at a point just south of where you reached it after walking from Copperbush Pond. Stay right, heading toward Evans Lake, on what is now the Fraser-Burrard trail, marked with round blazes. You'll drop through a mature stand of firs, but the rest of the way is mostly through juvenile trees. Descend 240 m (790 ft) in 1.1 km (0.7 mi) to a 3-way junction. The left fork, over the bridged creek, leads directly to the forestry camp. To avoid the buildings, turn sharply right, cross the bridge over a dry gully, and take the Blue Lake trail. Then take the second left, along the north shore of Evans Lake. You'll come out at a private road. Turn right and you're quickly back at your vehicle.

Trip 51

Cheakamus Lake

Location	Whistler, Garibaldi Provincial Park
Round trip	12.8 km (8 mi)
Elevation gain	negligible
Time required	3 to 5 hours
Available	early June through late October
Maps	BC Parks brochure; ITM Whistler and Region

OPINION

In a hurry? Welcome to God's take-out window, where you can grab a luscious natural feast—to go. "Ancient forest, please, with cedars. Awesome mountains, and uh, make that with glaciers...and a long, turquoise lake. Throw in a few creeks too, will ya?"

Kids, grandparents, wimps… everyone enjoys this walk, even experienced hikers. You can get a satisfying taste in a couple hours, or make it an ultra-easy overnighter by pitching your tent at one of the superb lakeshore campsites.

The broad, meticulously maintained trail undulates gently, dishing up sumptuous servings of mammoth cedars. Few places allow you to savour B.C.'s original forest so easily. On clear, summer evenings, reflections from the lake shimmer magically, like auras, on the trunks of the great trees.

Slowpokes can reach the glacier-fed lake in an hour. From there on, you get continuous views across the water to ice-laden peaks—piled-high sundaes that make mountain connoisseurs salivate for the next visual feast. The surrounding summits tower nearly a mile (1600 m / 5250 ft) above the shore. Curious how the lake looks from above? Hike the Musical Bumps (Trip 2) and peer down from 1900 m (6230 ft).

If you don't feel like walking the lake's entire 5.5-km (3.4-mi) length, turn around near 5 km (3 mi), where the trail rises onto a small cliff. After that, the forest loses its appeal; the trees are scrawny.

Bikes are allowed as far as the lake, so don't expect a placid walk. Be ready to step aside for swift or inconsiderate cyclists. Dogs, however, are not permitted in Garibaldi Park, which includes Cheakamus

Cheakamus Lake

Lake. Open fires are also prohibited, so bring a stove if you camp. Rangers patrol the trail.

FACT

By Car

Drive Highway 99 north 9.8 km (6.1 mi) from Brandywine Falls Provincial Park, or 7.7 km (4.8 mi) south from the big, brown sign WELCOME TO WHISTLER. A BC Parks sign warns of the turn east onto a logging road. Near the beginning, stay right where a road forks left. At 0.4 m (0.25 mi), turn left onto dirt. Drive another 7.1 km (4.4 mi) on the good gravel road to the trailhead at road's end, 838 m (2750 ft).

On Foot

In about 15 minutes, reach a junction at 1.5 km (0.9 mi). Continue straight. The right fork crosses the Cheakamus River, climbs beside Helm Creek (Trip 31), and eventually leads to Black Tusk Meadows and Garibaldi Lake.

Within earshot of the river, pass ancient cedars and Douglas firs. The platter-size, 6-pointed leaves that seem to float are devil's club; they dominate the understory. About 5 minutes beyond the first junction, the wide, energetic Cheakamus River is visible. After it heaves up a big rapid, you can see the calm, deep water flowing quietly from the lake. Reach the northwest end of the lake, 3.2 km (2.0 mi) from the trailhead, in 45 minutes to 1 hour. A sign with a map points to a pit toilet and food cache (bear pole). There are others farther along the shore. From here on, you'll pass many campsites—flat, bare spots, not designated by signs or platforms.

At 3.8 km (2.4 mi), the trail narrows, gets rootier, and runs closer to the tree-lined lakeshore. Views of snow-covered peaks expand. Castle Towers (2625 m / 8600 ft) is south. Mt. Davidson (2500 m / 8200 ft) is southeast. The roar of a waterfall might be audible; its origin is Corrie Lake, high on the slopes to the south.

Reach a campsite reserved for rangers at 4.2 km (2.6 mi). Cross a little creek tumbling down from the Fitzsimmons Range, north of you. Near 5 km (3.1 mi), the trail is about 10 to 15 meters above the lake, allowing you to gaze into its depths. Then, after ascending 15 m (50 ft), enter a dark, tight forest of scrawny trees. Pass through what could be a brushy area in summer, if BC Parks didn't have it cleared. Again encounter big trees. During spring runoff, all the minor, braided creeks are less of a threat, thanks to numerous boardwalks.

Reach the two forks of Singing Creek and the end of constructed trail at 6.4 km (4 mi)—about 2 hours from the trailhead. You'll find a couple campsites here, near the bigger fork, as well as a toilet, lines for hanging food, and a gravel beach. Peaks of the McBride Range are visible southeast above the Cheakamus valley.

Trip 52

Eagle Bluff

Location	West Vancouver, Cypress Provincial Park
Round trip	12 km (7.4 mi)
Elevation gain	974 m (3195 ft)
Time required	5 hours
Available	March through November
Maps	BC Parks brochure; ITM Vancouver's Northshore; North Vancouver 92 G/6

OPINION

Black Mountain is the southwest terminus of the B.C. Coast Mountains. At its base are Burrard Inlet to the south, and Howe Sound to the west. On its southwest shoulder is Eagle Bluff, where you can exercise your summit-ascending muscles while other trails are snowed under.

Ho-hum forest and rough trail make the climb a chore. The views are typical for this corner of the range. You can look down on the islands in the sound and across Georgia Strait toward Vancouver Island. But because you have to earn it, the scenery feels special from Eagle Bluff.

Before mid-May, snow is likely to keep you from pushing past the bluff, to the summit of Black Mountain. By mid-June, it's best to forget this long slog from the sea, because then you can probably zip up to Black Mountain quickly and easily (Trip 14) by starting at the Cypress ski area. Only then, when the weather is warm and you might muster the courage to dive into Cabin Lake, is the summit a worthwhile destination anyway.

FACT

By Car

Drive Highway 1/99 through West Vancouver. Slow down at the fork to Horseshoe Bay. Stay right toward Squamish and drive only 100 m farther. Just before a yellow-and-black striped sign on the cement wall, turn right into the parking lot, signed BLACK MOUNTAIN TRAIL. The elevation here is 120 m (395 ft). After your hike, you can return south on Highway 99 by first driving 200 meters north, then turning left toward Horseshoe Bay.

On Foot

The trail is initially an old road. Ascend 5 minutes to a junction with the Baden Powell Trail (BPT), which at this point is also an old road. Go left. (Right leads in about 15 minutes to Eagleridge Drive.) Pass through a mixed forest with bigleaf maples. Flat stretches of trail moderate the steep ones. About 15-20 minutes up, just past the power poles, reach a viewpoint. Pass the watershed signs and stay left. About 35 minutes up, there's a picnic table where the road tapers to trail. It's then a gradual 10-minute ascent to a junction at 395 m (1295 ft) where an older trail (now blocked) went left. Go right, crossing a creeklet—possibly dry.

After 1 hour of hiking, come to a broad stretch of trail at 478 m (1570 ft). Curve right, following orange blazes and a sign BP TRAIL TO EAGLE RIDGE. Ignore an old trail forking left here. Soon enter scraggly, regrowing forest. About 10 minutes beyond the last sign, cross a log over a small drainage. Another sign warns BPT VERY STEEP BEYOND THIS POINT. The trail tilts skyward, becoming rooty instead of rocky as it threads through some beautiful trees.

Within 1 ½ hours, at 628 m (2060 ft), reach a sign BPT, EAGLE RIDGE 60 MINUTES. The trail becomes faint and more challenging. You must clamber over a few very steep sections tangled with roots. Be extra careful when all is wet. Stay right (ignoring the route left to Do-Nut Rock), then cross Nelson Creek. Head generally southeast. Cross a talus slope, followed by a rockslide. The trail steepens before swinging north and topping Eagle Bluff at 1094 m (3588 ft).

To reach Black Mountain, stay right as you continue beyond the bluff. (Left leads to Do-Nut Rock again.) Just over 1 km (0.6 mi) from the bluff, pass Cougar Lakes, followed by Owen Lake. Intersect the Black Mountain Loop trail (Trip 14) 1.7 km (1.1 mi) from the bluff.

Trip 53
Brothers and Lawson Creeks

Location	North Shore
Loop	10 km (6.2 mi)
Elevation gain	437 m (1433 ft)
Time required	3 hours
Available	June through November
Maps	BC Parks brochure of Cypress Provincial Park; ITM Vancouver's Northshore; Vancouver 92 G/6

OPINION

You're a wimp. Or it's the weekend, and you didn't roll out of bed until 10 A.M. Or you're a keen hiker seeking a short, uncrowded trail for a mid-week evening workout. Or maybe you're just curious about the few remaining ancient cedars you've heard about on the North Shore mountains. These are reasons to try the short, easy hike up Brothers Creek. The water courses through an engaging gorge with a couple cascades. Here's your chance to gawk at big cedars without bushwhacking or driving for hours. Lost Lake and Blue Gentian Lake are mere ponds. They're simply openings in the forest where you can stretch your eyes. Think of them as turn-around points at the top of the loop, not significant destinations.

FACT

Before your trip

Pick up the brochure *Brother's Creek Forestry Heritage Walk* from the West Vancouver Parks & Recreation Department. They're on the second floor of the municipal building at 750 17th Street.

By Car

Driving Highway 1 through West Vancouver, take the Taylor Way exit north. If you're coming over the Lions Gate Bridge from the south, proceed into West Vancouver. At the intersection by Park Royal Shopping Centre, turn right on Taylor Way and continue uphill. For all approaches, drive into British Properties and turn left at the T-intersection. Take Highland Drive until you can turn left onto Eyremount

Drive. Continue to where it curves back sharply right and becomes Millstream Road. Park next to a gated forest road, at the top of Eyremount Drive. The elevation here is 375 m (1230 ft).

On Foot

Walk west on the gated road. It's marked with orange blazes. In about 5 minutes, turn right uphill. You've gone a bit too far if you reach Lawson Creek. You'll be heading north to the Baden Powell Trail (BPT) and Brothers Creek Forest Heritage Walk. In 15 minutes, take the right fork toward Brothers Creek and Lost Lake. If you make the loop using the BPT as the downhill leg, you'll return to this junction. In a few minutes, cross a powerline right-of-way where the BPT traverses west to Lawson Creek.

The trail is a mix of roots and needles. In a few more minutes, after crossing a boardwalk, stay straight (left), ascending Brothers Creek trail on the west side of the narrow creek gorge. Notice the big cedars. Near 600 m (1968 ft), after about 45 minutes of hiking, ignore the Crossover trail. It forks right and crosses the creek. Stay west of the creek and continue straight uphill, soon passing another signpost for the Crossover trail (left) and Lawson Creek Heritage Walk. You'll see many more giant cedars.

Almost 1½ hours from the trailhead, at 665 m (2180 ft), reach a 25-m high waterfall with two tiers. Just after the falls, a trail forks left. Signed WESTLAKE LODGE, it heads northeast, reaching Blue Gentian Lake in about 30 minutes. Ignore it. Instead, notice a metal sign on a tree: THIRD BRIDGE. Brothers Creek is no longer bridged here, but it's easy to rockhop across in fall. On the other side of the creek, high on a tree, is a wood sign LOST LAKE. That's the way. Cross to the east side of the creek to proceed to Lost Lake.

Immediately after crossing the creek, take the trail curving left, upstream. Ignore the blazed trail to the right. In 5-10 minutes, reach Lost Lake. It's nestled in trees, at 735 m (2410 ft). A rock slab in a bare spot, back from the lakeshore, is the only decent place to sit.

You can return to Eyremount Drive the way you came. Or, to complete the loop, bear left around the west end of Lost Lake, passing short paths to the shore. Cross the outlet stream on a slick footbridge. Head west and negotiate lots of muddy, boggy areas. This rooty and rough trail is not shown on the 1992 Cypress Park map. AREA CLOSED signs are posted to keep people from tumbling down the cliff. Rockhop across an unbridged creek. The trail starts descending. Then cross a bridged creek and reach a junction just above it. Straight ahead is Blue Gentian Lake, at 812 m (2663 ft). There's a picnic table here. You've now hiked about 20 minutes from Lost Lake.

To continue the loop, stay right. (Left cuts back to the unbridged crossing of Brothers Creek.) At the north end of Blue Gentian Lake, bear left where a right fork proceeds to West Lake and Hollyburn Lodge (Trip 65). Head southwest, roughly paralleling the west side of Blue Gentian Lake, and within 10 minutes reach a junction with the BPT.

Go left (southeast) on the BPT for about 30 minutes. Cross Lawson Creek en route. Where the BPT meets the Skyline trail, stay left. In a few minutes, stay right at the next junction. Then go right again onto the trail you initially ascended to the BPT. Descend about 15 minutes to meet the Millstream trail. Go left (east) back to Eyremount Drive.

Trip 54
Lynn Valley

Location	North Vancouver, Lynn Headwaters Regional Park
Loop	9.5 km (5.9 mi)
Elevation gain	160 m (525 ft)
Time required	2 ½ to 3 ½ hours
Available	all year, except after a snowstorm
Maps	Park brochure (at trailhead kiosk); North Vancouver 92 G/6

OPINION

Lynn Valley allows you to easily sample the North Shore mountains. Notice that the previous sentence is devoid of drooling adjectives ardently describing the trail. That's because it's merely a pleasant place to keep in shape and clear the city dust from your head. The scenery is unimpressive; the trees unremarkable. The moss-cloaked, second-growth forest allows only a few, forgettable views across the valley. The trip highlights? Initially, the silence of the forest; later, walking the Cedar Mill trail beside boisterous Lynn Creek. Giant stumps along the way are all that's left of the ancient cedars that thrived here before shortsighted loggers and home owners plundered them, starting in the early 1900s.

Here in the south end of Lynn Headwaters Regional Park, trails are well-signed and maintained. Yet every year many people get lost; some are even stranded overnight. That's because the park's accessibility lures newborn hikers, with little or no outdoor sense, into the mountains. If you're a newborn, read our *Preparation* chapter.

FACT

By Car

From Highway 1 in North Vancouver, take Exit 19 and follow Lynn Valley Road north. About 2.3 km (1.4 mi) from the highway overpass, continue straight, ignoring the turnoff to Lynn Canyon Suspension Bridge. At 3.2 km (2 mi) enter Lynn Headwaters Regional Park. Slow down and proceed 1 km along the narrow road. Be wary of the sheer drop on your right. At 4.7 km (2.9 mi) reach the road's end parking lot. The elevation here is 207 m (680 ft).

On Foot

From the parking lot, cross the bridge over Lynn Creek. Turn right (southeast). In about 100 meters, turn left onto the signed Lynn Loop trail. (Straight on the gravel path leads to Rice Lake.) In about 300 meters, a minor trail to Lynn Peak forks right. Continue straight on the Lynn Loop trail. About 15 minutes beyond here, you'll see fewer people.

The trail climbs to and maintains a fairly constant elevation, around 366 m (1200 ft). At about 2.5 km (1.6 mi), after roughly 45 minutes of hiking, take the short spur trail right, marked by a POINT OF INTEREST sign, to see the big boulders. Soon after, reach a junction at 3.2 km (2.0 mi). There are signs and a map here, next to huge cedar stumps. The Lynn Loop trail drops left, switchbacking comfortably to reach Lynn Creek at 3.9 km (2.4 mi). From there it's 1.8 km (1.1 mi) left (south) back to the parking lot. Go that way if you want to shorten the loop to a total of 5.7 km (3.5 mi).

At the 3.2 km (2.0 mi) junction, stay high and continue straight (north) on the Headwaters trail if you want to complete the longer, 9.5-km (5.9-mi) loop. About 5 minutes beyond the junction, take the short spur trail descending left to a platform providing a view of the valley and forested Mt. Fromme. Proceeding north on the Headwaters trail, at 4 km (2.5 mi) gradually descend to the first of two debris chutes. Reach the second, larger one at 5.6 km (3.5 mi). There's a junction here.

The Headwaters trail continues straight (north) to Norvan Creek (See Trips 16 and 34.) West, across the valley is Grouse Mountain. To return to the parking lot, go left (west). Cross the open, rocky area, head down to the creek, and go left (south) on the Cedars Mill trail paralleling the creek. At 7.7 km (4.8 mi) pass the trail that ascends left (east), switchbacking up to the Headwaters trail. Proceed straight (south) on the Lynn Loop trail, often close to the creek. Cross the bridge over Lynn Creek and reach the parking lot at 9.5 km (5.9 mi).

Trip 55

Dennett Lake / Burke Ridge

Location	Fraser Valley North
Round trip	10 km (6.2 mi) to Dennett;
	15 km (9.3 mi) up Burke Ridge
Elevation gain	860 m (2820 ft) to Dennett;
	1120 m (3675 ft) up Burke Ridge
Time required	5 ½ hours for Dennett; 7 for Burke Ridge
Available	early June through late October
Map	Coquitlam 92 G/7

OPINION

"Jesus Died for You" is spray-painted on a boulder near the trashed trailhead. It's a disheartening sight. The beginning of a hike should be a glad departure from urban dissonance. Here we were creeped-out. But the urgency to escape helped us meet the challenge of this bitterly steep ascent. The gain is headstrong from the start, clearing 610 m (2000 ft) in 3.5 km (2.2 mi) before reaching Munro Lake. That's about a 40% grade.

Soon, the beauty of a hardwood forest splashed with the greenery of giant ferns makes the task bearable. Just don't expect inspiring views on the way up. Seeing the Pitt River lowlands is hardly worth pausing for and losing momentum. Munro Lake, however, deserves appreciation. Surrounded by heather, muskeg and forest, it could pass for a scene on the Halifax peninsula or in Nova Scotia's Kejimkujil Provincial Park. Dennett Lake is pretty too, with a narrow band of rock rampart on one side that adds character to its visage, like the furrowed brow of a wise elder.

Fit, eager, capable hikers who make it to Dennett should press on to the summit of Burke Ridge and enjoy the view. This is a much more agreeable approach than via the messy southwest slope (Trip 69). The initial climb out of the Dennett Lake bowl seems twice as steep as the climb from the trailhead. Once you're on Burke Ridge, the grade eases. Having already ascended 860 m (2820 ft) to Dennett Lake, it's worth climbing an additional 260 m (850 ft) in 2.5 km (1.5 mi) to see nearby Widgeon Peak (north), Coquitlam Mountain (northwest), and Golden

Munro Lake

Ears (east). None are spectacular, but they *are* peaks. They add drama to an otherwise sparkless trip.

Dennett Lake will likely be snow-free by the end of May, but snow might cling to the ridge until the end of June. If you're an experienced snow tromper, give it a go earlier. By mid-July, when other summits are attainable, consider this one a Don't Do.

Start hiking early. The trail near the lakes and on the ridge is faint and narrow—difficult to follow at twilight. Fog is possible here too, which is another reason to allow sufficient time to stay on track or get your bearings if you stray. Unless it's a bombproof clear day, bring a headlamp, full rain gear, and gaiters for the mud and wet brush.

FACT

By Car

On the east side of Port Coquitlam, turn north off Lougheed Highway 7, onto Coast Meridian Road. In 2.4 km (1.5 mi), go right on Apel Road, then right again on Victoria Drive. After 2.1 km (1.3 mi) on Victoria, keep to the left fork at the top of a small rise. Follow signs to Minnekhada Regional Park. When the road turns to gravel, you're on Quarry Road. From the turn into Minnekhada Regional Park, drive 3.1 km (1.9 mi) farther to the potholed, bumpy, trashed trailhead on the left, at 100 m (328 ft).

On Foot

Thread through the trash and set out on a steep, old road. In 5 minutes, go right onto a trail. There might still be a big, red blaze on an alder. MUNRO is carved into a tree. Big rock slabs adorn the creek canyon. 10 minutes up, go left. 30 minutes up, reach a fork with a large diamond and directional arrows. Go right, toward Munro, on a trail that is not flagged. In another 2 minutes, a minor route with flagging descends left. Stay on the obvious main trail as it ascends right, heading generally northwest. You're now among hardwood trees beautifully covering an old burn. 45 minutes up, reach a fork; the paths rejoin in a couple minutes, but left, toward the reflector, is a bit easier. The main trail divides again in a few more places, but the paths always rejoin soon. Usually the right path ascends more gently; left is steeper, more direct.

Within 1 ¼ hours, strong hikers will arrive at the first viewpoint over the Pitt River and a golf course. After 1 ½ hours, reach a flat spot in trees where you can take a breather or munch a snack. The ascent is relentlessly steep to this point.

Several minutes beyond the flat spot, enter old-growth yellow cedar and mountain hemlock. Climbing more gradually now, skunk cabbage appears as you approach very muddy terrain. 15 minutes from the flat spot, reach a junction (possibly a quagmire) emblazoned with metal markers. Two orange signs are placed about 4 meters high on the trees (for skiers, not Bigfoot). Left leads west to the site of an old ski village. Proceed generally straight (northeast) another 10 minutes, following yellow blazes then red, to Munro Lake at 840 m (2755 ft). Hiking time from the trailhead to the lake is about 2 hours for strong hikers.

Up for Dennet Lake? Work your way around the boggy shore to the west end of Munro Lake. Leave the lake and enter what looks like Bullwinkle country. Cross a creeklet. Yellow flagging on the edge of the muskeg marks the route. After 8-10 minutes of bashing through bushes and marching through mud, cross a 2-meter wide, ankle-deep stream flowing into Munro Lake. 40 meters ahead, on the lone tree in the muskeg, is an orange flag. That's where you veer left, directly into the forest, toward old yellow flagging. The trail is steep here but well defined. Hike northwest through original forest for about the next 20 minutes, until reaching a pond on the left. The trail then meanders along a creeklet. The area seems to be a hummingbird haven; watch for them whirring about. In another 10 minutes, reach Dennett Lake at 960 m (3150 ft). Your total distance is now 5 km (3.1 mi).

Up for Burke Ridge? It's another 2.5 km (1.6 mi) and a gain of 260 m (850 ft) to the summit. Continue around the west side of Dennett Lake.

Near the end of the lake, look northwest for orange and blue flagging. The trail bolts up the ridge due west of where it leaves the lake. The flagged route is little more than a game trail—narrow and faint, but discernable. 20 minutes up from the lake, reach bogs and heather in a flatter area. A couple minutes farther, reach the main Burke Ridge trail and flagging of all colours everywhere. Take note of this area, so when you return off the ridge, you can remember where the faint trail (marked by a sign depicting a hiker) leads back to Dennett. To the left, visible if coming from the old ski village, is a big sign: DENNETT LAKE TRAIL, BMN. (BMN stands for Burke Mountain Naturalists.) Go right (northeast) to continue through heather and hemlocks up to the ridge summit, 7.5 km (4.7 mi) from the trailhead.

Trip 56

Mt. Agassiz

Location	Harrison Lake
Round trip	7.4 km (4.6 mi)
Elevation gain	700 m (2296 ft)
Time required	5 hours
Available	March through November
Map	Harrison 92 H/5

OPINION

Big trees are a loom. They spread their handiwork for the observant hiker to appreciate. And here, on the slopes of Mt. Agassiz, is a distinctly beautiful tapestry: decomposing, nitrogen-freeing deadfall, air freshening ferns, moisture conserving sphagnum moss, and the loose nonchalance of scattered twigs. Yet even if you're unimpressed by the biotic community, and you can't see the tapestry for the forest, you'll enjoy the culminating view of snowcapped mountains and the Harrison Lake inland fiord.

In spring, ascending Mt. Agassiz will challenge muscles allowed to atrophy during winter. The average grade is a huffing, puffing 16%. But the trail is short, and only the initial stretch—on an old road and along a cut line, within earshot of passing cars—is unaesthetic.

About 45 minutes up, you'll see the Cheam Range explode out of the Fraser Valley. The trail then dives into forest. It jibes through gullies, scampers over small logs, slips between larger ones, and dances around huge boulders.

Turn around at the helipad viewpoint. On a clear day, you might find more sunshine farther west, but that's all. The trail soon enters scraggly, second growth. The views diminish. And Campbell Lake is a dismal puddle. Its inhospitable shore provides almost no place to sit. And you're likely to find a truckload of yahoos there who've driven up on the logging road from Mt. Woodside. So instead of continuing, allow yourself more time to admire the forest tapestry on the descent.

Harrison Lake

FACT

By Car

Drive Lougheed Highway 7 east from Vancouver, or take Exit 135 off Highway 1, to Harrison Hot Springs. From the Highway 1 exit, drive 6.4 km (4.0 mi) north on Highway 9. Turn left on 7W & 9 toward Agassiz. At 10.3 km (6.4 mi) turn right on 9N. At 16.0 km (9.9 mi), as you approach the village of Harrison Hot Springs, park in the pullout on your left, opposite Balsam Avenue. The elevation here is 12 m (40 ft). The trailhead sign refers to Campbell Lake, but this is the trail that ascends Mt. Agassiz.

On Foot

Walk behind the signboard, around the chain-link fence, and go right on the gravel road. After 5-10 minutes, go right around the treatment plant. At the Forest Service sign, you're on trail, climbing steeply. Ascend what seems like a rocky streambed. At 1.5 km (0.9 mi) huge rock slabs at Tower 92 make for good relaxing, but the view is marred by powerlines. The Cheam Range is visible to the south. Leaving the man-made structures, the trail then enters wild forest. The trees aren't giants, but they are mature. Wood ladders assist you up the ribs of the mountain.

Just shy of 2.0 km (1.2 mi), the trail turns southwest and is level for a while. Near 3.3 km (2.0 mi), you'll probably encounter several long, downed trees. Look for a way across on the left. At 3.7 km (2.3 mi), reach the primitive helipad and an impressive view north up Harrison Lake to glacier-clad peaks. Hiking time here is about 2 hours. The slope above the helipad blocks the sun during spring, so this can be a chilly place to sit.

From the helipad, it's 1.3 km (0.8 mi) to Campbell Lake. The trail wends slightly downhill, around the north side of Mt. Agassiz. After crossing a rockslide, it spits you out onto an old, alder-lined road. Soon reach the lake, at 650 m (2132 ft).

Trip 57
Brigade Bluffs

Location	Fraser Canyon
Round trip	13 km (8 mi)
Elevation gain	780 m (2560 ft)
Time required	5 to 6 hours
Recommended	Early May through mid-June, mid-September through mid-November
Maps	Spuzzum 92 H/11, Boston Bar 92 H/14; ITM Lower Mainland

OPINION

The Brigade trail rockets out of the Fraser River Canyon, intent on its goal. Supermen built the trail and were using it by 1848. They were Hudson's Bay Company traders seeking a route from Ft. Yale, over Lake Mountain, to the Coldwater area (south of Merritt) and Kamloops. Wffeww! These days, most of us are victims of comfort. A journey like that can be daunting, even frightening. So, all we describe here is the first few miles—challenge enough for the average hiker. Though short, it's not sweet.

Technically, this historic trail isn't in the Coast Mountains. It's on the east wall of the canyon, which means it's on the west edge of the Cascades—a range that extends much farther north of the U.S./Canadian border than most people realize.

We've included the trip in this book, however, because it offers an unusual perspective of the Coast Mountains. Also, the Brigade trail is easier to access than others that are legitimately in the Coast Mountains, across the river.

"Shoulder season" is as much a warning as it is a recommendation for this trip. Unless you're a desert rat, heat exhaustion can be a real threat here during summer. Only if it's raining in the Coast Mountains, and at least cloudy over the Fraser Canyon, is this a sufferable summer hike. Whenever you come, pack two liters of water per person.

Traversing the first bluff, you can see the eastern Coast Mountains bursting from the recesses of the Fraser Canyon. Continuing beyond this 15-minute open stretch—to the second bluff, just past the junction with the 1858 trail—isn't worthwhile unless you're continuing to Gate Mountain. Return the way you ascended. The 1848 trail (the initial

Fraser Canyon

stretch of the Brigade trail) is steep, but the 1858 trail is even worse; rougher, too.

The intrepid (who aren't yet bored out of their gourd) might continue north, past the second bluff, to Gate Mountain. The trail winds through open, grassy, pleasant forest, but there are no terrific sights to punch up the scenery.

Consider the Brigade trail for an early-season, get-in-shape backpack trip. Haul lots of water. Set up camp along the first bluff, or in the open timber past the second bluff. From there, dayhiking to Gate Mountain and back would be quite enjoyable.

FACT

By Car

Drive Trans-Canada Highway 1 northeast through Hope. Cross the bridge over the Fraser River. Continue north 45.7 km (28.3 mi). Just beyond Alexandra Bridge, look for Alexandra Lodge on the right. Slow down. Proceed another 350 meters (0.2 mi) up a long hill, then turn off right (east). Park in the big pullout with garbage cans. The elevation here is 140 m (460 ft). The 1848 trail originally began at Alexandra Lodge, but this new trailhead provides easier access.

A one-way shuttle trip is possible, descending via the 1858 trail near 17 Mile Creek. To do this, you'll have to leave a second vehicle farther north. Drive 5 km (3 mi) north of the first trailhead to the rest area on the east side of the highway. But don't stop there. It's just a place to safely turn around, then drive slowly back south on the highway. Count 6 power poles (about 200 meters), then turn off right (west) into a pullout. Park here. From the north end of this pullout, the flagged 1858 trail is just across the highway.

On Foot

From the big pullout with garbage cans, walk about 50 meters south along Highway 1. Look on the east side, next to a rivulet. Marking the spot is a metal post (perhaps lying down) with red and white reflectors. The trail is initially overgrown with berry bushes. Flagging starts just above. About 40 m (130 ft) up, the older trail from Alexandra Lodge joins from the right. Continue ascending steeply, with few switchbacks, through forest with moss and salal undergrowth.

About 40 minutes up, highway traffic is no longer audible. Cross a small creek (unreliable in summer), then ascend beside a rockslide. Reach the bluff and views about 1 hour up. The Coast Mountains are visible to the west. The Fraser River is directly below. The ascent eases; level stretches provide relief. Tiger lilies and honeysuckle grace the forested slopes in early summer. About 1¼ hours up, there are bigger cedars, as well as ferns and devil's club.

You might not notice a trail forking right toward the Anderson River. That's fine. If you do, stay left, toward the bluff viewpoints. About 2 hours up, when it seems the trail should stay on the bluff, it descends steeply about 40-50 meters into the cedar-choked outlet of a small lake. The shore is 30 meters away, and you really have to thrash to get to it, and even then you won't find a comfortable place to sit. But this is probably your last water-refill opportunity. Be sure to purify. About 20 minutes from the lake, when the trail begins descending, directional signs on opposing trees confirm you're on the Brigade trail, with Alexandra Lodge behind you. Proceed straight north.

On the edge of the bluff, about 2½ hours up, is a campsite. There are signs BLUFFS TRAIL here, indicating north and south. Two minutes north you can look west, over the highway and the Fraser River, to the Westside Road contouring the mountainside about halfway up. Your trail, faint here, continues atop the open, rocky bluff, granting views for about the next 15 minutes. You can turn around anytime now, unless you've arranged a shuttle or you're going all the way to Gate Mountain.

The trail then descends to a junction in a bushy, overgrown area. It's easy to overlook the narrow 1858 trail dropping steeply west. It's 600 m (2000 ft) down to the highway. An old, wood sign on a big tree marks this junction; all three converging paths are flagged. The one rising steeply right reaches another bluff in about 10 minutes. No trail crosses this bluff, so watch carefully for flagging where a route resumes through brushy terrain. It leads to the east side of the ridge, then continues north approximately 5.5 km (3.4 mi), gaining 550 m (1800 ft), through semi-open timber to the rocky summit of Gate Mountain. There you can peer into the Fraser Canyon, and gaze east and south at the Cascade Mountains.

Trip 58
Skookumchuck Narrows

Location	Sechelt Peninsula
Round trip	8 km (5 mi)
Elevation gain	negligible
Time required	3 hours
Available	all year
Map	Sechelt Inlet 92 G/12

OPINION

Toddlers, waddlers, almost anyone can manage this short walk to see an astonishing tidal bore. Watching the water rush into and out of Sechelt Inlet is exhilarating. The surge through the narrows is strongest and most impressive when the tide is ebbing or flowing. Check a tidetable so you can be here then, and you'll see why it's called *Skookumchuck*, the Chinook word for *powerful water*. Even if your timing is off, the Sechelt Rapids and the surrounding mountains are plenty entertaining. And the narrows is an ideal habitat for colourful seastars and urchins. If you're traveling in the area, don't miss it. There's even a free campground nearby, at Klein Lake.

FACT

By Car

One kilometer (0.6 mi) southeast of the Earls Cove ferry terminal, turn east off Highway 101, toward Egmont. Drive 5.5 km (3.4 mi) to the trailhead pulloff on the right. It's before the road descends into Egmont.

Interested in the nearby, free Forest Service campground at Klein Lake? The turnoff is 1.7 km (1.1 mi) northeast of Highway 101, or 3.8 km (2.4 mi) west of the trailhead. It's on the south side of the road. Turn onto the signed NORTH LAKE FOREST SERVICE ROAD. Drive past the cottages. Near the end of North Lake, at 2.9 km (1.8 mi), take the right fork. Reach Klein Lake at 4.8 km (3.0 mi).

On Foot

The trail (initially a road) leads to a bridged creek crossing. It then climbs gently behind some cabins and enters mature second-growth forest. At about 1.6 km (1 mi) glimpse Brown Lake north of the trail. Reach a junction at 2.8 km (1.7 mi). North Point is left. Roland Point is right. Go either way.

Heading right, in 10 minutes you'll reach the rock slabs at Roland Point and a fine view of the narrows. From there, follow the coastal trail northwest about 1 km (0.6 mi) to North Point and another viewpoint of the narrows. Then walk the trail southwest 10 minutes to the junction where you previously went right to Roland Point. Retrace your steps to the trailhead.

Trip 59
Mt. Daniel

Location	Sechelt Peninsula
Round trip	5 km (3 mi)
Elevation gain	375 m (1225 ft)
Time required	2 hours
Available	all year
Map	Texada Island 92 F/9

OPINION

Mt. Daniel is the small, isolated mountain visible on the left as you drive north of Madeira Park on Highway 101. Dan offers you an easy opportunity to get out of your vehicle and enjoy a short, exhilarating, 2-hour workout. Not only will it assuage any guilt you might feel about sitting in your car most of the day, it will reward you with splendorous views north over Sakinaw Lake, southwest over the bays and peninsulas of Pender Harbour and Malaspina Strait, and southeast to the Caren Range. The hike begins on a nicely overgrown logging road beneath overarching alders. Big, beautiful ferns enhance the ascent. Arbutus don the bluff.

FACT

By Car

Drive Highway 101 northwest 38 km (23.6 mi) from Sechelt, or 5.8 km (3.6 mi) past the Madeira Park road. Turn left on Garden Bay Road. If you're heading south from Earls Cove on 101, continue 0.7 km (0.4 mi) beyond the Pender Harbour Secondary School, then turn right. From either approach, drive 3.3 km (2.0 mi) on Garden Bay Road. Slow down after you see Oyster Bay Road. Garden Bay Road curves left, then just as it straightens out, pull off left onto a rough road. Park there. A sign on a tree says MT. DANIEL TRAIL—TAKE A HIKE. The elevation here is 45 m (150 ft).

On Foot

About 3 minutes up the road, reach a fork. Ascend left. In another couple minutes, the road ends. Proceed on the trail, marked by red flagging. Pass through abundant, enormous ferns. The hike is steep and viewless all the way to the top. The trail is obvious. Pass a small, mucky pond on the right, just before reaching the first rocky outcropping. It's surrounded by trees, affording only a sliver view of the sea. The 420-m (1376-ft) summit is another 10 minutes farther.

From the outcropping, the trail cuts back left, descending a short way. It then resumes climbing steeply to the summit, which is marked by a huge rock cairn in a small, open area surrounded by trees. Still no views! Faint trails fan out from the cairn. They lead to a rocky bluff on the southwest side of the summit, where you'll find superb views south and west. Strong hikers can get here in 1 hour; others will take about 1 ½ hours.

Trip 60

Inland Lake

Location	Powell River
Loop	13 km (8 mi)
Elevation gain	negligible
Time required	3 to 4 hours
Available	all year
Maps	Powell River 92 F/15, Haslam Lake 92 F/16

OPINION

The 5.5-km long, forest-ringed lake, devoid of eye-lifting mountain scenery, is not unique. But the trail is special. The Powell River Forest Service constructed a 13-km, wheelchair-accessible trail around Inland Lake. The wide path is made of crushed limestone and never exceeds a 4% grade. Along the way are fishing wharfs, rest areas, outhouses, and three rustic log-cabins, all designed for the disabled. At the road's-end campground are two more cabins for the disabled and 16 free camp-sites a minute's walk from your vehicle. In summer a caretaker is there, ready to help anyone who needs it. This tranquil haven is a fine place to hike or canoe, whether you're disabled or not. It's especially attractive in shoulder season because the low elevation ensures snow is rarely present, and the limestone trail resists getting muddy despite all the coastal rain. Boat motors are allowed, but to keep the lake quiet they must be under 10 h.p.

FACT

Before your trip

Request the *Inland Lake Site and Trail System Interpretive Guide* from the Sunshine Coast Forest District (604-485-0700).

By Car

The road to the FS campground and trailhead at Inland Lake is well signed, and there are several access points from Highway 101 in Powell River. If approaching from the southeast, take Cassiar Manson Avenue toward Cranberry Lake. From the northwest, just south of the highway bridge over the Powell Lake outlet, look for the green highway sign directing you left (east) toward Cranberry Lake. From the northwest approach, reach Cranberry Lake's east side in about 3.7 km (2.3 mi). A sign here says Inland Lake Camping is 7.6 km (4.7 mi) farther. Head east on Haslam Street, and in 0.6 km (0.4 mi) go left. Farther along, where a road goes left to Haywire Bay Park, stay straight on Inland Lake Road. At the next minor junction, turn left and descend to the south end of Inland Lake. The elevation here is 122 m (400 ft).

From October 15 to April 15, to prevent vandalism, a locked gate blocks vehicles from driving the last couple hundred meters to the parking area. During those months, park near the gate, alongside the road, and walk 10 minutes to the lake.

On Foot

From the FS campground at the south end of the lake, start walking the lakeshore trail in either direction. Go out and back as far as you'd like, or all the way around. The path is easy to follow. If you walk the entire 13 km (8 mi), it loops back to where you started.

Trip 61

Deeks Bluffs

Location	Howe Sound
Round trip	9 km (5.6 mi)
Elevation gain	395 m (1296 ft)
Time required	4 hours
Available	most of the year
Maps	ITM Vancouver's Northshore; Squamish 92 G/11

OPINION

Why bother walking this often ill-natured trail, through unimpressive forest, over root-sewn slopes? Because it's early spring or late fall, when higher, more exciting trails are not hikeable. You need a quick escape after too many days indoors. And because here, on a clear day, at least you'll enjoy break-the-monotony views of Howe Sound, as the trail porpoises over the bluffs.

It's possible to make this a one-way shuttle trip, by linking up with the Deeks Lake section of the Howe Sound Crest trail, then rejoining Highway 99 about 5 km (3 mi) north of Deeks Creek bridge, near Porteau. Don't bother; you won't see anything new to make it worth the hassle.

It's also possible to make this a loop trip, by returning via the *old* Deeks trail. Again, don't bother. It adds variety, but the route can be perplexing and there's a drop-off that requires down-climbing. We recommend going out and back on the Bluffs trail, taking in the views both ways.

And in summer, when superior options are available, don't hike the Bluffs at all, except maybe as a training run after work. For that purpose, you'll certainly find it more peaceful than the Grouse Grind (Trip 66). Keep in mind, however, there's a rat's nest of old roads and trails in the Deeks Creek area. It's easy to get confused here. Even with our directions, you'll need good mountain sense.

If you have the four hours necessary to go all the way to the highest bluff and back, go for it. But if your time is limited, turn around at any of the viewpoints along the way.

FACT

By Car

Just outside West Vancouver, drive north on Highway 99. From the Horseshoe Bay turnoff, pass the Lions Bay north exit (Harvey Creek) at 11.6 km (17.2 mi). At 17.4 km (10.8 mi), slow down as you cross the Deeks Creek bridge. Immediately northwest of it, park on the left. The elevation here is 80 m (262 ft).

On Foot

The old Deeks trail ascends next to the creek. Don't go that way. The new trail is more gradual, less rugged, and easier to follow.

From the bridge over Deeks Creek, walk 150 m (490 ft) north along the highway. Look for blazes on the right. The trail is initially steep. In about 10 minutes, reach a narrow defile with a fixed rope to help you climb. About 5 minutes beyond, reach a level spot. After 20 minutes of earnest hiking, you'll elude the highway noise and hear a roaring creek.

Ascending, stay left on the Bluffs trail at each of three forks, ignoring the flagged or signed right branches that lead to the old Deeks trail. There's a series of viewpoints as the Bluffs trail surges over dry knolls and drops into wet hollows. After about 1 hour, it then descends past some ponds to an old cat track. Go left. The track soon reverts to trail. After rising onto an old road, go right. Shortly after, turn left and make the final 10-minute ascent to the highest of the bluffs, 475 m (1558 ft). Here, 1 ½ to 2 hours from the trailhead, you can savour views south and west over Howe Sound.

Trip 62
Petgill Lake

Location	Howe Sound
Round trip	11.5 km (7 mi)
Elevation gain	665 m (2181 ft)
Time required	5 hours
Available	most of the year
Map	ITM Garibaldi Region; Squamish 92 G/11

OPINION

The word *nice* is so cliche as to be almost denigrating. "Oh, he's such a nice man," really means, "He's just a typical guy." So when we say Petgill is a nice lake, we do so intentionally; it's no compliment. Petgill is a cliche lake.

The trail is nothing special either, just tolerably pleasant. And the lake is little more than a big pond, serving merely as a recognizable destination—a forest clearing that happens to be full of water. Trees and steep slopes prevent you from relaxing on the shore, except at a couple tiny worn-out spots. Where the path around the lake rises and affords views, the scenery is... well, nice.

Nevertheless, hiking to Petgill is worthwhile, because you can do it when other trails require skis or snowshoes. The lake elevation is only 755 m (2476 ft), so snow might only be an obstacle in the dead of winter. Any Coast Mountain trail that's walkable in November or March has to be a lot worse than nice before we'd rate it Don't Do.

On a rainy fall or spring day, Petgill is a reasonable destination. You won't miss any significant scenery. Still, don't expect solitude. This is a surprisingly popular trail. And should you backpack here (why would you want to?), don't count on finding a vacant tent site.

FACT

By Car

From the turnoff to Horseshoe Bay, just outside West Vancouver, drive 36 km (22.3 mi) north on Highway 99. Turn left into the parking lot at Murrin Provincial Park. This is 3 km (1.9 mi) north of Britannia Beach. Leave your car near the entrance.

On Foot

The trailhead is directly across the highway from the Murrin parking lot. Immediately north of the parking lot entrance, look up to the right (east). It's just after the third telephone pole.

The going is initially steep, switchbacking up through rocks, sometimes requiring handholds. But the trail is obvious, marked with orange metal blazes. The other splashes of orange you might notice are tiger lilies. Soon enter forest studded with an occasional big tree.

You'll dispatch the steepest section of trail in about 20 minutes. Your reward is a view across Howe Sound. The smoke-spewing Woodfibre mill dominates the scene. Then the trail is back in forest. Reach a second viewpoint in another 10 or 15 minutes, and a third 5 minutes beyond that. Both of these are signed and provide an interesting perspective of the Stawamus Chief and the Squamish Valley.

After 45 minutes, come to a T-intersection with an old road. Left is blocked with brush. Go right, ascending gently. Within 1 ½ hours you should reach a small hogsback ridge where you can glimpse Howe Sound through the trees. From there, the trail winds in and out, up and down, through pretty, forested hollows. After 2 ¼ hours arrive at a little pass, where a trail descends right. That's the way to Goat Ridge. Continue straight another 4 minutes to where the trail rises onto a rock overlooking Petgill Lake, 40 m (130 ft) below. A sign here states the elevation is 795 meters.

To continue around the lake, bear left. Other paths drop steeply. One is signed LAKE CIRCUIT. All will suffice, but the more gradual descent left is easier. Follow the orange blazes.

Hiking the lake circuit clockwise, you'll soon pass a tent site on the shore. A spur trail left leads 300 meters to a bluff and views of the mountains across Howe Sound. Continuing the circuit, pass another tent site on the north side of the lake.

Rounding the northeast shore, pass the signed Shannon Creek route, forking left. It offers the option of a one-way shuttle trip. As the name suggests, this blazed path crosses Shannon Creek above Shannon Falls. It eventually intersects the trail ascending the Chief, Trip 43.

Completing the lake circuit, you must negotiate a bluff, with the help of a ladder and fixed rope. A third flat area, back from the southeast corner of the lake, has room for 2 or 3 tents, near a brook. The circuit now forks. Go left and you're homeward bound. Right is a slight detour, leading onto a narrow ledge strung with a fixed rope, ascending to near where you first saw the lake.

Trip 63
Place Creek Falls

Location	Birkenhead Road
Round trip	3 km (2 mi)
Elevation gain	230 m (754 ft)
Time required	1 ½ hours
Available	mid-May through November
Map	Pemberton 92 J/7

OPINION

A walloping, wild waterfall like this would be a moving sight anywhere. But because Place Creek Falls is out of the way, unsigned, and seldom visited, you'll probably be here alone. It's so rare to experience anything in solitude these days that the event acquires instant significance. It will invigorate your spirit, just as the pounding roar and frigid spray will arouse your senses.

It's a stiff, 30-minute hike to the lower falls, and summer is hot here. But the trail is well shaded, and the water droplets ricocheting around the cataract will chill you quickly. Climbing above the lower falls is torturous. It's a punishing route, best left to keen climbers gunning for the Place Glacier, high above at 1830 m (6000 ft). See Trip 25 for details.

FACT

By Car

Drive Highway 99, from Lillooet or Pemberton, to the three-way junction in Mt. Currie. Head north toward D'Arcy. Cross the railroad tracks 20.8 km (12.9 mi) north of Mt. Currie, then slow down. At 21.4 km (13.3 mi), just west of Gates Lake, turn right on a minor dirt road. Follow it 1.5 km (0.9 mi). Park here before the railroad tracks, or if no gate bars your way, cross the tracks and continue about 350 meters on a dirt road through the trees. Pass under a powerline. Where a smaller road forks left, stay right. In the clearing, where there's a second powerline, park your car near a stump. Don't follow the road that curves right. The elevation here is 510 m (1673 ft).

Place Creek Falls

On Foot

From the stump in the clearing, head straight (south) to a flagged path in the brush. Proceed through the brush, then through trees on old logging road that tapers to trail. Ascend 100 m (330 ft), then contour southwest to reach Place Creek gorge in 15-20 minutes. You'll have to climb over or maneuver around deadfall. Then ascend steeply along the edge of the gorge. In another 5 minutes, glimpse the huge cascade. Already you can feel its cooling effect. To reach a better viewpoint, negotiate a big, fallen tree blocking the trail. A few minutes later, you can see the falls full-on. Here in the cool mist, more cedars inhabit the slopes. The trail snakes along the precipice where it's always slick. Be steady. A misstep could be fatal.

The steep ascent continues beside the falls. In another 5 minutes, there's an open view next to the flying plume of the spray, at about 740 m (2427 ft). You can look northwest to Mt. Ronayne and Sun God Mountain.

Trip 64
Birkenhead Lake

Location	Birkenhead Provincial Park
Round trip	3.5 km (2.2 mi)
Elevation gain	negligible
Time required	1½ hours
Available	mid-May through November
Map	Birkenhead Lake 92 J/10

OPINION

Birkenhead Lake is a beauty: 6-km-long, boldly guarded by Birkenhead Peak and its sentinel siblings along the ridge. But the lakeshore trail through ancient forest is so short it's not worth driving out of your way to hike. And for most of us, this little provincial park is definitely out of the way. Unless you're already in the area, or intent on exploring every crevice in B.C., don't rush to get here.

Cheakamus Lake (Trip 51) is more accessible than Birkenhead, and more crowded as a result. But it's also more enjoyable, with a longer trail and even grander scenery. Go there first.

If you make it to Birkenhead, include nearby Place Creek Falls (Trip 63) in your plans, and by all means hike the lakeshore trail. It's often within 4 horizontal meters of the water. The giant, deeply fissured Douglas firs and sensuous red cedars are a moving sight. Too bad the voracious mosquitoes will probably keep *you* moving.

Return via the lakeshore trail and commune with the big trees and lapping water again, rather than do a loop trip and be bored with the scrawny forest lining the Sockeye road/trail. A mountain bike is really the only form of locomotion to consider if you want to go the whole 8 km (5 mi) southwest on the old logging road to the end of the lake.

FACT

By Car

Drive Duffey Lake Road / Highway 99 to the three-way junction in Mt. Currie. Follow the road north toward D'Arcy. In 34.6 km (21.5 mi) turn left at the sign for Birkenhead Provincial Park. From there, it's

Birkenhead Lake

8.4 km (5.2 mi) to the free Blackwater Lake FS campground, on the left. Mt. John Decker is prominent straight west as you near Birkenhead Provincial Park. At 13.8 km (8.6 mi), go left to enter the park gate. Arrive at Birkenhead Lake at 15.6 km (9.7 mi). Don't turn left into the campground. Continue straight to the day-use parking area. The elevation here is 652 m (2140 ft).

When you leave, 300 meters before you reach the D'Arcy road, be sure to look south to Nequatque Mountain and southwest to Gates Peak. You'll see an inviting glacial bowl way up there. But think twice before you respond to that invitation: it demands a miserable 1200-m (3940-foot) climb.

On Foot

A post at the entrance to the day-use parking lot indicates it's 8 km (5 mi) to the Birkenhead FS Road, which you can reach by walking the Sockeye trail southwest, past the park boundary. That FS Road used to access the park 25 years ago. It came north, up the Birkenhead River, but frequent landslides forced BC Parks to abandon it. The Sockeye trail—no lake views, no impressive trees—is about 25 m (82 ft) above the shore.

Start on the lakeshore trail. Park rangers have cut away lots of deadfall, allowing easy hiking. In about 15 minutes, a rocky beach offers good views and a possible sunning spot. Within 30 minutes, cross a rocky alluvial fan and a bridge over a drainage that might be full during spring runoff. Then enter a cedar grove, followed by a stand of big Douglas firs. Go out to the shore to look northeast, beyond the end of the lake, to the 7500-foot (2287-m) unnamed peaks above the Blackwater FS Road.

You can tell this is a pampered, provincial-park trail: the minor creek beds are bridged. Apparently it gets pretty wet through here. About 35 minutes of hiking will bring you to a campground (pit toilet, makeshift table) in a large open area on a peninsula. Across the lake, there's a waterfall high on the slopes beneath 2524-m (8278-ft) Birkenhead Peak.

The lakeshore trail peters out beyond the campground, and there's no pretty, green understory to brighten the big fir forest. If you insist on a loop trip, return to the day-use parking lot via the Sockeye Creek trail, which leads northwest from the toilet's right side. (A sign points straight but should point right.) Within 5 minutes reach the Sockeye trail (actually a road). Right leads back to the parking lot in about 30 minutes. Left about 10 minutes is roaring Sockeye Creek. Just before it, cross a bridge over a tiny creek. Don't mistake this one for the longer, higher, log bridge with a railing that spans Sockeye Creek.

Trip 65
Lower Hollyburn Lakes

Location	West Vancouver
Loop	11 km (7 mi)
Elevation gain	427 m (1400 ft)
Time required	5 hours
Available	late May through mid-November
Maps	BC Parks brochure of Cypress Provincial Park; ITM Vancouver's Northshore; North Vancouver 92 G/6

OPINION

Hiking this trail was no fun. Writing about it is painful. The reason it's in the book is to warn you away from an area that's enticing but disappointing: the loop (roughly a square) linking the lakes on the lower slopes of Hollyburn Mountain. We've described it in detail because many people will hike here despite our advice. The second side of the square, following Brothers Creek upstream (Trip 53), is worthwhile. Check it out. The rest is everything hikers hate. Roads. Ski trails. Confusing junctions. Deep mud. Shallow ponds. (Who ever called them lakes, anyway?) Private land. Girl Guide cabins. Boy Scout cabins. Ma & pa cabins. Industrial junk. Bogus historical sites. Dismal, scraggly, ruthlessly-logged forest. And no views.

Sure, it's a long enough loop for a decent shoulder-season work-out, but you can get that in Lynn Valley (Trip 54). Lynn is just as convenient and offers a more pleasing experience. On lower Hollyburn, you'll never drift into that incredible lightness of being that distinguishes a hike from a trudge. The scenery is too grating, the tangle of routes too obnoxious.

If you come, bring a Cypress Park map to help you stay oriented. If you wander off this loop, you can probably get back on track farther along; some of the trails are signed, and there are often several ways to reach the same destination.

FACT

By Car
Driving Highway 1 through West Vancouver, turn off at Cypress Bowl, Exit 8. Continue up Cypress Parkway to Hi-View Lookout, at the second hairpin turn. Park in the gravel lot in the middle of the hairpin, across from the paved lookout. The elevation here is 412 m (1350 ft).

You can also start this loop at the top of Eyremount Drive, in British Properties. See Trip 53 for directions.

On Foot
Heading northeast from the toilet, walk across the road to the end of the cement retaining wall. You'll see a sign NO TRAIL BIKES, but stay alert for bikers anyway.

Immediately there's a choice of three trails. Don't take the rocky path descending right. The dirt path ascending left is the way you'll complete our proposed loop. Start on the dirt path straight ahead. It's signed TO MILLSTREAM ROAD 45 MINUTES. In 30 meters, ignore a minor trail ascending left. Stay right on the main trail dropping northeast to cross a bridged creek. Soon cross an intermittent creek drainage, then cross four creeks in the next 15 minutes. The old Millstream Road becomes your trail as you continue east, descending slightly.

Pass the trail forking left (north) to the Skyline trail. Pass signs for the short Heritage Walks. About 30 minutes along, immediately after crossing Lawson Creek, at 385 m (1263 ft), go left (north) toward the Baden Powell Trail (BPT) and Brothers Creek Forest Heritage Walk. Heading uphill, reach another junction in 15 minutes. Take the right fork toward Brothers Creek and Lost Lake. In a few minutes cross a powerline right-of-way where the BPT traverses west to Lawson Creek.

The trail, now marked with red blazes, is a mix of roots and needles. In a couple minutes, after crossing a boardwalk, stay straight (left), ascending Brothers Creek trail on the west side of the narrow creek gorge. Notice the big cedars. Near 600 m (1968 ft), after about 1 ¼ hours of hiking, ignore the Crossover trail. It forks right and crosses the creek. Stay west of the creek and continue straight uphill, soon passing another signpost for the Crossover trail (left) and Lawson Creek Heritage Walk. You'll see many more giant cedars.

About 1 ¾ hours from Hi-View Lookout trailhead, at 665 m (2180 ft), reach a 25-m high waterfall with two tiers. This is a good rest stop. Just after the falls, a trail forks left. Signed WESTLAKE LODGE, it heads northeast, reaching Blue Gentian Lake in about 30 minutes. For the full loop, ignore it. Instead, notice a metal sign on a tree: THIRD BRIDGE.

Brothers Creek is no longer bridged here, but it's easy to rockhop across in fall. On the other side of the creek, high on a tree, is a wood sign LOST LAKE. Cross to the east side of the creek to proceed to Lost Lake.

Immediately after crossing the creek, take the trail curving left, upstream. Ignore the blazed trail to the right. In 5-10 minutes, reach Lost Lake. It's nestled in trees, at 735 m (2410 ft).

To continue, bear left around the west end of Lost Lake, passing short paths to the shore. Cross the outlet stream on a slick footbridge. Head west and negotiate lots of muddy, boggy areas. This rooty and rough trail is not shown on the 1992 Cypress Park map. Rockhop across an unbridged creek. The trail starts descending. Then cross a bridged creek and reach a junction just above it. Straight ahead is Blue Gentian Lake, at 812 m (2663 ft). You've now hiked about 20 minutes from Lost Lake.

Stay right at Blue Gentian Lake. (Left cuts back southeast to the unbridged crossing of Brothers Creek.) At the north end of the lake, the trail forks. Left goes southwest to intersect the BPT in 5-10 minutes. If you decide to return that way, see the Brothers and Lawson Creeks description (Trip 53) for details. For the full loop, go right (northwest) toward West Lake and Hollyburn Lodge.

In about 10 minutes, take the right fork. Reach West Lake in another 10 minutes. The trail then improves. Go left around the south side of the lake, past a bare spot, to meet the BPT. The elevation here is 838 m (2750 ft). Go right on the old road to the top of the rise, where there are signs high on trees for skiers. Head toward Hollyburn Lodge. Pass the Jack Pratt Memorial Ski Jump and, down to the left, a small, locked cabin signed NOOTKA LODGE. After gaining 50 m (160 ft), intersect another old road where there's a map/sign. Go right. You're on the BPT, but this section is also called the Grand National ski trail. In a couple minutes, reach a 4-way junction. Stay straight on the far left road to Hollyburn Lodge and First Lake. (The middle trail, the BPT, was the only way to access the summit of Hollyburn Mountain before construction of the Cypress Parkway.) Reach First Lake about 3½ hours from the trailhead, or 1¼ hours from Lost Lake.

The Forest Service has a cabin here, on the west side of the outlet stream. There's a drinking water faucet beside it. Brothers Creek brochures are available from the notice board in front of the cabin. A map illustrates the maze of trails on Hollyburn Mountain. Just north of the Forest Service cabin is the old Hollyburn Lodge, now closed. To complete the loop back to your vehicle, go left (south) between the notice board and the Forest Service cabin. On the map displayed on the back of the notice board, this trail is labeled MAIN; on the park map, it's OLD FORKS. You'll pass many private cabins, a Girl Guide cabin, and Challenger Inn.

About 10 minutes below First Lake, where you pass a Boy Scout cabin, take the right fork. When the main trail intersects a 4WD road, go right. Descend 5 minutes to another road. Go right again. About 30 minutes below First Lake, reach yet another road junction, at 762 m (2500 ft). Go right again, on Cypress Park Resort Road. In 5 minutes, pass a log home with a stunning view of English Bay and downtown Vancouver. About 75 meters beyond the log home, look for a small, flagged trail descending left. A short way in, a couple trees are blazed.

The descent is rough and steep, through scrawny forest. In 15 minutes, meet the Skyline trail under powerlines, at 625 m (2050 ft). Make a short right into a shallow gully to cross beneath the powerlines and continue the descent. Don't ascend left. The roar of traffic on the Trans-Canada Highway is now audible. Where a minor trail goes left, stay on the larger trail between two blazes, dropping farther into dark forest. Cross bridged Marr Creek. Just afterward, take the right trail steeply descending a bluff to Hi-View Lookout on Cypress Parkway.

Trip 66
Grouse Grind ✓

Location	North Shore
Round trip	5 km (3.2 mi)
Elevation gain	854 m (2800 ft)
Time required	1 ½ to 2 ½ hours
Available	April through mid-November
Maps	Grouse Mountain Hiking Trails, available at the base office; ITM Vancouver's Northshore; North Vancouver 92 G/6

OPINION

Hearing Vancouverites talk, you'd think this was *the* trail in the Coast Mountains. It's laughable, like a kid wearing water wings bragging about how well he swims. But many Grinders haven't hiked elsewhere in the range. The Grind is all they know. So don't let them sucker you into wasting a sunny, summer weekend day on this outdoor treadmill.

Short, steep and accessible, the Grind has become a rite of passage for the pseudo outdoor crowd. Many Grinders compete with each other, clocking their ascents. The attraction of Grinding, however, isn't just the activity itself. For some, it's the other Grinders—lean, energetic, athletic singles. You won't experience the Coast Mountains here, but you might get a date.

After work, and especially on weekends, the Grind is usually congested. The trail is viewless until you pop out of the trees near the Grouse Mountain Chalet. The hum of the city is always noticeable, except where the trail briefly sidles up to a creek. On top, you're greeted by a gondola station, restaurant, bar, tourist shop, paved walkways, and absurdities like a giant wood carving of a basketball player. So bringing neophyte hikers here is a mistake: you'll turn them off. And this is obviously no place for anyone with an affinity for wilderness.

The Grind, nevertheless, is a good place to get some exercise and fresh air. In that regard it's way better than going to a gym. But do it mid-week. Weekends are your opportunities to enjoy *real* hikes. And when you do come here, make the Grind more worthwhile; allow time to continue to Goat Mountain (Trip 16).

Volunteers have recently improved the Grind trail, so it's in excellent condition. Just don't assume this is typical of the range. Coast Mountain trails are generally much rougher. If you're uncomfortable here, you'll find other trails harrowing.

FACT

By Car

Drive or catch the bus up Capilano Road in North Vancouver. Follow the signs: GROUSE MOUNTAIN SKYRIDE. Capilano Road eventually becomes Nancy Green Way. Approaching the upper, paved parking lot at Grouse, look on your right for the signed trailhead: GROUSE GRIND, BADEN POWELL TRAIL. If you arrive by bus, walk back 30 meters from where you disembarked. If you plan to Grind regularly, and you prefer to take the gondola down, buy a Skyride Pass ($50 in 1997) for unlimited rides all year. A descent ticket is $5.

On Foot

If you plan to hike up *and* down the Grind, be sure to allow enough time to get back to the parking lot before dark. In the forest, light diminishes about 45 minutes earlier than it does in the open. And the average hiker takes about 1 hour to descend the Grind. (Fast, confident hikers do it in 40 minutes.) That means you should begin hiking down 2 hours before sunset.

Here's another consideration before starting. Though the Grind is easier to descend, for variation we describe the BCMC trail as a return route. Built by the B.C. Mountaineering Club in 1900, it's a bit rougher and longer, requiring about a 1 ⅓-hour descent for an average hiker. Like the Grind, it's completely in trees, so it offers no change of scenery, but it's less popular, so it might grant you a few moments of solitude.

The Grind trailhead elevation is 275 m (900 ft). A big, blue sign suggests that the ascent of 854 m (2800 ft) in 2.5 km (1.6 mi) will take you 1 ½ hours. For the average hiker, that's probably true. Strong, determined hikers do it in 55 minutes, maybe less.

In case you're planning a longer foray across the North Shore mountains, here's the rest of the data on the trailhead signpost. Heading east: DEEP COVE 21.6 KM (7 HRS), SKYLINE DRIVE 2.6 KM (1 HR), MOUNTAIN HIGHWAY 7 KM (2.5 HRS), LYNN CANYON SUSPENSION BRIDGE 10 KM (3.5 HRS). Heading west: CYPRESS PROVINCIAL PARK (SOME HIGH ELEVATION TRAVEL) 11.6 KM (4 HRS); EAGLE DRIVE, HORSESHOE BAY 23.3 KM (8 HRS).

Now, up you go, but you really don't need these directions. The Grind is exceptionally well-marked. The times we state are cumulative, from the trailhead, and are valid for fit, fast hikers. In about 3 minutes, go left at the well-signed junction. The Baden Powell Trail continues straight, following orange blazes. In 10 minutes, amid ferns, go either way. The diverging paths marked with blue arrows rejoin shortly.

At a junction in 15 minutes, go left onto a log bridge over a gully. Right is for the BCMC trail. About 35 minutes up, having gained 425 m (1395 ft), the trail swings close to the gondola. Here you can go left to look down on Capilano Lake and West Vancouver. The gondola tower and cables, however, partially obstruct the view, so unless you're getting claustrophobic in the forest, just keep climbing.

About 45 minutes up, reach a creek cascading through a gorge. Another burst of effort and you'll top out at the Chalet. The elevation here is 1128 m (3700 ft).

To descend via the BCMC trail, return to where you emerged from the trees at the top of the Grind. Facing the Chalet, go right on the road. In 20 meters, across from propane tanks, you'll see an unmarked trail dropping to your right. That's the way. About five minutes down, where the trail briefly widens to what feels like a road, look for pink flagging on your right; follow it back onto trail. (If you continue straight, you'll soon reach a ski run.) You should also see an orange blaze and a blue sign: BCMC TRAIL. After a stretch that's often muddy, be careful on the small, slippery rock slabs. Initially the grade is moderate, but then becomes steep, heading down the fall line. After about 20 minutes, reach a three-way junction. Continue descending to your right, following the sign for the BCMC Cabin and Skyline Drive.

You'll reach a viewpoint where the cabin once stood. Go right here, descending to a junction with the Grind where you crossed a gully on a log bridge. You should now be on familiar ground. Go left, descending to the Baden Powell Trail, where a right turn leads you quickly back to the Grind trailhead.

Trip 67
Mt Fromme

Location	North Shore
Round trip	15 km (9.3 mi)
Elevation gain	866 m (2840 ft)
Time required	5 hours
Available	mid-May through mid-November
Maps	ITM Vancouver's Northshore; North Vancouver 92 G/6

OPINION

Mt. Fromme is the Rodney Dangerfield of mountains. It don't get no respect. People have humiliated it—building pipeline roads, service roads, logging roads, butchering the trees, and now rampaging mountain-bike routes every which way. The wretched forest that remains is further disfigured by a perplexing mess of markers: orange flagging, and splashes of paint, some orange, others blue.

Stay away. Let the pathetic hulk suffer in silence.

Endure these ravaged slopes and your only significant view will be from the summit. Meslilloet Mountain is visible northeast over the Seymour River valley, Coliseum Mountain is nearby northeast, Mt. Garibaldi and Mamquam Mountain are far north, and the peaks of Mt. Seymour are east. The same scenery is available elsewhere, at the end of more enjoyable hikes.

Almost any North Shore trail is better: Hollyburn for an easy trip, Mt. Seymour for a more difficult trip, Coliseum Mountain for a tough trip. Fromme might be worthwhile only if you bike the gated road from the north end of Mountain Highway in Upper Lynn. Then hike the trail departing from the old Grouse Mountain Highway.

FACT

By Car

In North Vancouver, follow Lonsdale Road all the way north. Jog left onto Prospect Road and follow it up to where it ends near Mosquito Creek. Park along the residential roadside, at 305 m (1000 ft).

On Foot

Start at the gated end of Prospect Road. Stay right along the fence and pass the water towers. The trail then splits into three branches. Ascend right. Soon go left toward the old Grouse Mountain Highway (GMH). A sign says you'll reach it in 50 minutes.

Descend briefly and hit another 3-way junction. Go left, ascending on a rocky surface that looks like water might course over it. In 15 meters, stay left on the smoother path. When you get up on the old road, notice the foundation of a long-gone cabin. That's where the route curves right. Follow orange blazes and blue spray paint on trees. Turn left, ascending past a VW-bus sized boulder. About 20 meters farther reach another old road. See more blue paint on trees. Go left, following blazes. You'll continually recross remnants of an old road.

The old road turns into a trail. Mosquito Creek canyon is to your left. There's a newer mountain-bike trail going right. Straight ahead is a signed junction: VIEWPOINT 10 MINUTES, CASCADES 15 MINUTES. Leave the Pipeline trail where there's a huge Douglas fir on your left. Go right, away from the creek, following more blue paint and orange blazes. Ascend steeply, then see orange paint on trees and a sign on the right: OLD MTH HWY 30 MIN. Go right, still climbing. Keep following trees daubed with orange paint. Turn left onto the road. In 30 meters, reach a fork where a minor road heads northwest toward Grouse ski area. Walk just right of the minor road, onto the Per Gynt trail. The ascent is now more gradual, through second growth forest.

Having gained 365 m (1197 ft), reach a good gravel road (the GMH) still used by service vehicles. Turn left. Proceed 15-20 minutes north on the road. Just before a big, sweeping left-hand turn, look right: orange paint on a low rock indicates where the trail surges skyward. About 45 minutes up, reach a buggy subalpine bog. Angle right to the ridge. From the road, it's a 305-m (1000-ft) ascent to the 1171-m (3841-ft) south knob of Mt. Fromme. Rock slabs on the subalpine summit create an open vantage point.

Instead of about-facing, loop back to the GMH. Follow the sign to Senate Peak—the north knob of Mt. Fromme. The blazed route hurtles into a defile. After a 15-meter drop, regain that elevation and confront a rock knob. From the west side of the knob, descend 5 minutes down the forested gully. Hit a T-intersection at a small rock band where there's a sign TO SENATE PEAK for people ascending. The left fork quickly leads to Meech Lake. Descend right (northwest) on the main trail to Pipestone Pass and a junction. Right goes to Goat Mountain via Thunderbird Ridge. Go left to the GMH. From there, it's 15 minutes south to where you first intersected the road on your way up.

Trip 68

Lynn Peak

Location	Lynn Headwaters Regional Park
Round trip	7.2 km (4.5 mi)
Elevation gain	714 m (2340 ft)
Time required	2 hours
Available	early May through early November
Maps	Park brochure (at trailhead kiosk); North Vancouver 92 G/6

OPINION

Only measured by a heart-rate monitor is this a worthwhile hike. You can get a good, short workout here, but the emotional reward is minimal. For a spring-training dash, it's fine. In late fall, the trail might be one of the few snow-free options. Otherwise, forget it.

The peak itself is an insignificant bump on a trivial ridge. Below, the city and harbour are visible, but that's to be expected on any North Shore summit. The other views, into Lynn Canyon and across at the forested Mt. Seymour peaks, are unmoving. Though the trail leads you into pockets of old-growth trees, the forest is mostly typical second-growth—too young to be interesting.

Beyond Lynn Peak are the Needles, a name that conjures images of Kangaroo Ridge in North Cascades National Park, or Howser Spire in the Bugaboos. But the reality falls disappointingly short. So don't continue, unless all you're seeking is further challenge. A better destination would be nearby Coliseum Mountain (Trip 34). It too will test your mettle, but the enormous, relatively flat summit is an alpine playground with wandering and camping possibilities you won't find at the Needles.

FACT

By Car

See Lynn Valley (Trip 54) for directions to the trailhead.

On Foot

From the parking lot, cross the bridge over Lynn Creek. Turn right (southeast). In about 100 meters, turn left onto the signed Lynn Loop trail. In about 300 meters, turn right on a minor trail signed LYNN PEAK. Ascend a broad swath of boulders that soon narrows to a trail. After a steep 1 km (0.6 mi), Mt. Seymour is visible to the east. Proceed through impressive, old firs. The ascent eases in scrubby regrowth. Reach a better viewpoint. The trail swings back west, climbing moderately to a viewpoint over Lynn Canyon.

On a typical weekend, you'll know you've topped out at 921 m (3020 ft) on Lynn Peak when you see all the hikers hanging around the rocky platform on the east side of the ridge. Burnaby and the Fraser lowlands are visible below. The minor peaks on the ridge directly east are Mt. Elsay and Mt. Seymour.

Still haven't reached your maximal heart rate? Push on. A faint, narrow route (marked by flagging) continues ascending north through forest. It rides the ridge over three more "peaks," repeatedly losing and regaining 75 to 150 m (250 to 290 ft) in the next several kilometers, until hitting the first rocky bump of The Needles.

Trip 69
Burke Ridge

Location	Fraser Valley North
Round trip	20 km (12.4 mi)
Elevation gain	880 m (2885 ft)
Time required	too much (7 to 8 hours)
Available	mid-June through mid-November
Map	Coquitlam 92 G/7

OPINION

No truth or beauty here. Just disappointment. The summit scenery doesn't justify the miserable approach: old logging roads and a mish-mash of trails. You can do without seeing Widgeon Peak and insignificant Coquitlam Mountain easier than you can tolerate the long slog up Burke Ridge.

Scratching up the side of this ravaged mountain are "trails" that spit in the face of what a trail should be. They drag you under power-lines, across roads, into logging slash, through ugly, chewed up land. It's a long trudge to the top, too, and viewless the whole bummed-out way. Hike elsewhere. Even nearby Dennett Lake (Trip 55), on the other side of Burke, is a better choice. Hollyburn Mountain (Trip 39) and Eagle Ridge (Trip 17) are way better.

Another black mark against this trail is the local Gun Club. You'll hear the obnoxious, bam-bam-bam of rifles during the initial ascent. Then, just when you think you've escaped the noise, you cross to the east side of the ridge, where you're likely to hear more gun nuts blasting away in the Pitt River valley. People who enjoy tranquility will be incensed by this madness. Our sense of adventure here was nil. Our feeling of unease was intense.

If you insist on hiking Burke Ridge, stay on the road (despite the ankle-gobbling rocks) to the site of the defunct ski chalet. You'll get there faster with less trouble navigating. The only noteworthy sight along the trail to that point is a small cascade in mossy, Pritchett Creek canyon. The pinched canyon itself is gloomy and depressing, and the trail is in horrid shape through there. Beyond the canyon, the South

Slope trail dumps you into a nasty jumble of old roads in a clearcut. Witnessing such a pillaged landscape is like finding the carcass of a bear slaughtered for its gall bladder; both experiences evoke feelings of sadness and disgust.

FACT

By car

From Highway 7, just east of Port Coquitlam, drive Coast Meridian Road north 5.2 km (3.2 mi). Turn right on Harper Road and proceed 2 km (1.2 mi) on gravel. Park near the Hunting and Fishing Club entrance, at 320 m (1050 ft) elevation.

On Foot

Cross the road to the trailhead sign and map. If you want to try the trail, walk the road beyond the gate for a couple minutes and go left onto a minor trail marked by flagging. This is before the first fork in the road. If you choose to walk the road (avoiding the dark, scraggly forest, messy trail, and tangle of old skid roads), when you reach a fork about 10 minutes up, stay left on the higher road. At another minor fork, stay left on the main road. After about 1 ¼ hours, come to where the trail (actually a skid road at this point) meets the main road, which you're on.

If you hike the trail from the start, you'll reach a fork in about 10 minutes. Left is the Woodland Walk loop. Go right to continue up Burke. Cross a creek in about ½ hour. At a fork where the Coquitlam Lake View trail goes left, stay right. Then stay left past a sawdust pile. Look for red flagging as you near Pritchett Canyon. Continue through an area of decimated forest where all the crisscrossing roads can be confusing. Go right when you hit the first road, then curve left, then go right, then left. Head east toward the main road. Then go left (northeast) uphill to the road's end and what used to be the site of a ski chalet, at 1020 m (3346 ft). The view here, over the Fraser Valley, is uninspiring.

From here, a rough trail heads right. It passes ponds and crosses heather meadows. About ½ hour from the road, a trail from Dennett Lake (Trip 55, the way we recommend accessing Burke) joins from the right. Continue straight for the summit. Just before topping out, pass a trail heading left. It leads to another viewpoint, about 1 hour distant.

Trip 70

Gambier Island / Mt. Liddell

Location	Howe Sound
Round trip	14 km (8.7 mi) up Mt. Liddell;
	15 km (9.3 mi) to Gambier Lake
Elevation gain	903 m (2963 ft) up Mt. Liddell;
	475 m (1550 ft) to the lake
Time required	6 to 7 hours
Available	May through November
Maps	North Vancouver 92 G/6,
	Squamish 92 G/11

OPINION

Like the plot of a horror movie, this trip begins with a deceptively pleasant powerboat ride on the *Dogwood Princess*, from Langdale to Gambier Island. All seems well as you walk past a cute country store and cottages, on a lovely lane beneath overarching trees. The new subdivision foreshadows a turn for the worse. Soon the route to Mt. Liddell reveals its true malevolence. Like young hoods, tight bunches of immature pines have overtaken the path, standing in your way, forestalling passage. It becomes a ghastly trek as the gentle island roads morph into wickedly steep, ankle-gnashing bedrock. Before the summit, every view reveals yet another haunting clearcut on the grisly, shorn Sechelt mountains. Industrial noise from the Port Mellon mill seems inescapable. It's enough to make you flee.

If you attempt Liddell despite our dire warning, and your resolve to continue is dashed, return to the harbour and find a place to enjoy the beautiful water. The vantage atop Liddell is nothing special. The Howe Sound Crest looks just as good from the deck of a B.C. Ferry.

Mid-winter, if you're desperate for a diversion, consider Gambier Lake. It's nowhere near as steep as Liddell and the striding is easier, though it's essentially a road walk. Another, more accessible, shoulder-season option is nearby Petgill Lake (Trip 62). It's not wildly scenic either, but at least it's a real hike on a genuine trail.

Finally, mountain bikes are not allowed on the powerboat shuttle to Gambier Island. Even if they were, the bouldery bedrock route up Liddell is unrideable. So don't think your bike will make this trip worthwhile.

FACT

By Car and Ferry

West of Vancouver, Highway 1 turns north and becomes Highway 99. Near here take the Horseshoe Bay exit and drive down to the ferry. Or, from the traffic light by McDonald's in Squamish, drive south 44.5 km (27.6 mi). Leave your car at Horseshoe Bay. Walk on the BC Ferry to Langdale. If you're coming from the Sunshine Coast, park in the public parking lot (a few dollars a day). Go to the well-signed boat dock immediately north of the big ferry landing. Take the *Dogwood Princess* powerboat across Thornbrough Channel to New Brighton and Gambier Harbour. Hurry to make the connection; the *Dogwood* leaves soon after the ferry disembarks. It costs $6.50 to $7 (1997) per person round trip and takes 10 minutes one way.

On Foot

Walk straight uphill from the pier, past the public telephone. In a couple minutes, turn left at a junction by the sign COMMUNITY CENTER. Pass the Gambier Island General Store. Pass the community center and The Farm, then walk uphill through new subdivisions. At the top of the hill, the road forks. Go left, soon descending. Then the way is flat through a mature, regrown forest of giant, bigleaf maples and cedars. About 30 minutes from the harbour, reach a lone ancient tree, standing in a cutblock. Foxglove is profuse here in early summer.

About 15 minutes beyond the lone tree, reach a junction. Go left, then left again 2 minutes later at the next junction, where a sign points left to Gambier Lake. Walk downhill toward the audible creek. About 10 minutes beyond the Gambier Lake sign, reach a fork at the top of a small rise. Andy's Bay is left. Cut back sharply right, uphill, if you're heading to Mt. Liddell or Gambier Lake. From here it's about 1 ½ hours to the lake. You're now on a rougher old road marked with orange flagging. Exposed bedrock soon makes walking more difficult. The route heads northeast through young, short hemlocks.

About 1 ½ hours from the harbour, you can hear Mannion Creek on the right as you approach a junction of overgrown logging roads at 280 m (918 ft). Flagging tied to an alder might still have directions written on it. Go left to Mt. Liddell; right to Gambier Lake. Orange flagging marks the way to the lake.

Heading left to Mt. Liddell, watch your footing before you cross Mannion Creek; don't step into the hole on the old bridge. Soon you must bushwhack through thick evergreens. The young hemlocks grow so tightly together you have to shove your way through the interlocking branches. Again watch your footing when you cross a dry drainage. At aptly named Muskeg Lake, a flat area on the left is a possible campsite. From here you can see Port Mellon to the west and Mt. Liddell northeast. Your goal still looks far away, and it is. Stay left at the next junction and keep trudging steeply up the unstable bedrock. Pass through another almost impenetrable wall of hemlocks and continue ascending without views.

Three hours into the horror hike, see another clearcut mountain ahead as you proceed north. Bedrock rubble still poses difficulties. Cross a crumbling old bridge. From its northeast course, the rugged route circles the mountain, curving southwest to make the final approach. To expand your view to include Howe Sound east of Liddell, you must bushwack south, gaining another 50 m (165 ft) to the top of a 903-m (2962-ft) knoll.

Back at the junction of overgrown logging roads, if you go right, heading to Gambier Lake, the route rises steadily. After passing a reedy pond, go right at the fork, then left at the next fork. Finally descend 100 m (330 ft) to tree-ringed Gambier Lake, at 375 m (1230 ft). If camping, pitch your tent on one of the already worn-out sites.

Trip 71

Marion and Phyllis Lakes

Location	Howe Sound
Round trip	16 km (10 mi)
Elevation gain	490 m (1607 ft)
Time required	too much (4 hours)
Available	most of the year
Map	Squamish 92 G/11

OPINION

In a good thesaurus, you'll find more than 130 synonyms for *ugly*. On this hike, you'll find occasion to use lots of them. It's a dismal, disturbing tour of clearcuts, logging slash, powerlines, and wretched forest struggling to regenerate. Calling it a hike is an exaggeration. The route is on trail only long enough to link up with the next available logging road. And there are plenty of those in this beaten, bruised landscape.

You'll see nothing noteworthy here. The view of Howe Sound is easily shrugged off. There are dozens of superior vantage points along the Sound. Though you'll walk up the Phyllis Creek valley, the creek is out of sight and sound most of the way. And the lakes are a big SO WHAT? They skulk in a narrow forested cleft. Reaching their shorelines is difficult. You have to strain just to glimpse them.

Stay away. Choose any other shoulder-season trail in this book. Nearby Petgill Lake (Trip 62) is a better option.

FACT

By Car

From the turnoff to Horseshoe Bay, just outside West Vancouver, drive 25 km (15.5 mi) north on Highway 99 to the parking lot at Porteau Provincial Park.

On Foot

From the park, cross to the east side of the highway and walk 50 meters back (south). At the end of the concrete retaining wall, a small sign BETH LAKE marks the trail. Follow the flagged route east into forest. Ascend 0.4 km (0.25 mi) to an old logging road and turn left. Near the end of this road, turn right on a flagged route and continue ascending. Cross a log-filled gully and proceed on another old logging road. Howe Sound is visible left, Mt. Capilano right.

Descend to the Phyllis Creek logging road. Turn right and ascend to a fork near 358 m (1175 ft) where you're almost under powerlines. The left fork descends to cross Phyllis Creek and eventually provide access northeast to Beth Lake and the route up the north side of Mt. Capilano. Bear right (southeast), staying on the west side of the creek.

Soon cross from the west to the east side of bridged Phyllis Creek. Continue southeast, still on logging road ascending moderately. There are powerlines nearby, paralleling the road. The forested flank of Mt. Capilano is to your left (east).

About 2¼ hours from the highway, reach Marion Lake at 503 m (1650 ft), with the cliffs of Deeks Peak rising above it. Phyllis Lake is 10 minutes farther.

Trip 72

Stawamus Squaw

Location	Squamish
Round trip	14.5 km (9 mi)
Elevation gain	570 m (1870 ft)
Time required	5 hours
Available	March through November
Map	Squamish 92 G/11

OPINION

Only Stephen King would find inspiration among the dark, mean, snarly little trees en route to the Squaw. A fine viewpoint awaits you atop this minor summit, but only if you endure a depressing trail that skulks through humiliated forest.

The sensitive person will quickly weary and want to turn back, discouraged by what the slash-happy logging companies have left in their wake. We hope your discouragement ferments and eventually hardens into determination to save the few ancient forests still standing in B.C.

So it's good that people hike here. We shouldn't ignore a rape victim, whether human or environmental. If you're open to the concept of nature spirits, you'll agree there's reason to recognize the forest's pain and affirm its worth during this difficult stage of renewal. If you're not feeling magnanimous, however, this trudge is not worthwhile.

FACT

By Car

Drive Highway 99 to the Chief viewpoint or the Shannon Falls trailhead. For directions, see Stawamus Chief (Trip 43).

On Foot

Initially, follow our *On Foot* description for the Chief (Trip 43). At the fork where right leads to Upper Shannon Falls, continue straight. In a couple minutes you'll come to a signed junction. Go right, toward the

Squaw. The trail ascends a forested gully beneath the cliffs of the three Chief summits (high above, to your left.) When the trail gets brushy and seems to peter out, proceed upward, northeast, with a granite wall nearby on your left.

About 15-20 minutes beyond the last signed junction, watch closely for a fork. Bear right at the sign: SQUAW 2 HOURS. Left leads to a log ladder and onward to the North and Center summits. Glimpse cliffs out to the right above a swath of downed trees that look like matchsticks. The trail then drops. A waterfall across the canyon is now audible.

Where the trail used to continue straight, go right. A sign directs you onto a new trail winding down through second growth, away from the cliffs. You're soon heading northeast. Come to a moss-splotched rock that affords a view and is a good place to take a break. The descent continues. You might have to negotiate a massive blow-down before reaching the marshy low point where there's a pond. Beyond, the trail gradually ascends through prettier forest—mostly alders, with a few bigger firs and cedars. To your right, about 120 m (394 ft) above the pond, is a viewpoint. Then come to a creeklet.

The trail steepens. You'll know you're on an old logging road when the forest becomes scraggly again. After passing through another stand of alder, reach a 3-way junction. Go left onto yet another old log-ging road. Before the road reaches the crest, look left. A white sign and blazes mark a faint route climbing steeply above the road. That's the way. In about 10-15 minutes, step onto the treed, brushy 610-m (2000-ft) summit of the Squaw.

Check out the open views on both the north and south sides. Mt. Garibaldi and Mamquam Mountain are bold in the northeast. Southeast is nearby Mt. Habrich. Goat Ridge is south, a bit farther away. West across the Squamish River estuary are Mounts Murchison and Lapworth.

PREPARING FOR YOUR HIKE

Hiking in the Coast Mountains is an adventure. Adventure involves risk. But the rewards are worth it. Just be ready for more adventure than you expect. The weather here is constantly changing. Even on a warm, sunny day, pack for rain or snow. Injury is always a possibility. On a long dayhike, be equipped to spend the night out. If you respect the power of wilderness by being prepared, you'll decrease the risk, increase your comfort and enjoyment, and come away fulfilled, yearning for more.

The following recommendations will help you know what's best to pack for mountain conditions. If you don't own or can't afford some of the things listed, make do with what you have. Just be sure to bring warm clothing that insulates when wet. Cotton is terrible. Wool is good. Lighter, softer, synthetic fabrics are better. When upgrading or buying new equipment, consult this section so you don't waste money on something inefficient or inappropriate.

THE FIRST THING TO PACK

Even with all the right gear, you're ill-equipped without physical fitness. If the weather turns grim, the physical capability to get out of the wilderness fast might keep you from being stuck in a life-threatening situation. If you're fit, and a companion gets injured, you can race for help. Besides, if you're not overweight or easily exhausted, you'll have more fun. You'll be able to hike farther and reach more spectacular scenery. So if you're out of shape, work on it. Everything else you'll need is easier to acquire, but still essential.

TRAVEL LIGHT

Weight is critical when backpacking. The lighter you travel, the easier and more pleasant the journey. Carrying too much can sour your opinion of an otherwise great trip. Some people are mules; they can shoulder everything they want. If you'd rather be a thoroughbred, reduce your load and get lighter gear. You might have to sacrifice a little luxury at the campsite in order to be more agile, fleet-footed and comfortable on the trail, but you'll be a happier hiker.

If you've been using an external-frame pack, consider a lighter, internal-frame model. A palatial dome tent is probably overdoing it. Check out the smaller, lighter, anthropomorphic designs. Down sleeping bags generally weigh less, stuff smaller and last longer than synthetic-filled sleeping bags. You can also cut weight and volume with a shorter, inflatable sleeping-pad instead of a full-length one made of thick foam. Forget that heavy, bulky, fleece jacket. If you get really cold at camp, you can dive into your bag. And on any trek less than four days, it's possible to pack only real food and leave all that clunky cooking equipment at home. Try it. Hot meals aren't necessary. Playing outdoor chef and dishwasher is a time-consuming hassle. Select the right foods and you'll find they weigh no more than a stove, fuel, pots, and freeze-dried meals that always turn out gloppy.

These reductions long ago revitalized our interest in backpacking. Now we revel in going light. Lighter equipment is more expensive because the materials are finer quality and the craftsmanship superior. But it's definitely worth it. Consult reputable backpacking stores for specific brands.

UNNECESSARY STUFF

It's amazing how much unnecessary stuff a lot of hikers carry. Unless you're in terrific shape, have a high pain threshold, or don't mind creeping along at a slug's pace, think about everything you pack. Jettisoning preconceptions will lighten your load.

Do you really need the entire guidebook? Take notes, or photocopy the pages of your book. Carrying the whole thing is like dragging an anchor up the trail.

Unless you're a fanatic naturalist, you probably don't need a wildflower book either. In the field, you can take photos, draw sketches, or fire-up your powerful memory. Consult the book when you get back to the car.

An extra pair of shoes? No way. Even river sandals are heavy. Either bring a pair of beach flip-flops, or just change into dry socks and clomp around camp (not on grass) in your unlaced boots.

Jeans are ridiculous. They're heavy, restrictive, and don't insulate. Cotton sweatpants are almost as bad. Anything 100% cotton is a mistake, as explained below.

LAYERING WITH SYNTHETICS

Don't just wear a T-shirt and throw a heavy sweatshirt in your pack. Cotton kills. It quickly gets soaked and takes way too long to dry. Wet clothing saps your body heat and could lead to hypothermia, a leading cause of death in the outdoors. Your mountain clothes should be made of synthetic fabrics that wick sweat away from your skin, insulate when wet, and dry rapidly. Even your hiking shorts and underwear should be at least partly synthetic. Sports bras should be entirely synthetic.

There are now lots of alternatives to the soggy T-shirt. Many outdoor clothing companies offer short-sleeve shirts in superior, synthetic versions. Unlike cotton T-shirts, sweat-soaked synthetics can dry out during a rest break.

For warmth, several synthetic layers are more efficient than a single parka. Your body temperature varies constantly on the trail in response to the weather and your activity level. With only one warm garment, it's either on or off, roast or freeze. Layers allow you to fine tune for optimal comfort.

In addition to a synthetic short-sleeve shirt, it's smart to pack two long-sleeve tops of different fabric weights: one thin, one thick. Wear the thin one for cool-weather hiking. It'll be damp when you stop for a break, so change into the thick one. When you start again, put the thin one back on. The idea is to always keep your thick top dry in case you really need it to stay warm. Covered by a rain shell (jacket), these two tops can provide enough warmth on summer hikes. You can always wear your short-sleeve shirt like a vest over a long-sleeve top. For more warmth on the trail, try a fleece vest. For more warmth in camp, try a down vest or down sweater. Don't hike in down clothing; it'll get soaked and be useless.

For your legs, bring a pair of tights or long underwear, both if you're going overnight. Choose tights made of synthetic fabric with a small percentage of lycra for stretchiness. These are warmer and more durable than the all-lycra or cotton/lycra tights runners wear. You'll find tights way more efficient than pants. They stretch and conform to your body movements. They're lighter and insulate better. You can wear them for hours in a drizzle and not feel damp. If you're too modest to sport this sleek look, just wear shorts over them. Shorts also protect tights from snagging when you sit down.

You'll be smiling too if you're prepared for inclement weather.

RAINGEAR

You need a full set of raingear: pants, and a shell (jacket) with a hood. Fabrics that are both waterproof and breathable are best, because they shed rain and vent perspiration vapor.

Wearing coated nylon, you can end up as damp from sweat as you would from rain. If you can't afford technical raingear, use a poncho. It allows enough air circulation so you won't get sweat soaked.

Raingear is necessary even when it's not raining. A shell and pants, worn over insulating layers, will shed wind, retain body heat, and keep you much warmer.

BOOTS AND SOCKS

Lightweight fabric boots with even a little ankle support are more stable and safer than runners. But all-leather or highly technical leather/fabric boots offer superior comfort and performance. For serious hiking, they're a necessity. Here are a few points to remember while shopping for a pair.

If it's a rugged, quality boot, a light- or medium-weight pair should be adequate for most hiking conditions. Heavy boots will slow you down, just like an overweight pack. But you want boots with hard, protective toes, or you'll risk a broken or sprained digit.

Lateral support stops ankle injuries. Stiff shanks keep your feet from tiring. Grippy outsoles prevent slipping and falling. And sufficient cushioning lessens the pain of a long day on the trail.

Out of the box, boots should be waterproof or at least very water resistant, although you'll have to treat them often to retain their repellency. Boots with lots of seams allow water to seep in as they age. A full rand (wrap-around bumper) adds an extra measure of water protection.

The most important consideration is comfort. Make sure your boots don't hurt. If you wait to find out until after a day of hiking, it's too late; you're stuck with them. So before handing over your cash, ask the retailer if, after wearing them in a shopping mall, you can exchange them if they don't feel right. A half-hour of mall walking should be a reliable test.

Socks are important too. To keep your feet dry, warm and happy, wear wool, thick acrylic, or wool/acrylic-blend socks. Cotton socks retain sweat, cause blisters, and are especially bad if your boots aren't waterproof. It's usually best to wear two pairs of socks, with a thinner, synthetic pair next to your feet to wick away moisture and reduce friction, minimizing the chance of blisters.

GLOVES AND HATS

Always bring gloves and a hat. You've probably heard it, and it's true: your body loses most of its heat through your head and extremities. Cover them if you get chilled. Carry thin, synthetic gloves to wear while hiking. Don't worry if they get wet, but keep a pair of thicker fleece gloves dry in your pack. A fleece hat, or at least a thick head-band that covers your ears, adds a lot of warmth and weighs little. A hat with a long brim is required equipment to shade your eyes and protect your face.

TREKKING POLES

The relentlessly long, wickedly steep ascents and descents in the Coast Mountains make trekking poles vital. Hiking with poles is easier, more enjoyable, and less punishing to your body. If you're constantly pounding the trails, they could add years to your mountain life.

Working on a previous guidebook, we once hiked for a month without poles. Both of us developed knee pain. The next summer, we used Leki trekking poles every day for three months and our knees were never strained. We felt like four-legged animals. We were more sure-footed. Our speed and endurance increased.

Studies show that during a typical 8-hour hike you'll transfer more than 250 tons of pressure to a pair of trekking poles. When going downhill, poles significantly reduce stress to your knees, as well as your lower back, heel and forefoot. They alleviate knee strain when you're going uphill too, because you're climbing with your arms and shoulders, not just your legs. Poles also improve your posture. They keep you more upright, which gives you greater lung capacity and allows more efficient breathing.

The heavier your pack, the more you'll appreciate the support of trekking poles. You'll find them especially helpful for crossing unbridged streams and negotiating muddy, rooty, rough stretches of trail, both of which are frequent obstacles in the Coast Mountains. Poles prevent ankle sprains—a common hiking injury. By making you more stable, they actually help you relax, boosting your sense of security and confidence.

On every trail, someone asks about our poles. Yet we rarely see others using them. A few people carry those big, heavy, gnarled wood staffs, which are a joke. Some hike with old ski poles, which are better, but not nearly as good as poles designed specifically for trekking. To get the full benefit, invest in a pair of true trekking poles made of aircraft-quality aluminum, with adjustable, telescoping shafts and anti-shock springs.

FIRST AID

Someone in your hiking party should carry a first-aid kit. Pre-packaged kits look handy, but they're expensive, and some are inadequate. If you make your own you'll be more familiar with the contents. Include an anti-bacterial ointment; pain pills with ibuprofen, and a few with codeine for agonizing injuries; regular bandages; several sizes of butterfly bandages; a couple bandages big enough to hold a serious laceration together; rolls of sterile gauze and absorbent pads to staunch bleeding; adhesive tape; tiny fold-up scissors or a small knife; and a compact first-aid manual. Whether your kit is store bought or home made, check the expiration dates on your medications every year and replace them as needed.

Instead of the old elastic bandages for wrapping sprains, we now carry neoprene ankle and knee bands. They slip on instantly, require no special wrapping technique, keep the injured joint warmer, and stay in place better. They're so convenient, we sometimes slip them on for extra support on long, steep descents.

BANDANAS

A bandana will be the most versatile item in your pack. You can use it to blow your nose, mop your brow, or improvise a beanie. It makes a colourful head band that'll keep sweat or hair out of your eyes. It serves as a bandage or sling in a medical emergency. Worn as a neckerchief, it prevents a sunburned neck. If you soak it in water, then drape it around your neck, it'll help keep you from getting overheated. Worn Lawrence-of-Arabia style under a hat, it shades both sides of your face, as well as your neck. For an air-conditioning effect, soak it in water then don it à la Lawrence. But in the Coast Mountains, your bandana will be particularly useful for fending off flies and brush. Read *Scourge of the Coast Range* and *Battling Brush* sections for details. Always bring at least two bandanas on a dayhike, more when you're backpacking.

SMALL AND ESSENTIAL

Take matches in a plastic bag, so they're sure to stay dry. It's good to have a Bic lighter, too. A fire starter, such as Optimus Firelighter or Coghlan FireSticks, might help you get a fire going in an emergency when everything is wet. Buy the finger-size wands, not the type for a barbecue.

Pack an emergency survival bag on dayhikes. One fits into the palm of your hand and could help you survive a cold night without a sleeping bag or tent. The ultralight, metallic fabric reflects your body heat back at you. Look for the survival bags you crawl into; they're more efficient than survival blankets.

Bring several plastic bags in various sizes. Use the small ones for packing out garbage. A couple large trash bags could be used to improvise a shelter.

A headlamp or flashlight, and extra batteries, are always necessary for safety. If you have to hike at night, you'll need one to stay on the trail. If you know how to use it, carry a compass. Most people find bug repellent indispensable for flies and mosquitos. For those dreaded blisters, pack Moleskin or Spenco jell. Cut it with the knife or scissors you should have in your first-aid kit.

Wear sunglasses for protection against glare and wind. Your eyes won't get nearly as tired. A few hours in the elements can strain your eyes. People who don't wear sunglasses are more prone to cataracts later in life.

Bring sunscreen and a hat with a brim. High-altitude sun can fry you fast. The Coast Mountains aren't exempt from holes in the ozone layer.

And don't forget to pack lots of thought-provoking questions to ask your companions. Hiking stimulates meaningful conversation.

KEEPING IT ALL DRY

To protect your gear from rain, bag it in plastic bags, or use a pack cover. Rain is a constant likelihood, so you might as well start hiking with everything in bags. That's easier than wrestling with it in a storm. For added assurance, use plastic bags *and* bring a pack cover.

WATER

Giardia lamblia is a waterborne parasite that causes severe gastrointestinal distress. It's transported through animal and human feces, so never poop or pee near water. To be safe, assume giardia is present in all surface water in the Coast Mountains. Don't drink any water unless you're certain it's from a pure source, like a glacier or spring, or until you've boiled, disinfected, or filtered it. Boiling is an immense hassle. Killing giardia with iodine tablets can be tricky and it makes the water smell and taste awful, unless you use a brand that comes with neutralizing pills. Carrying a small, light filter (some simple models weigh only 240 grams / 8 ounces) is the most practical solution. To strain out giardia cysts, your filter must have an absolute pore size of 4 microns or less. To strain out cryptosporidium cysts, which are increasingly common and cause physical symptoms identical to giardiasis, your filter must have an absolute pore size of at least 2 microns. Iodine has no effect on crypto.

Drink water frequently. Keeping your body hydrated is essential. If you're thirsty, you're probably not performing at optimal efficiency. But water is the heaviest thing in any pack. A litre (quart) weighs almost one kilogram (two pounds). Although every hiker should bring a water bottle, it's not always necessary for each member of a group to keep his or her bottle full. Over the period of several hikes, pay attention to how much you drink and how often water is available. You'll find it's abundant along most trails on the wetter, west side of the Coast

Mountains. For the two of us, filling a single bottle is usually sufficient. We make sure we're totally hydrated before we start hiking, then guzzle and refill at every water source. Leaving our extra bottle empty lightens our load, helping us hike faster and farther. But if the trail you're on has long dry sections, the weather is hot, or you're uncertain how much water you'll need, carry a litre (quart) per person.

Filtering water from Widgeon Creek (Trip 40)

BODY FUEL

When planning meals, keep energy and nutrition foremost in mind. During a six-hour hike, you'll burn 1800 to 3000 calories, depending on terrain, pace, body size, and pack weight. You'll be stronger, and therefore safer and happier, if you fill up on high-octane body fuel.

A few candy bars and a white-flour bun with a slab of cheese or meat on it won't get you very far up the trail. Refined sugars give you a brief spurt that quickly fizzles. Too much protein or fat will make you feel sluggish and drag you down.

For sustained exercise, like hiking, you need a little protein and fat to function normally and give you that satisfying full feeling. But protein and fat are hard to digest. Your body takes three or four hours to assimilate them, compared to one or two hours for carbohydrates. You don't want your blood supply diverted to your stomach. You need it hustling oxygen to your legs.

Toiling muscles crave the glycogen your body manufactures from complex carbos. So load your pack with foods made of whole wheat flour, rice, corn, oats, potatoes, and legumes. The ideal ratio is roughly 70% carbos, 10% protein, 20% fat.

You'll find natural or health-food stores a reliable source of hiking food. They even stock energy bars, which are superior to candy bars because they're rich in carbos and low in fat. Whether dayhiking or backpacking, always bring extra energy bars for emergencies.

On dayhikes, carry dried fruit; whole-grain pita bread filled with tabouli, hummus, avocado, cucumbers, sprouts; whole-grain cookies made with natural sweeteners (brown rice syrup, cane sugar, fruit juice, molasses); whole-grain crackers; or sesame sticks. We often pack a bag of unsalted, organic corn or mixed-grain tortilla chips prepared in high-oleic, expeller-pressed safflower or canola oil.

For a backpacking breakfast, try spreading margarine, maple syrup and cinnamon on hearty, whole-grain bread or in pita pockets. Or why not whole-grain cookies in the morning? They're like cereal, only more convenient. The backpacking lunch menu is the same as for dayhiking. For dinner, try bean salad, or pre-cooked pasta with dressing and pre-steamed vegetables. Tofu that's been pressed, marinated, baked, and vacuum-packed is delicious and lasts about three days. Cold burritos you make ahead of time are great, too. To get enough fresh veggies, bring whole carrots and sweet, red bell-peppers; they travel well and stay fresh for several days.

Real meals are heavier than freeze-dried, but they make up for it by eliminating the weight of cooking equipment and the hassle of cooking. Plus they're tastier, more filling, cheaper, and better for you.

Most backpackers carry a stove. In addition to using it to cook meals, they say it'll help keep them warm in an emergency. Which is true. Warm liquids can help revive someone slipping into hypothermia. But we prefer to reduce our load and go without, risking the small chance that we'll ever need a stove. In case our survival depends on it, we carry tiny, lightweight fire starters to help us light a fire.

Fresh food tends to be too heavy, bulky and perishable for trips longer than four days. A stove makes sense then. But for shorter trips, don't adhere blindly to tradition. Carry a stove only if cooking significantly increases your enjoyment.

Information Sources

Maps and current trail reports are available at these offices. Park offices are open 8:30 A.M. to 4:30 P.M. weekdays year-round.

B.C. Mountaineering Club
Box 2674, Vancouver, B.C. V6B 3W8

Cypress and Mt. Seymour Provincial Parks
ph: (604) 924-2200   fax: (604) 924-2244
BC Parks Regional District Office
1610 Mount Seymour Road
North Vancouver, B.C. V7G 1L3

Federation of Mountain Clubs of British Columbia
ph: (604) 737-3053
1367 W. Broadway, Vancouver, B.C. V6A 4H9

Garibaldi Provincial Park
ph: (604) 898-3678   fax: (604) 898-4171
District Manager, Alice Lake Provincial Park
Box 220, Brackendale, B.C. V0N 1H0

Golden Ears Provincial Park
ph: (604) 463-3513   fax: (604) 463-6193
Box 7000, Maple Ridge, B.C. V2X 7G3

Lynn Headwaters Regional Park
Parks Dept., Greater Vancouver Regional District
ph: (604) 224-5739
4330 Kingsway, Burnaby, B.C. V5H 4G8

North Shore Hikers
Current phone number is in the telephone directory.
Box 4535, Vancouver, B.C. V6B 4A1

Western Canada Wilderness Committee
ph: (604) 683-8220   fax: (604) 683-8229
20 Water Street, Vancouver, B.C. V6B 1A4

The Authors

Besides each other, hiking is Kathy and Craig's greatest passion. Their second date was a 32-km (20-mile) dayhike in Arizona. Since then they've never stopped for long.

They've trekked through much of the world's vertical topography, including the Himalayas, Pyrenees, Alps, Dolomites, Sierra, North Cascades, and Rockies, as well as the mountains of New Zealand and the canyons of the American Southwest. They moved from the U.S. to Canada so they could live near the Canadian Rockies, the range that inspired their highly unconventional *Don't Waste Your Time*® guidebook series. *Camp Free in B.C.* was their next book. They then devoted two years to hiking the North Cascades, the subject of their second *Don't Waste Your Time*® guidebook. They now live on Kootenay Lake, between B.C.'s Purcell and Selkirk mountains. Their new book *Premier Hikes*™ *in B.C.* touches on these ranges. You'll find comprehensive coverage in their next book: *Don't Waste Your Time*® *in the West Kootenays*.

Their enthusiasm for the joys of hiking and their colourful, unflinchingly honest writing make this an unusually compelling guidebook. To complete the research, they hiked 1200 kilometers (745 miles) and ascended elevation equivalent to climbing from sea level to the summit of Mt. Everest 6½ times.

Joyful moment during the authors' odyssey

Other Titles from Voice in the Wilderness Press

Look for these and other titles by the Copelands in outdoor shops and book stores. You can also order them by sending a cheque to Voice in the Wilderness Press, P.O. Box 71, Riondel, B.C. V0B 2B0 Canada. The prices include shipping and GST. If you order more than one book or cassette, deduct the following amount from the total cost: CDN $3 for shipments within Canada, or US $3 to the States. Allow 2-3 weeks for delivery in Canada, 3-4 weeks to the States.

Camp Free in B.C. Volume I.........CDN $17   US $15
   ISBN 0-9698016-7-x   1999, 3rd edition, 320 pages
Precise directions to over 260 official, free campgrounds accessible by two-wheel drive. Covers southern BC, from Trans-Canada Hwy 1 to the U.S. border, from Vancouver Island to the Rocky Mountains.

Camp Free in B.C. Volume II.......CDN $17   US $15
   ISBN 0-9698016-6-1   1999, 1st edition, 368 pages
Precise directions to over 225 official, free campgrounds accessible by two-wheel drive. Covers central BC, from Trans-Canada Hwy 1 north past Hwy 16, from the Coast Range to the Rocky Mountains.

Bears Beware! Warning Calls You Can Make to Avoid an Encounter...CDN $11   US $ 9
   ISBN 0-9698016-5-3   1998 edition, audio cassette
30 minutes that could save your life. Find out why pepper spray, talking, and bells are not enough. Follow these strategies for safer hiking and camping in bear country.

Premier Hikes™ in British Columbia.........CDN $18   US $15.50
   ISBN 0-9698016-8-8   June 1999, 208 pages,
   16 pages of colour photos
The only book you need to enjoy the most spectacular, exhilarating hikes in the province. Discerning trail reviews help you choose your trip. Detailed route descriptions keep you on the path. Includes dayhikes and backpack trips. Covers the Coast Mountains, Cascades, Selkirks, Kootenays, and Rockies.

More Voice titles on page 272

PREMIER   OUTSTANDING   WORTHWHILE   DON'T DO

The Don't Waste Your Time® *hiking guidebook series rates and reviews trails to help you get the most from magnificent wilderness areas. Route descriptions are comprehensive. Includes shoulder-season trips for more hiking opportunities. Offers wisdom on mountain travel.*

Don't Waste Your Time®
   in the Canadian Rockies........CDN $19 US $16
      ISBN 0-9698016-4-5   1998 edition, 392 pages
125 hikes in Banff, Jasper, Kootenay, Yoho and Waterton national parks, plus Mt. Robson and Mt. Assiniboine provincial parks.

Don't Waste Your Time®
   in the North Cascades................CDN $20 US $17
      ISBN 0-89997-182-2   1996 edition, 364 pages
110 hikes in southern BC and northern Washington. Includes North Cascades National Park, Mt. Baker and Glacier Peak wilderness areas, plus BC's Manning and Cathedral parks.

Don't Waste Your Time®
   in the West Kootenays..........CDN $19 US $16
      ISBN 0-9698016-9-6   April 2000, approx. 320 pages
70 hikes in the Selkirk and Purcell ranges of southeast B.C. Includes Valhalla, Kokanee Glacier, Goat Range, West Arm, and St. Mary's Alpine parks.

What's Your Opinion?

A guidebook is never finished. It continues to evolve, like the landscapes it describes. Please contribute to the evolution of this book by answering the following questions. Then put this form in an envelope, stamp it and mail it. Thanks. We value your comments.

What did you like most about this book?

_____

_____

What did you like least?

_____

_____

How can this book be improved?

_____

_____

Were any of the directions inaccurate or difficult to follow? ____yes ____ no
If so, which trip? Please explain.

_____

_____

_____

Name_____ Phone_____

Address _____

Age_____ Occupation _____

How many years have you been a hiker?_____

How often do you dayhike?_____

How often do you backpack?_____

What's Your Story?

What's the most memorable hiking or camping experience you've ever had? It could be romantic, frightening, challenging, exhausting, spiritual, beautiful, moving, mysterious, disgusting, instructive, or bizarre. Write your story in complete detail and send it (with this form) in an envelope. Be sure to give us your name, address and phone number. **If we include it in an upcoming book, we'll give you full credit and send you a free copy.**

Put this form in an envelope, stamp it
and mail it to:

Voice in the Wilderness Press, Inc.
P.O. Box 71
Riondel, B.C., Canada V0B 2B0